SEASON 2024/25

The fascinating story of the Deeside Ducks' first – and only - season in the NIHL Laidler Division, as told in the Flintshire & Wrexham Leader newspaper and on the Ice Hockey Review website.

#keepquacking #fowlnotfoul

Published in Great Britain in June 2025 by Ice Hockey Review
which is an imprint of Posh Up North Publishing, Beckenham Road, Wallasey

The majority of the stories and reports in this book have been previously published on
the Ice Hockey Review website and in part or in full in the Flintshire & Wrexham
Leader newspaper.

The league tables and player statistics shown are based on information taken from the
England Ice Hockey website Gameday data, www.nihlstats.com, Elite Prospects and
other sources.

Gamesheets for individual matches are taken from the "Box Scores" section on
www.nihlstats.com where they are available or generated using EIH(A) / Gameday
data when not.

ISBN: 978-1-909643-68-0

Front Cover Images:
Deeside Ducks Logo
Ducks team - for names see page 170 (Photo by Paul Breeze)

Back Cover Image:
Author / Editor Paul Breeze (Photo by Chris Jones)

CONTENTS

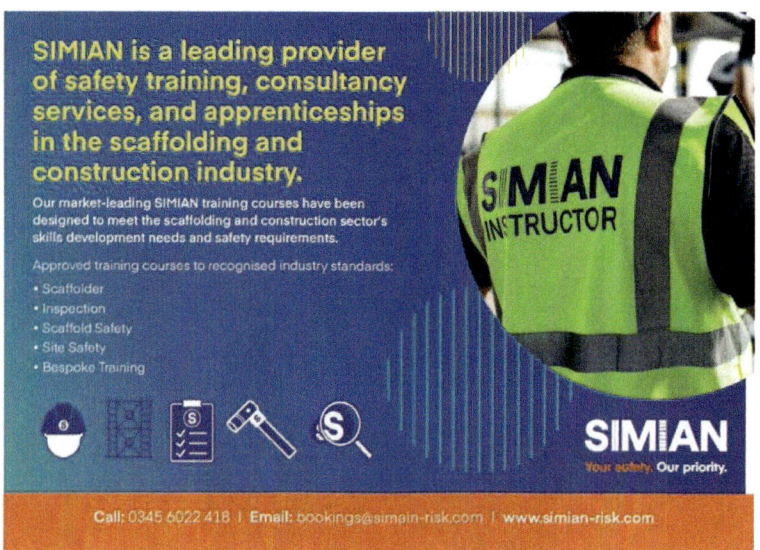

PB multi-tasking at a Deeside Ducks game
(Photo by Chris Jones)

From The Editor

I first started following British ice hockey in the 1982/83 season when the Peterborough Pirates team started up in my home town (yes – I agree, I don't look old enough...) and they used to beat the Deeside Dragons in the British League on a regular basis.

I played a bit of rec hockey – very badly, and only for a very short while (total career stat - 1 assist) - and then decided that I could better serve the game from off the ice rather than on it.

I was involved with a couple of international tournaments and eventually volunteered at other clubs – Altrincham

Aces, Blackburn Hawks, Fylde Flyers, Blackpool Seagulls - after I moved up north with my job.

When I moved to the Wirral in the spring of 2015, I had actually arranged with Peter Sheffield and Ian Foster to write the match reports for the Dragons website for the following season.

Unfortunately, this all coincided with the Red Hockey takeover and the Dragons' home games got moved to Saturday evenings – which I couldn't manage - so I ended up going to Widnes instead and helped them out for a number of years.

SO, I was very pleased when, in the summer of 2024, I was asked to help out with the media for the new Deeside Ducks team.

I immediately started working on news stories and the player announcements for the lead-up to the new season and have been producing match reports and news items ever since.

Now, the majority of what you will be reading in this book is already freely available on the Ice Hockey Review website, the Ducks Facebook page and in the Leader newspaper and their website.

But, even so, I think it is nice to have it all in one place – and it is a great souvenir of the Deeside Ducks' debut season in the NIHL Laidler Division. So I hope you enjoy it.

Paul Breeze - *Wallasey, June 2025*

As reported on www.icehockeyreview.co.uk

28th May 2024: New Ducks Set To Soar In Deeside

Deeside have announced that a new "Deeside Ducks" team will play in the NIHL Laidler Division for the 2024/25 league season.

The idea of the team is to offer a stepping stone between the highly successful Deeside junior development system – who operate teams at various age groups from Under 10s to Under 18s - and the senior Dragons team who play in the NIHL Moralee Division.

The aim is allow younger players to continue to play competitive league ice hockey after they have "aged out" of the junior system and gain experience at senior level in the hope of eventually breaking through to the Dragons Moralee side.

The Ducks have arranged two open player trials – on Monday 10th June and Monday 17th June from 9.30 to 10.30pm at Deeside Leisure Centre. Anybody interested in taking part is asked to contact James Parsons by email at James.Parsons@aura.wales

Ducks' Head Coach Gary Shaw & Lead Coach Peter Bleackley

2nd July 2024: Deeside Ducks Announce Lead Coach Staff For Debut Season

The Deeside Ducks are pleased to announce their lead coaching staff for their debut 2024/25 NIHL season.

The Head Coach will be Gary Shaw backed up by Peter Bleackley as a lead coach, who both have long associations with the Deeside club in playing and coaching capacities.

Shaw was a highly rated player with the Deeside Dragons and Flintshire Freeze ENL/NIHL teams over a 20 year period and was more recently Head Coach of the Dragons for the 2018/19 and 2019/20 seasons. Last season, he was Head Coach of the Dragons Under 18 team that finished 6th in the U18 North 2 league table.

Peter Bleackley also has a huge amount of experience, having played and coached at Blackpool, Fylde, Blackburn, Widnes and Deeside over the years. He is a specialist netminding coach and has also been Head Coach of junior teams at Widnes and Deeside.

Talk about coaching the new team, Gary Shaw said:

"I am pleased to be given this opportunity to help develop the players from their current levels to enhance their skills, knowledge and experience and to push forward and advance their opportunities to play in the senior Dragons team."

"This Ducks team will be predominantly U23 with at least a third being U19. Some older players will be asked to play and their role will be to support the youth of the team and help with their progression. The aim is to ultimately push for places in the Dragons senior team and on to higher levels such as England and Premier."

"While winning is the aim of all teams, there are many different ways to win, so we will focus on all aspects required to advance our squad and, if we achieve the win on the scoreboard, it is a bonus for the team."

Peter Bleackley added:

"I'm really looking forward to getting back to coaching after a few years' break. Gary, Simon and I have all coached and played hockey together, so as a coaching team we have a good understanding of our joint goals for the season ahead."

"A Deeside D2 development team is a great opportunity for our juniors to gain a pathway into senior hockey. Many juniors - especially those that start playing hockey in their teens - aren't ready for D1 and either drop out of the sport or play Recreational hockey when they age out of our junior system."

"There's a good buzz around the rink for the upcoming season and the new team will be an opportunity for players to showcase their skills and get valuable experience of regular competitive hockey at a senior level."

Simon Hughes, Stewart Cutting and Angela Wilkes

3rd July 2024: Deeside Ducks Complete Coaching Staff For Debut Season

Following the appointment of Gary Shaw as Head Coach and Peter Bleackley as Lead Coach, the Deeside Ducks are pleased to announce that Simon Hughes and Stewart Cutting are joining the staff as Assistant Coaches.

Hughes is a former Deeside Demons, Dragons and Altrincham Aces player and currently a Deeside junior coach while Cutting previously played for Slough Jets and Swindon Wildcats in ENL South and currently plays for the Deeside based Connah's Quay Cobras recreational side. Cutting will also turn out as a player for the Ducks team

Talking about his appointment, Cutting said:

"I am delighted to be asked to be an Assistant Coach for this exciting new team in Deeside. Having coached the junior club, it's going to be rewarding to see these young talented players come through the system and transition into adult hockey"

The Team Manager for the new Ducks team will be Angela Wilkes, who also has a long affiliation with the Deeside club and was the Manager for the Under 18 team last season.

Wilkes said: "After many months of planning, it is amazing to see this team come together. I am excited to be working with a passionate team to build a solid foundation to secure the future of ice hockey at Deeside, giving local talent the pathways and opportunities to develop their game to Division 1 level and beyond. I am hoping to make our inaugural season one to remember."

Introducing himself, Simon Hughes said:

"I was born and lived within a mile of the Deeside Ice Rink. Ice skating and hockey has been an interest since the rink opened in 1974. First as a figure skater, then hockey fan (Deeside Dragons) and player from 1984 to 1995.

"I was a product of the Deeside Juniors, although it was nowhere near as well structured as it is nowadays. Then I progressed to senior hockey with the Deeside Demons and was flattered to be chosen to wear the C in the first home game of the newly formed team (1987).

"At 18 I was training with the Dragons and occasionally playing up (4th line if I was lucky). Practicing and icing with the Dragons veterans I had supported as a kid and legendary imports and coaches was a fantastic experience, finally making the squad for the Dragons in the British League (Heineken) until the team sadly folded in the early 1990's.

"A few of us had the opportunity to play in Manchester for Altrincham Aces/Trafford Metros, which I did until 1992. Hockey has changed, it was certainly less skilful and more physical, than the modern game, however this was a part of the game I particularly enjoyed.

"After redundancy from my fulltime job, I returned to Deeside to work alongside Gary Shaw as assistant coach with the Demons. I later continued playing recreational hockey until a knee injury ended my playing days in 1995.

"I have remained a life-long hockey fan and enjoy following all aspects of the sport in the UK and internationally, including trips to North America to watch live NHL games.

"Following a 25+ year hiatus, I have returned to the ice as an assistant coach for the Deeside Dragons Junior Ice Hockey Club. I have also started officiating as a Level 1 Referee for Ice Hockey UK (IHUK) 2023-24. I am really pleased to be working with the new Deeside Ducks as an assistant coach, helping young players progress and hopefully seeing future success of this new NIHL D2N setup."

Left to right: Cody Ogden, Henry Phillips and Daniels Fadejevs will all play for the Deeside Ducks this season (Photo by Dragons IHC)

5th July 2024: Deeside Ducks Announce Talented Trio

The Deeside Ducks have announced the signing of three promising junior players for the forthcoming NIHL Laidler Division season.

The idea of the Ducks team is to offer a stepping stone between the Deeside Junior development system and the senior Dragons team who play in the NIHL Moralee Division and regulations in place from the sport's governing body - England Ice Hockey – allow for players under the age of 23 to "play up" for different teams in order to gain more experience and help with their development.

This arrangement means that promising Deeside junior players will be able to gain experience of regular senior hockey with the Ducks on a regular basis and also train and play with the senior Dragons team on suitable occasions.

The first of this trio of Ducks player signings is 17 year old Cody Ogden, who is a former Widnes Wild junior but switched to the Dragons U18s last season. He also made one appearance for the senior Dragons in the Moralee Division.

Cody said: "Last year [making my senior Dragons debut] was a really big opportunity for me. I was nervous, but everyone was really encouraging, and I seemed to fit in pretty well. I felt really welcomed to the team. This season I feel great, I'm really excited for it. I can't wait!"

16 year old Daniels Fadejevs played at U16 and U18 level for both the Deeside juniors and Manchester Storm Academy last season and was captain of the Storm U16 team.

16 year old defenceman Henry Phillips also played for both Deeside and Manchester at U16 and U18 level last season. He was also selected to play in the Longstaff U16 team at this year's national Showcase tournament.

Looking ahead to the new season, Phillips said: "I really appreciate the opportunity and am so grateful for it. Being on a two-way contract with the Ducks also gives me a chance to develop with the Ducks and translate that to the Dragons. It's a massive opportunity for me and the atmosphere around the team is great to be around. Everyone's been so supportive and welcoming, I can't wait to get started!"

Chris Jones (Photo by Keith & Jenny Davies)

9th July 2024: Chris Jones Joins Deeside Ducks

The Deeside Ducks have announced the signing of experienced player Chris Jones for the forthcoming NIHL Laidler Division season.

The idea of the new Ducks team is to provide regular senior hockey for young players coming out of the Deeside junior programme and to act as a stepping stone towards the senior Dragons team.

While the majority of the team will be Under 23s, a number of older more experienced players are also being added to the roster to bring stability and wisdom to the mix.

Deeside supporters won't need any introduction to Chris Jones who has been a long term favourite at the North Wales rink.

He was a Flintshire junior player and has enjoyed 19 seasons of senior hockey – mainly with the Flintshire Freeze and Deeside Dragons but with brief sojourns at Telford and Blackburn as well.

In that time he has played some 460 competitive games, scoring 314 goals, 231 assists and amassing 1628 penalty minutes.

Talking about joining the Ducks, Chris Jones said:

"I am pleased to join Deeside Ducks for the coming season and for the new challenge in my hockey career. I feel that being part of the team as a player will be a great experiences for me - as will helping build the team and assisting in developing the juniors through the club."

"The Ducks team is exactly what Deeside needs to create a pathway into senior hockey. There is a strong D1 team at Deeside and this new team gives the younger players a stepping stone to that league in their future hockey careers."

Ducks' Head Coach Gary Shaw said of Jones' signing:

"I have known Chris for many years from juniors to seniors and had a lot of time coaching his progression as a player. I now have asked him to give back to this new team and help me prepare the new talent for the next step up to senior hockey. Chris's knowledge and experience will be vital to help the coaching team develop the next generation. Welcome on board, Chris."

11th July 2024: Charlie Spridgeon

The Deeside Ducks are pleased to announce the signing of another experienced NIHL player – Charlie Spridgeon - for the forthcoming Laidler Division season.

Spridgeon is a product of the Deeside junior system and has played over 130 competitive games at NIHL level over 5 seasons.

He has played most of his career at Deeside – apart from the 2021/22 season, when the rink was closed and he won the Laidler Division title with Telford.

Talking about joining the Ducks, Spridgeon said:

"I am really excited to start playing hockey again after missing all of last season through injury. I think that we can have a really competitive season in this league and I'm looking forward to it."

Ducks Lead Coach Peter Bleackley said of Spridgeon:

"It's great to have Charlie on the squad this season. Having coached him as a junior, we know he brings good energy to a team with his work rate and net drive. Recently, injury has plagued his seasons at D1 but now he is back to fitness, we are hoping for big things from him with the Ducks."

Spridgeon will also continue to be an important member of the Dragons organisation and will train regularly with the senior team.

Kenny Williams (Photo by Peter Sheffield)

12th July 2024: Kenny Williams

The Deeside Ducks are pleased to announce the signing of Kenny Williams for the forthcoming Laidler Division season.

Williams was a highly popular player for both the Flintshire Freeze and Deeside Dragons over a 10 year period and was a member of the Dragons side that won the Laidler Division League and Play Off double in 2016.

He is a veteran of over 200 games at NIHL level and has most recently been playing for the Deeside-based Connah's Quay Cobras recreational team.

Talking about joining the Ducks, Williams said:

"I am really grateful to be given the chance to play at Deeside again with the new team. It has a brilliant coaching team and it will be great to see the junior step up into senior hockey and hopefully, make the move to the Dragons in the future."

Ducks Assistant Coach Stewart Cutting said of Williams:

"Kenny has been a fantastic voice and guide for the younger members of this team already, and has a wealth of knowledge and experience to bring to the table. His presence on the ice this season will be key to the success we are looking to achieve, not only this season, but for the future of the Ducks."

Callum Preston with his father – former Blackburn and Widnes player Chris Preston (Photo by Donna Preston)

16th July 2024 Callum Preston

The Deeside Ducks are pleased to announce the signing of promising 17 year old netminder Callum Preston for the forthcoming Laidler Division season.

Callum is a former Widnes, Blackburn and Bradford junior and played last season for the Manchester Storm Under 18 team that finished 5th in EIHA Division 1 North.

He already has some NIHL level experience as he dressed for Widnes Wild as a back-up netminder for 4 Moralee Division games in the 2022/23 season and played a 20 minute shift in a North West Cup game, during which he achieved a 6-shot shut out.

Talking about joining the Ducks, Callum said:

"After 15 years of juniors and a handful of senior appearances under my belt, I am keen to make my step up to senior hockey full time. This is something everybody can look forward to and, of course, I have heard great things about the fans in Deeside."

"I can't wait to play in front of the crowds at this rink. The team is fast approaching its inaugural season and I am honoured to be here for it. With all eyes on the team being new to the league, I am excited to bring experience and energy and provide support wherever I can".

Ducks Lead Coach Peter Bleackley said of Preston:

I am excited to have Callum as one of our netminders this year. He started his journey playing U10's back in Widnes in 2014 and stood out back then. I've followed his junior career and seen him go from strength to strength. He stood out in the trials and all the coaching staff immediately voiced their opinions that Callum was a solid choice for us between the pipes."

Lucy - Poet in Residence

Lucy loves a good sports mascot and she was especially impressed with Duck Ed's on-screen debut in the recent Deeside Ducks' promotional video.

He is now having a well earned pamper at Deeside's Afon Spa and Lucy felt moved to pen a few lines about it:

There's a new ice hockey team called Deeside Ducks
Icing in Deeside and slicing pucks.
The Ducks have a mascot called Duck Ed
When Ed wants to relax he doesn't get into bed
Oh no! Instead -
He goes along to the beautiful Spa facility
At Deeside Leisure Centre and assures his continued mobility.

Lucy London, 5th July 2024

20th July 2024: The 2024/25 Laidler Division Explained.

The Deeside Ducks will play in the Laidler Division (NIHL North 2) for the 2024/25 season. It will be a 10-team league and, in a departure from previous seasons, it will be split into two regional sections with 5 teams in each.

The Deeside Ducks will play in the same regional group as Altrincham Aces, Bradford Bulldogs, Coventry NIHL Blaze and Telford Tigers 2.

The other group will comprise: Billingham Buccaneers, Kingston (Hull) Sharks, Nottingham Lions 2, Sheffield Titans and Sutton Sting.

Each team will play the other teams from their own group twice home and twice away and the teams from the other group once home and once away for a 26 game league season.

Cup Competition

There will also be a Laidler Cup competition, with two qualifying groups of 5 teams each feeding into knockout semis and a final.

Rather than playing separate cup games for the qualifying stage, the first league meeting home and away between the participating teams will be counted towards the cup group table and this will decide who goes through to the latter stages.

Play Offs

The end of season Play Offs also have a change of format for this year. The top 8 teams in the final Laidler Division table will qualify for the Play Offs and two groups of four will play each other home away*.

The top two finishers in each group will meet in 2 legged semi-finals played on a home and away basis.

The winners of the two semi finals will then meet in the Laidler Division Play Off final, which will be held as part of a bigger NIHL Finals Weekend – at a venue yet to be announced - over the weekend of 12th & 13th April 2025.

All four NIHL divisions – Moralee (North 1), Laidler (North 2), Britton (South 1) and Wilkinson (South 2) will have their respective play off finals held on the Saturday and the winners of each will meet in North v South national finals on the Sunday.

(Note*: this is per the graphic announcement by EIH made on social media on 29th June 2024 and differs from the official Rules of Competition, which state that QFs are to be a two legged home and away tie played over one weekend)

League Points

Another important development for the new season is the change in the allocation of points for league and cup qualifying tables.

In order to encourage teams to push for a win in regulation time, rather than hold out for a draw and overtime, 3 points will be awarded for a win in regular time for the 2024/25 season.

2 points will be awarded for a win in Overtime or by Penalty Shoot Out and 1 point for an OT / PS loss. A loss in regulation time will yield 0 points as before.

Imported Players

A further rule change sees the number of imported players allowed on the team roster for any one game reduced from three last season to two this season, and both being allowed on the ice at the same time.

SEASON 2024/25

NIHL NORTH DIVISION 2

LEAGUE SCHEDULE
Teams split into two regional groups
2H 2A in own group, 1H 1A in other
26 league games

LAIDLER CUP
Teams split into two groups of five
First league game H&A counts to Cup
Knockout games in Jan & Feb 2025

PLAY-OFFS
Top eight teams qualify
Two groups of four play 1H 1A
Top two sides qualify for two legged semi-finals

Post season note:

For some reason, this Play Off format did not happen and the top 8 teams played knockout home and away quarter final ties instead....

Laidler Division information graphic published by England Ice Hockey on 29th June 2024

Deeside Ducks Announce First Signings.

(Rehash of previous stories for Wrexham Leader newspaper).

The Deeside Ducks ice hockey team have announced the signing of highly experienced Dragons player Chris Jones as part of their roster for the new NIHL season.

The Ducks are a new team in the Laidler (North 2) Division for the 2024/25 season and the aim is to provide regular senior hockey for young players coming out of the Deeside junior programme and to act as a stepping stone towards the senior Dragons team.

While the majority of the team will be Under 23s, a number of older, more experienced, players are also being added to the squad to bring stability and wisdom to the mix.

Deeside supporters won't need any introduction to Chris Jones who has been a long term favourite at the North Wales rink.

He was a Flintshire junior player and has enjoyed 19 seasons of senior hockey – mainly with the Flintshire Freeze and Deeside Dragons, but with brief sojourns at Telford and Blackburn as well – and is a veteran of over 460 competitive games at NIHL level.

Jones is joined on the Ducks roster by another Dragons player from last season – Charlie Spridgeon – as well as long standing Deeside favourite Kenny Williams, who has most recently been playing recreational hockey with the Connah's Quay Cobras.

Former Slough Jet Stewart Cutting – another current Cobras player – has also joined the Ducks as a player and assistant coach.

The sport's governing body - England Ice Hockey – allows for players under the age of 23 to "play up" for different teams in order to gain more experience and help with their development.

This arrangement means that promising Deeside junior players will be able to gain experience of senior hockey with the Ducks on a regular basis and also train and play with the Dragons Moralee Division team on suitable occasions.

The first of the junior players who will benefit from playing for the Ducks team this season have also been announced.

The talented trio of 17 year old Cody Ogden, 16 year old Daniels Fadejevs and 16 year old Henry Phillips all played regularly for the Deeside Under 18 team last season and Ogden also made one appearance for the Dragons.

Ducks Head Coach Gary Shaw said of the new team:

"This Ducks team will be predominantly U23 with at least a third being U19. Some older players will be asked to play and their role will be to support the youth of the team and help with their progression. The aim is to ultimately push for places in the Dragons senior team and on to higher levels such as England and Premier."

"While winning is the aim of all teams, there are many different ways to win, so we will focus on all aspects required to advance our squad and, if we achieve the win on the scoreboard, it is a bonus for the team."

Kieran Clarkson (Photo by Mark Ray)

19th July 2024: Kieran Clarkson Joins Deeside Ducks

The Deeside Ducks have announced the signing of Kieran Clarkson as part of their roster for the new NIHL season.

The 22 year old defenceman is a former Deeside and Manchester junior and has also played 4 seasons of Laidler Division hockey for Altrincham Aces and Bradford Bulldogs.

In that time he has made some 70 competitive appearances at NIHL level and has most recently been playing for the Connah's Quay Cobras recreational team.

Ducks Lead Coach Peter Bleackley said of Clarkson:

"Kieran started his hockey at Deeside and moved to Manchester. We have watched his career with interest and he was on our wanted list as soon as the D2 team was in its early stages. A solid player with a cool attitude, we are really glad for him to be playing at Deeside again."

Talking about joining the Ducks, Kieran said: "I'm so glad to be back where it all started. I'm looking forward to the new season and can't wait to hit the ice with the team."

Story Written - But This Didn't Happen...

The Deeside Ducks Ice Hockey Club have unveiled a number of sponsorship packages to allow businesses and individuals to support them during their debut 2024/25 NIHL.

The Title Sponsorship Package includes sponsor's name prominently displayed on all social media posts and advertising related to the team, sponsor's name featured on the front of the team jerseys, 5 season tickets to enjoy the action-packed games and a personalised team jersey to show your support in style.

The Match Night Sponsorship Package includes 15 tickets for the match, puck drop opportunity, company logo featured on the match night and photos with the MVP.

The Jersey Sponsorship Package includes your logo showcased on the team jerseys for maximum visibility, logo displayed on social media platforms and match night posters and 2 season tickets to witness the thrilling matches live.

Anybody interested in becoming a sponsor of the Deeside Ducks Ice Hockey Club and joining them on their exciting journey is asked to contact james.parsons@aura.wales.

ICE HOCKEY: A NEW TEAM IS SET UP IN DEESIDE

BY SHAUN DAVIES

shaun.davies@newsquest.co.uk

Ducks seek to make a splash!

THE newly-formed Deeside Ducks have announced their first signings.

Highly experienced Deeside Dragons player Chris Jones has been confirmed as part of their roster for the new National Ice Hockey League season.

The Ducks are a new team in the North 2 Division for the 2024/25 season and the aim is to provide regular senior hockey for young players coming out of the Deeside junior programme and to act as a stepping stone towards the senior Dragons team.

While the majority of the team will be under-23s, a number of older, more experienced, players are also being added to the squad to bring stability and wisdom into the mix.

Deeside supporters won't need any introduction to Chris Jones who has been a long-term favourite at the North Wales rink.

He was a Flintshire junior player and has enjoyed 19 seasons of senior hockey - mainly with the Flintshire Freeze and Deeside Dragons, but with brief sojourns at Telford and Blackburn as well - and is a veteran of over 460 competitive games at NIHL level.

Jones is joined on the Ducks roster by another Dragons player from last season - Charlie Spridgeon - as well as long standing Deeside favourite Kenny Williams, who has most recently been playing recreational hockey with the Connah's Quay Cobras.

Former Slough Jet Stewart Cutting - another current Cobras player - has also joined the Ducks as a player and assistant coach.

The sport's governing body, England Ice Hockey, allows for players under the age of 23 to "play up" for different teams in order to gain more experience and help with their development.

This arrangement means that promising Deeside junior players will be able to gain experience of senior hockey with the Ducks on a regular basis and also train and play with the Dragons Division One team on suitable occasions.

The first of the junior players who will benefit from playing for the Ducks team this season have also been announced.

The talented trio of 17-year-old Cody Ogden, 16-year-old Daniels Fadejevs and Henry Phillips, also 16, all played regularly for the Deeside under-18 team last season and Ogden also made one

PROMISE: Cody Ogden, Henry Phillips and Daniels Fadejevs, and, below, Kenny Williams (left) and Chris Jones. Pictures: Deeside IHC, Keith / Jenny Davies and Peter Sheffield

appearance for the Dragons.

Ducks' head coach Gary Shaw said: "This Ducks team will be predominantly U23 with at least a third being U19.

"Some older players will be asked to play and their role will be to support the youth of the team and help with their progression.

"The aim is to ultimately push for places in the Dragons senior team and on to higher levels such as England and Premier.

"While winning is the aim of all teams, there are many different ways to win, so we will focus on all aspects required to advance our squad and, if we achieve the win on the scoreboard, it is a bonus for the team."

Wrexham and Flintshire Leader, 17th July 2024 - Page 36

Ducks In The Newspaper For the First Time!

33

Ducks Poems

Guess who's
In the news
Hitting the headlines, cutting a dash –
"The Leader" says they're making a splash!
Deeside Ducks are a very special team –
Helping young ice hockey players to live the dream.

Lucy London, 17th July 2024

Introducing the Deeside Ducks,
We're ice hockey players - we're not quackers,
Nor are we cricket batters.
We shoot with pucks
And we're an exciting new venture.
We play our home games at Deeside Leisure Centre.

Lucy London, 19th July 2024

Alfie Kelly (Photo by Manchester Storm Academy)

23rd July 2024: Deeside Ducks Sign Alfie Kelly

The Deeside Ducks have announced the signing of Alfie Kelly as part of their roster for the new NIHL season.

The 17 year old defenceman is a former Manchester junior and was captain of the Storm Under 18 team last season.

He also made 22 appearances for the Altrincham Aces in the Laidler Division in what was his breakout senior season.

Talking about his move westwards Kelly said

"I am really grateful for the opportunity to come and play for the Deeside Ducks and am looking forward to the coming season."

"I am excited to work with the coaching group and within the pathway for juniors to progress into senior hockey. I played for Altrincham Aces last season and gained some experiences in this league and I am keen to gain more here at Deeside. I can't wait to get started!"

James Parsons, Head Coach of the Deeside Juniors, said of Kelly:

"Alfie came to our open trials in June, and what stood out right away was his fantastic attitude and work ethic."

"Alfie already has a good amount of games played in NIHL 2, which I feel will benefit the team as they enter their first season. Not only that, but Alfie will also get to train and play with our junior team. Welcome, Alfie!"

30th July 2024: Jack Davies

Jack Davies
(Photo by David Tattum)

The Deeside Ducks have announced the signing of Jack Davies to boost their roster for the forthcoming 2024/25 Laidler Division season.

The 19 year old forward is a former Widnes junior and also played for the Manchester Storm Under 18 team during the 2021/22 season.

He has most recently been playing for the Widnes-based Halton Huskies recreational side.

Talking about joining Deeside, Davies said: "I'm excited for the opportunity to play for the Ducks and to develop my game at the senior level"

Ducks Lead Coach Peter Bleackley said of Davies:

"Jack started his career at Widnes and he always stood out as a junior whenever Widnes have played against Deeside."

"He's a good reader of the play and his composure on the puck made Jack a solid pick for us all here."

Luke Wainwright (Photo by Mark Ray)

2nd August 2024: Luke Wainwright

The Deeside Ducks have announced the signing of Luke Wainwright to add to their roster for the forthcoming 2024/25 Laidler Division season.

The 22 year old defenceman is a former Deeside junior and was captain of both the Under 15 and Under 18 Dragons sides.

He has played over 70 competitive matches for Deeside Juniors and is currently a member of the Connah's Quay Cobras recreational team that has won through to the Summer Cup Play offs.

Talking about joining the Ducks, Luke said:

"I'm very excited to be joining this hockey team for the next season and am looking forward to competing at a high level and improving as a player."

Ducks Assistant Coach Stewart Cutting said of Wainwright:

"Players like Luke are exactly what the Ducks team has been created for - junior players who aged out during covid and did not get the opportunity to develop their game in the adult leagues. Now he gets that opportunity."

"The speed and skill he has when moving up the ice, and his work ethic and commitment when defending, make him an asset to the team. I'm looking forward to watching his development over the coming season."

Max And The Ducks

A very dear friend of ours
A successful businessman we got to know -
Often used to say to us
"Always get your Ducks in a row."

And look who's in the news again:
Deeside Ducks!
Hitting the headlines
as though they were pucks.

Lucy London – 27 & 30.07.2024

Ben Roscoe (Photo by My Team Photo)

26ᵗʰ July 2024: Ben Roscoe

The Deeside Ducks have announced the signing of Ben Roscoe to add to their roster for the forthcoming 2024/25 Laidler Division season.

The 17 year old forward is a product of the Deeside junior system and was Alternate Captain for the Dragons Under 18 team last season

Talking about joining the Ducks, Ben said:

"I love ice hockey and I am thrilled to have been given the opportunity to play with this fantastic new senior team, the Deeside Ducks."

"I'm excited to start the season and can't wait to play alongside these talented players."

Assistant Coach Simon Hughes said of Roscoe:

"If you are looking for an example of commitment and enthusiasm for Ice Hockey, then they would be wearing #29. Ben was a latecomer to the sport at 14 and played one season at U16 which was cut short by the pandemic."

"With the reopening of the Den in December 2022, he returned to the ice with gusto for the newly formed U18 squad. The pace of his skill development has been impressive."

"Ben is now a promising addition to the Ducks and also helps out with coaching the Juniors. I look forward to seeing him progress into senior hockey, guided by more experienced players."

"I'm sure he will continue to learn and develop further in a challenging D2 league. There will be some hard lessons and my best piece of advice for this fearless Duckling is 'keep your head up, Roscoe'."

Newspaper Round-Up Story: Four More Sign For Ducks

The Deeside Ducks are continuing to assemble an exciting roster for their debut season in the NIHL Laidler Division and have announced the signing of four more promising young players

The most experienced of the quartet is 22 year old defenceman Kieran Clarkson, who is a former Deeside and Manchester junior and has also played 4 seasons of Laidler Division hockey for Altrincham Aces and Bradford Bulldogs.

In that time he has made some 70 competitive appearances at NIHL level and has most recently been playing for the Connah's Quay Cobras recreational team.

Another Deeside junior, 17 year old Ben Roscoe only has two seasons of hockey under his belt - due to the Covid pandemic lockdowns and the closure of the North Wales rink – but he was an Alternate Captain for the Dragons Under 18 team last season.

The other two players come from further afield and were selected after their participation in the open player trials in June.

17 year old defenceman Alfie Kelly is a former Manchester junior and was captain of the Storm Under 18 team last season. He also made 22 appearances for the Altrincham Aces in the Laidler Division in what was his breakout senior season.

17 year old netminder Callum Preston is a former Widnes, Blackburn and Bradford junior and also played last season for the Manchester Storm Under 18 team.

He already has some NIHL level experience as he dressed for Widnes Wild as a back-up netminder for 4 Moralee Division games in the 2022/23 season and played a 20 minute shift in a North West Cup game, during which he achieved a 6-shot shut out against the Blackburn Hawks.

ve/ SPORT

ICE HOCKEY: SEASON COUNTDOWN

Quartet sign up with the Ducks

THINGS are shaping up nicely for the recently formed Deeside Ducks.

The determined Ducks are continuing to assemble an exciting roster for their debut season in the NIHL Laidler Division and have announced the signing of four more promising young players.

The most experienced of the quartet is 22-year-old defenceman Kieran Clarkson, who is a former Deeside and Manchester junior.

He has also played four seasons of Laidler Division hockey for Altrincham Aces and Bradford Bulldogs.

In that time, he has made some 70 competitive appearances at NIHL level and has most recently been playing for the Connah's Quay Cobras recreational team.

Another Deeside junior, 17-year-old Ben Roscoe, only has two seasons of hockey under his belt - due to the Covid pandemic lockdowns and the closure of the North Wales rink - but he was an alternate captain for Deeside Dragons U16s last season.

The other two players come from further afield and were selected after their participation in the open player trials in June.

Seventeen-year-old defenceman Alfie Kelly is a former Manchester junior and was captain of the Storm U18 team last season.

He also made 22 appearances for the Altrincham Aces in the Laidler Division in what was his breakout senior season.

Netminder Callum Preston, also 17, is a former Widnes, Blackburn and Bradford junior and also played last season for the Manchester Storm U18 team.

He already has some NIHL level experience as he dressed for Widnes Wild as a back-up netminder for four Moralee Division games in the 2022/23

IN THE RANKS: Kieran Clarkson has joined Deeside Ducks.
Picture: MARK RAY

season and played a 20-minute shift in a North West Cup game, during which he achieved a six-shot shut out against the Blackburn Hawks.

People can follow the progress of the new Deeside Ducks team as they prepare for their first season of competition on their Facebook page.

Meanwhile, Deeside Dragons have announced long-time defenceman Billy Perks will be in the ranks for the 2024-25 season.

Perks has been a Dragon since playing for the U16s in 2014, when he was only 13, and since then he has only ever suited up in a Deeside jersey.

Since taking two years out when the team was inactive

6th August 2024: Thomas Milnes

Thomas Milnes
(Photo by Manchester Storm Academy)

The Deeside Ducks have announced the signing of Thomas Milnes to add to their roster for the forthcoming 2024/25 Laidler Division season.

The 17 year old forward is a former Blackburn and Manchester junior player and has over 70 competitive games under his belt at Under 15 to Under 18 level, with 92 goals and 33 assists to his record.

Talking about joining the Ducks, Thomas said:"I am really looking forward to my first season with the Deeside Ducks. I have been playing hockey for 7 years at Manchester Storm and Blackburn Hawks Academy.

"I'm really grateful to have been given the opportunity to be able to play for the club this season for the D2 team and also excited for the great experience that comes with it. I'm ready to give all I can offer and can't wait to see you all at games in the new season."

James Parsons, Head Coach of the Deeside Juniors, said of Milnes: "Thomas also came to our open trial in June, and you could see right away that he had a great skill set and fitted in well with the team. I look forward to seeing how he develops in his first season of senior hockey. Welcome, Thomas!"

9th August:
Heather Clarkson

Heather Clarkson (Photo by Widnes Wild Academy)

The Deeside Ducks have announced the signing of Heather Clarkson to add to their roster for their debut 2024/25 Laidler Division season.

The 18 year old defender is a former Manchester juniors player, was captain of the Manchester Storm Under 16 girls team for two seasons and has also played Women's Elite League hockey for the Hull-based Kingston Diamonds.

Heather spent last season playing for the Widnes Wild Under 18 team. She was also selected as a reserve for the Great Britain women's Under 18 squad that played in the 4 Nations tournament in Spain in November 2023 but did not actually get called up to play.

Talking about joining the Ducks, Heather said:

"I am honoured to get the opportunity to train and play alongside everyone. I feel that it's going to be a good season and I can't wait to see where it goes."

Ducks' Assistant Coach Stewart Cutting said of Clarkson:

"Heather is a bright young hockey player joining from Widnes. She sees the game well and isn't afraid to get stuck in. I am looking forward to seeing this talented individual develop her game further with the Ducks."

Josh Jones (Photo by Drew Brown Official)

13th August: Josh Jones

The Deeside Ducks have announced the signing of Josh Jones to add to their roster for their debut 2024/25 Laidler Division season.

The 20 year old forward is a long term member of the Deeside junior development system and has played for the junior club at every level from Under 10s upwards.

He is one of a number of players who "aged out" of the junior system during the Covid lockdowns and was also affected by the continued closure of the Deeside rink afterwards.

He has most recently been playing for the Deeside based Chester Road Reapers recreational team.

Talking about joining the Ducks, Josh said:

"I played as a Dragons junior from the Under 10s all the way through until Covid hit and we lost the rink. I came back and played for a year of rec hockey for the Reapers at Deeside and now I am a Duck. I cannot wait to get started playing league hockey again."

Ducks' Assistant Coach Simon Hughes said of Jones:

"If you're looking for the epitome of a Deeside Ducks player, it is Josh Jones."

"Coming up through the ranks of the Juniors, his ice hockey career started as an 8 year old icing for the Dragons U10's, highlighted by selection with England U13 showcase. With the reopening of the rink, Josh resorted to recreational hockey with the Chester Road Reapers."

"As a forward with a keen eye for goal, from his preferred position of right wing, he is an agile skater with an unwavering enthusiasm for the sport. I am confident that the coaching team at the Ducks will harness his boundless energy and hone his skill set into a fully rounded member of this new senior NIHL D2 team."

"Josh has ambition to progress to D1 with the Dragons before he's 25 and who knows where his career may peak."

"Selection in the Ducks squad and securing his number 73 means a lot to him personally (chosen by his late Grandmother), so I am looking forward to seeing him develop and progress as a competitive senior player to do the jersey proud."

Newspaper Story: Four More Sign For Ducks

The Deeside Ducks are continuing to assemble an exciting roster for their debut season in the NIHL Laidler Division and have announced the signing of four more promising young players

22 year old defenceman Luke Wainwright is a former Deeside junior and was captain of both the Under 15 and Under 18 Dragons sides.

He has played over 70 competitive matches for Deeside Juniors and is currently a member of the Connah's Quay Cobras recreational team that won through to the Summer Cup Play offs.

17 year old forward Thomas Milnes is a former Blackburn and Manchester junior player and has over 70 competitive games under his belt at Under 15 to Under 18 level, with 92 goals and 33 assists to his record.

19 year old forward Jack Davies is a former Widnes junior and also played for the Manchester Storm Under 18 team during the 2021/22 season. He has most recently been playing for the Widnes-based Halton Huskies recreational side.

Last - but, certainly, not least - 18 year old defender Heather Clarkson is a former Manchester mixed juniors player, was captain of the Manchester Storm Under 16 girls team for two seasons and has also played Women's Elite League hockey for the Hull-based Kingston Diamonds.

Heather spent last season playing for the Widnes Wild Under 18 team. She was also selected as a reserve for the Great Britain women's Under 18 squad that played in the 4 Nations tournament in Spain in November 2023 but did not actually get called up to play.

The Deeside Ducks team will be playing in the Laidler (North 2) Division for their debut NIHL season.

The Laidler Division for this season comprises 10 teams, split into two regional groups of 5 and also has a cup competition.

The NIHL season starts in early September and finalised fixture lists will be published shortly.

Busy time for Deeside duo

DEESIDE DUCKS are continuing to assemble an exciting roster for their debut season in the National Ice Hockey League Laidler Division.

Defenceman Luke Wainwright, 22, is a former Deeside junior and he was captain of both the Deeside Dragons' U15 and U18 sides.

Pictured above, Wainwright has played over 70 competitive matches for Deeside juniors and is currently a member of the Connah's Quay Cobras recreational team that made it through to the Summer Cup play-offs.

Forward Thomas Milnes, 17, is a former Blackburn and Manchester junior player and has over 70 competitive games under his belt at U15-U18 level, with 92 goals and 33 assists to his name.

Nineteen-year-old forward Jack Davies is a former Widnes junior and also played for the Manchester Storm U18 team during the 2021/22 season. He has most recently been playing for the Widnes-based Halton Huskies recreational side.

Meanwhile, 18-year-old defender Heather Clarkson is a former Manchester mixed juniors player, was captain of the Manchester Storm U16 girls team for two seasons and has also played Women's Elite League hockey for the Hull-based Kingston Diamonds.

Clarkson was also selected as a reserve for the Great Britain women's U18 squad that played in the Four Nations tournament in Spain last November.

Deeside Ducks are preparing for their bow in Division Two North.

It comprises of 10 teams, split into two regional groups of five and the division also has a cup competition.

Fixtures for the new Division One North season have also been

Ducks In The Newspaper!

Flintshire & Wrexham Leader (14th August, p34) about the latest Deeside Ducks signings – Luke Wainwright, Thomas Milnes, Jack Davies and Heather Clarkson – as well as a brief intro to the new Laidler Division season.

16th August: Rory Sillery

The Deeside Ducks are pleased to have announced the signing of Rory Sillery to add to their roster for the 2024/25 Laidler Division season.

Rory Sillery (on the right)
(Photo by Paul Breeze)

The 19 year old defenceman is a former Widnes junior player and has recently been playing for the Riverside Raiders recreational team.

Talking about joining the Ducks, Rory said:

"I am honoured to get the opportunity to train and play alongside everyone. I feel that it is going to be a good season and I can't wait to see where it goes."

Deeside Juniors Head Coach James Parsons said of Sillery:

"Rory wasn't able to make it to our trials in June, but he jumped in with us for a session and fit right in with the team. Rory has a great work rate and can play both forward and defence, which will be a massive help for the team this season. He is another player who has joined us with a great attitude and the drive to transition to league hockey. Welcome, Rory!"

Michael Speare (Photo by Peter Sheffield)

20th August: Michale Speare

The Deeside Ducks have announced the signing of Michael Speare to add to their roster for their debut 2024/25 Laidler Division season.

The 22 year old defender is a long term Deeside junior from Under 10s upwards and was an Alternate Captain for the Dragons Under 15 and Under 18 teams

He made his senior debut last season with the Bradford Bulldogs in the Laidler Division, making 24 appearances and scoring 11 goals and 6 assists.

Talking about joining the Ducks, Michael said:

I am excited to be back at the Den where my career began, following an excellent season with the Bradford Bulldogs where I developed so much as a senior player. I am looking forward to the coming season and to growing and evolving my game with the Ducks. I am eager to be part of the exciting new team dynamic. I relish this opportunity and will strive to make this team the very best it can be.

Commenting on Speare's signing, Ducks' Lead Coach Peter Bleackley said:

"Mikey started at Deeside juniors as an U10 and has always had a strong work rate. He was our Junior Captain and last season he made the step up to Division 2 playing for Bradford Bulldogs under the watchful eye of their head coach Andy Brown.

He is a solid player with a great attitude and I am expecting lots of points from Mikey this season.

George Spofforth
(Photo by Lewis Cleveland)

23rd August:
George Spofforth

The Deeside Ducks have announced the signing of George Spofforth to add to their roster for their debut 2024/25 Laidler Division season.

The 22 year old defenceman is a former Dragons Under 18 player and has most recently been playing for the Chester Road Reapers recreational team.

Talking about joining the Ducks, George said:

"I have played hockey since U18s but it was cut short due to Covid. I went on to play a year at Widnes and a year of rec but I'm now ready to get back to League."

Commenting on Spofforth's signing, Ducks' Lead Coach Peter Bleackley said:

"George is a product of our junior club. He is always hard working and a good skater and penalty killer. I am looking forward to working with him this season."

Newspaper Story: Ducks Roster Nears Completion

The Deeside Ducks' playing roster for their debut season in the NIHL Laidler Division is nearing completion following the signing of four more promising young players.

20 year old forward Josh Jones is a long term member of the Deeside junior development system and has played for the junior club at every level from Under 10s upwards.

He is one of a number of players who "aged out" of the junior system during the Covid lockdowns and was also affected by the continued closure of the Deeside rink afterwards. He has most recently been playing for the Deeside based Chester Road Reapers recreational team.

22 year old Michael Speare defender is another long term Deeside junior and was an Alternate Captain for the Dragons Under 15 and Under 18 teams. He made his senior debut last season with the Bradford Bulldogs in the Laidler Division, making 24 appearances and scoring 11 goals and 6 assists.

19 year old defenceman Rory Sillery is a former Widnes junior academy player and has recently been playing for the Widnes-based Riverside Raiders recreational team.

22 year old defenceman George Spofforth is a former Dragons Under 18 player and – like Josh Jones - has also been playing for the Chester Road Reapers recreational team.

The opening fixtures of the new season have now been announced and the Deeside Ducks will play their first ever match at home to Kingston (Hull) Sharks on Saturday 14th September at Deeside Leisure Centre – 5pm face off.

Ducks Poems

Don't forget to drop the puck
Not the Duck …
To be a Deeside Duck
You need a heap of luck
And a great deal of pluck

Lucy London, 10th August 2024

Deeside Ducks are quacking on compiling their Team List
Here's a reminder of why the Deeside Ducks Ice Hockey
team exists -
They're a stepping stone for youngsters coming through
The Deeside Junior Development System – helping them
to
Progress to higher levels of ice hockey when they are
good enough.

Lucy London, 11th August 2024

There's not a great deal of space
Between a Duck and a hard place –
That's the ice pad on which they skate
For the season to start the Ducks cannot wait …
Deeside Ducks have added to their roster with Michael
Speare
Keep up with all the Duck news via Facebook here:
https://www.facebook.com/profile.php

Lucy London, 27.08.2024

First Public Outiung For Ducks
(Facebook-only post due to short notice)

Members of the new Deeside Ducks squad will be appearing in a public "on ice" session this Saturday 31st August at Deeside Leisure Centre - 5pm start.

The event will take the format of an "informal scrimmage" – along with a group of Deeside-based rec players and a few other personalities - and this will be an ideal opportunity for fans to see the Ducks playing together before their NIHL Laidler Division season debut.

Admission is free for all spectators and doors open at 4.15pm

Mackenzie Wilkes (Photo by RDG Digital) & Deacon Wilkes (Photo by Angela Wilkes)

30th August 2024: Ducks Sign Two Sets Of Brothers

Following a relatively quiet week at Ducksmedia HQ, we now have not ONE but FOUR – yes, FOUR! - player signings to announce in advance of tomorrow's keenly anticipated public "On-Ice" session at Deeside Leisure Centre.

All four players are products of the highly respected Deeside junior development system and they are two sets of brothers!

20 year old forward Mackenzie Wilkes is a former Deeside junior player who "aged out" during the Covid closure period. He has recently been playing for the Connah's Quay Cobras and was a member of the successful squad who were runners up in the Summer

Classic Cup and winners of the Sheffield RecFest Plate this summer.

Mackenzie will be wearing shirt number 19 for the Ducks this season.

His younger brother is 16 year old defenceman Deacon Wilkes who played for the Dragons Under 16 and Under 18 teams last season and was an Alternate Captain for the U16s. Deacon is the youngest member of the Duck's squad for this season and will wear number 13.

The other pair of brothers are the Morgan brothers Louis and James.

Despite being only 23, defenceman Louis Morgan already has an impressive senior career having played Moralee Division hockey for 4 seasons with the Dragons senior team.

Add to that brief stints with Telford Tigers 2, Dragons 2 and the 2018/19 season with the senior Dragons in the Laidler Division and Louis has over 80 NIHL appearances to his record. Louis will wear shirt number 8 for the Ducks this season

His older brother James Morgan – a 27 year old defenceman - played for the Dragons juniors for a number of years and was captain of the Under 20 team during the 2016/17 season.

James took a break from playing for a few years but is pleased to be back in action with the Ducks for their debut NIHL season. He will be wearing number 31.

Louis Morgan (Photo by Deeside Dragons)

DON'T FORGET – you can see the Ducks for the first time tomorrow when they take part in a public "On-Ice" session at Deeside Leisure Centre. Admission is free for all spectators. Doors open at 4.15 and the fun starts at 5pm.

#keepquacking #fowlnotfoul

Deeside Ducks Team – 31st August 2024 (Photo by Paul Breeze)

Back Row: James Morgan, Gary Dixon, Charlie Spridgeon, Chris Jones, Kieran Clarkson, Callum Preston, Heather Clarkson, Paul Jones, Luke Wainwright. Front Row: Michael Speare, Mackenzie Wilkes, Jack Davies, Rory Sillery, Cody Ogden, Josh Jones, Ben Roscoe, Deacon Wilkes.

31st August 2024: Deeside Ducks 6 – Not Ducks 8

The Deeside Ducks made their first public appearance on Saturday as fans were invited to watch an "On Ice Session" at Deeside Leisure Centre.

Members of the Ducks squad were joined on the ice by a group of local recreational players and a number of former Dragons to bring an air of "realism" to the training session as they continue to prepare for their debut league season.

This wasn't actually a "game" as such (for various legal reasons...), so the first ever Ducks goal wasn't scored by Josh Jones at 13.36 and subsequent goals weren't scored by Charlie Spridgeon (2), Jack Davies (2) and Chris Jones (1).

And Josh Jones, Kieran Clarkson and Mackenzie Wilkes didn't get an assist each, either.

But, looking on the bright side, this means that the 8 goals that the "Not Ducks" opposition team scored also didn't happen – so all is good at the Pond!

The Ducks' first league game is at home to Kingston Sharks on Saturday 14th September at Deeside Leisure Centre, 5pm face off.

Not Ducks Team (Photo by Paul Breeze)

Not in order: Leo Hyman (NM), James Parsons, Steve Fellows, Sam Plant, Chris Keating, Oli Howells, James Shaw, Anrich Landmann, Brad Commins, Jared Dickinson, Brad Bannon, Tomas Mitrik, Oli Fellows, Libor Krempasky, plus 3 more...

ENGLISH ICE HOCKEY ASSOCIATION LIMITED
OFFICIAL GAME SHEET

Not-a-Game Details

Home Team:	Deeside Ducks
Away Team:	Not Ducks
Date:	31st August 2024 Time: 5.00pm
Venue:	Deeside Leisure Centre
Competition:	Not A Game

Period Scores	1	2	3	OT	Tot
Ducks	1	2	3		6
Not Ducks	4	2	2		8

Penalty Minutes	1	2	3	OT	Tot
Ducks	0	0	0		0
Not Ducks	2	0	0		2

Netminders	TOI	1	2	3	OT	Tot
Jones (DEE)	30.15	10	0	3		16
Preston (DEE)	29.45	0	12	6		18
Hyman (NOT)	60.00	12	7	10		29

Time Outs:	Home:	Away:

Referee:	
Signature:	Disc:
Timekeeper:	Dave Billingsley
Scorer:	Paul Breeze
Goal Judge:	David Jones
Goal Judge:	Eve Brown
Penalty Box (H):	Dan Roscoe
Penalty Box (A):	Ellie Baker
Attendance:	

Deeside Ducks Players

NM	#	Player	G	A	PIM
NM	1	Paul Jones			
	3	James Morgan	2		
	4	Charlie Spridgeon			
	5	Heather Clarkson			
	6	Joshua Jones	1		
	7	Chris Jones	1		
	9	Gary Dixon			
	12	Michael Speare			
	13	Deacon Wilkes*			
	14	Jack Davies	2		
	15	Rory Sillery			
	17	Kieran Clarkson		1	
	18	Luke Wainwright			
	19	Mackenzie Wilkes		1	
NM	20	Callum Preston			
	29	Ben Roscoe*			
	40	Cody Ogden*			

Ducks Goals

Time	Type	G	A	A
13.36	E	6	19	
30.00	E	4	17	
36.25	E	14		
38.03	E	4		
52.32	E	14	6	
58.29	E	7		

Ducks Penalties

No	PIM	Offence	Given	Start	End

Not Ducks Players

NM	#	Player	G	A	PIM
NM	1	Leo Hyman (NM)			
	2	James Parsons			
	6	Steve Fellows			
	8	Sam Plant	1		
	10	Chris Keating	2		
	11	Oli Howells			
	14	James Shaw		1	
	15	Anrich Landmann	1		
	16	Brad Commins			
	17	Jared Dickinson	1		
	18	Brad Bannon		1	
	20	Tomas Minik	1		2
		Oli Fellows	1		
		Libor Krempasky	1		
	22	Player?			
		Player?			
		Player?			

Not Ducks Goals

Time	Type	G	A	A
6.01	E	10		
15.58	E	10		
16.14	E	Libor	14	
17.38	E	8		
24.00	E	22	18	
32.32	E	15		
50.00	E	17		
56.56	E	20		

Not Ducks Penalties

No	PIM	Offence	Given	Start	End
20	2	TRIP	9.37	9.37	11.37

Not a gamesheet – 31st August 2024

Condensed Report For Newspaper

The Deeside Ducks made their first public appearance on Saturday as fans were invited to watch an "On Ice Session" at Deeside Leisure Centre.

Members of the Ducks squad were joined on the ice by a group of local recreational players and a number of former Dragons to bring an air of realism to the training session as they continue to prepare for their debut league season.

The Ducks further strengthened their roster during the week with the signing of 4 new players – all of whom are products of the highly respected Deeside junior development system and are, indeed, two sets of brothers!

20 year old forward Mackenzie Wilkes is a former Deeside junior player who "aged out" during the Covid closure period and has recently been playing for the Connah's Quay Cobras recreational team while his younger brother - 16 year old defenceman Deacon Wilkes - played for the Dragons Under 16 and Under 18 teams last season.

The other pair of brothers are the Morgan brothers, Louis and James.

Despite being only 23, defenceman Louis Morgan already has an impressive senior career having played Moralee Division hockey for 4 seasons with the Dragons senior team, while his older brother James Morgan – a 27 year old defenceman - played for the Dragons juniors for a number of years before taking a break from the sport.

Deeside Ducks

Laidler Division Fixtures - Season 2024/25

14th Sept: home v Kingston	15th Dec: away @ Billingham
21st Sept: away @ Coventry*	**21st Dec: home v Altrincham**
28th Sept: away @ Kingston	4th Jan: away @ Sutton
29th Sept: home v Sheffield	**5th Jan: home v Altrincham***
5th Oct: home v Bradford*	12th Jan: away @ Bradford
20th Oct: away @ Sheffield	26th Jan: away @ Telford
26th Oct: away @ Telford*	**1st Feb: home v Sutton**
3rd Nov: away @ Bradford*	2nd Feb: away @ Altrincham
17th Nov: home v Telford*	**8th Feb: home v Nottingham**
23rd Nov: away @ Coventry	**16th Feb: home v Coventry**
30th Nov: home v Coventry*	**1st Mar: home v Billingham**
8th Dec: away @ Altrincham*	**8th Mar: home v Telford**
14th Dec: home v Bradford	23rd Mar: away @ Nottingham

Home games face off at 5pm / doors open 4.15
*Matches marked * are combined league and cup games*

3rd September 2024: Deeside Ducks Laidler Division Fixtures Announced

The Deeside Ducks have announced their full list of Laidler Division fixtures for their first ever season on NIHL ice hockey.

The first league game is on Saturday 14th September at home to Kingston Sharks and the regular NIHL season runs through until March, finishing up with a Play Off Finals weekend in April.

Ducks home games face off at 5pm at Deeside Leisure Centre with doors opening at 4.15.

Ticket prices are: Adults - £7.00, Children - £5.00, Dragons season ticket holders - £5.00 (must show season ticket to qualify), Concessions - £5.00, Junior Dragons - free entry with Junior Dragons pass.

ICE HOCKEY: SEASON SET TO START

LOOKING FORWARD: Deeside Ducks. Picture: Paul Breeze

Ryan remains with Dragons

A KEY defensive unit is remaining with the Deeside Dragons ahead of the big skate-off.

The club has announced that Ryan Brauler Jones is to remain with the seam for the forthcoming season, which gets underway this weekend.

Action opens for the Dragons with Saturday's Welsh Cup showdown at home to Cardiff Fire on Saturday, followed by Sunday's league opener at home to the Nottingham Lions.

Brauler Jones' prowess in defence is marked by his sharp tactical play and consistent performances on the ice.

Meanwhile, the Dragons have announced the departure of Dalton Thompson ahead of the start to the season.

Dalton signed for the Dragons last season on a two-way contract with the Altrincham Aces and he proved to be a great fit for the Deeside team.

The newly-formed Deeside Ducks made their first public appearance last week as fans were invited to watch an on-ice session at Deeside Leisure Centre.

Members of the Ducks squad were joined on the ice by a group of local recreational players and a number of former Dragons to bring an air of realism to the training session as they continue to prepare for their debut league season.

The Ducks further strengthened their roster during the week with the signing of four new players - all of whom are products of the highly respected Deeside junior development system and are, indeed, two sets of brothers!

Twenty-year-old forward Mackenzie Wilkes is a former Deeside junior player who "aged out" during the Covid closure period and has recently been playing for the Connah's Quay Cobras recreational team while his younger brother, 16-year-old defenceman Deacon Wilkes, played for the Dragons U16 and U18 teams last season.

The other pair of siblings are the Morgan brothers - Louis and James.

Despite being only 23, defenceman Louis Morgan already has an impressive senior career having played Moralee Division hockey for four seasons with the Dragons senior team, while his older brother James Morgan, a 21-year-old defenceman, played for the Dragons' juniors for a number of years before taking a break from the sport.

In what has been a busy spell for the side, the Ducks have also announced the acquisition of a number of other players.

Twenty-year-old forward Josh Jones is a long-term member of the Deeside junior development system and has played for the junior club at every level from U10s upwards.

He is one of a number of players who "aged out" of the junior system during the Covid lockdowns and was also affected by the continued closure of the Deeside rink afterwards.

He has most recently been playing for the Deeside-based Chester Blatt Reapers recreational team.

Defender Michael Spears, 22, is another long-term Deeside junior and was an alternate captain for the Dragons U15 and U18 teams.

He made his senior debut last season with the Bradford Bulldogs in the Laidler Division, making 24 appearances and scoring 11 goals and six assists.

Defenceman Rory Sibery, 19, is a former Widnes junior academy player and has recently been playing for the Widnes-based Riverside Raiders, while 25-year-old defenceman George Spofforth is a former Dragons U18s player and he has also been playing for the Chester Bratt Reapers recreational team.

Ducks' first league game is at home to Kington Sharks on Saturday, September 14 (6pm face-off).

Josh gets call at The Oval

LEICESTERSHIRE bowler Josh Hull will make his England Test debut against Sri Lanka at The Oval.

The 20-year-old left-arm seamer will replace Matthew Potts for tomorrow's third Test.

Hull, who made his first class debut last year, was added to the squad ahead of the second Test following an injury to Mark Wood.

England will be looking to complete a series clean sweep after winning the opening two matches.

Pictured above, Hull, who stands 6ft 7in and is capable of generating good pace, has made only 10 first-class appearances, with his 16 wickets coming at 62.75.

However, his rising stock was confirmed when he earned an England Lions call-up to face Sri Lanka in a pre-Test warm-up last month, taking five wickets, including experienced duo Angelo Mathews and Dinesh Chandimal.

Stand-in England skipper Ollie Pope said: "When you're 6ft 7in and you can get it down, pushing up to the 85-90mph mark with a bit of swing and the left-arm angle, there's a lot to like."

After a keenly-fought first

Test at Old Trafford, England wrapped up the series with a comprehensive 190-run victory at Lord's on Sunday.

England are now just one win away from completing a clean sweep of home Test triumphs for the first time since 2004, having moved on emphatically from a disappointing 4-1 defeat by India in the winter.

Dom Sibley and Sean Curran shared a stand of 95 as Surrey reached finals day with a five-wicket win over Durham in the T20 Blast.

Sibley hit 67 in 46 balls while Curran added 52 in 34, including four sixes, as the hosts chased down a target of 163 with 12 balls to spare.

In tonight's quarter-final, Northamptonshire host Somerset.

Ducks In The Newspaper!

There's another great Deeside Ducks story in today's Flintshire & Wrexham Leader (5th September 2024 – page 35), looking at the public "on Ice" session at the weekend, plus the signings of the Wilkes and Morgan brothers.

You can read the story in full on the highly informative grass roots "Ice Hockey Review" website: http://www.icehockeyreview.co.uk/2024/09/deeside-ducks-first-public-appearance.html

Gary Dixon playing for Flintshire Freeze (Photo by Peter Sheffield)

6th September 2024: Gary Dixon

The Deeside Ducks have announced the signing of Gary Dixon to further boost their squad for their debut 2024/25 Laidler Division season.

The 38 year old forward is a highly experienced player who has spent most of his 22 year senior career at Deeside playing with the Flintshire Freeze and the Dragons.

Dixon has played some 320 competitive games at NIHL level, scoring 49 goals and 138 assists and picking up 488 penalty minutes.

He was part of the Dragons team that won the Laidler Division league and Play Off double in the 2015/16 season and last season he played 20 league games in the Moralee Division helping the team to a well-earned 4th place in the league table.

Talking about joining the Ducks, Gary said:

"One of my main reasons for supporting this exciting project is to help the club create a pathway for our home-grown generation of junior Dragons players to progress into senior hockey."

"I feel this has been lost over the last few years, though not due to any fault of its own, and the club is currently thriving as a whole under Snip (Junior Head Coach James Parsons)."

"There has been a lot of positive feedback regarding the club's name and branding so I am looking forward to seeing how far this club can grow. It's time to play two-way hockey!"

Commenting on Dixon's signing, Deeside Juniors Head Coach James Parsons said:

"Dicko brings a wealth of experience not only on the ice but also in the dressing room. He has played in N1 and N2 for many years, and I am looking forward to him sharing his experience and guidance with the younger players. Welcome to the team, Ham!"

The Ducks' first league game is at home to Kingston Sharks this Saturday 14th September at Deeside Leisure Centre, 5pm face off.

then scored his first Deeside goal in the closing four minutes to confirm victory.

Assistant head coach Matt Compton said: "It was good to see the team celebrate when Jayson got his first goal.

"He is another young guy working hard."

Deeside Ducks have announced the signing of Gary Dixon to further boost their squad for their debut 2024/25 Laidler Division season.

The 38-year-old forward is a highly experienced player who has spent most of his 22-year senior career at Deeside playing with the Flintshire Freeze and the Dragons.

Dixon has played some 320 competitive games at NIHL level, scoring 49 goals and 138 assists and picking up 488 penalty minutes.

He was part of the Dragons' team that won the Laidler Division league and play-off double in the 2015/16 season and last season, he played 20 league games in the Moralee Division, helping the Deeside team to a well-earned fourth place in the league.

Deeside Ducks' first league game is at home to Kingston Sharks on Saturday (5pm).

Deeside Ducks In The Newspaper!

There is a small piece about the Ducks in today's newspaper (Flintshire & Wrexham leader, 10th September p36) about the recent signing of Gary Dixon.

You can read the full story on www.icehockeyreview.co.uk

Callum Preston receives the MVP award from sponsor Richard Beevers (Photo by Paul Breeze)

Saturday 14th September 2024 – NIHL Laidler Division
Deeside Ducks 4 - Kingston Sharks 5

The Deeside Ducks put in a plucky performance in their first ever league game, only narrowly losing out 4-5 to the Kingston Sharks at Deeside Leisure Centre on Saturday.

The Ducks team has been set up this season to provide a stepping stone between the highly regarded Deeside junior set up and the senior Dragons side and comprises mainly younger players with a few older heads to offer experience and stability. As such, the game saw NIHL debuts for 12 players who had never played at this level before.

Before the face-off, there was a minute's applause in memory of Ken Taggart - the former player, referee and long time Chairman of the English Ice Hockey Association – who died earlier in the week at the age of 78.

Once the puck had dropped, the visitors were quickest out of the blocks and took an early lead after just 42 seconds. However, the Ducks managed to settle down and their first ever league goal came on 12 minutes 32 seconds scored by Thomas Milnes, assisted by Charlie Spridgeon.

The score remained 1-1 at the first period break and although they had been outshot by almost 3 to 1, the Ducks had given a good account of themselves.

The second period saw 2 unanswered goals for the Sharks and they edged further ahead early in the third period to lead 1-5 with 15 minutes left to play.

The Ducks' second goal of the game came on 50 minutes with team captain Chris Jones firing in a delayed penalty strike punishing a Sharks tripping call and this served to spark a late Deeside fightback.

Further goals for the Ducks – from Cody Ogden on 54 minutes and the same player on 57 minutes - drew the home side to within one goal of their opponents.

Both teams called timeouts in the latter stages to discuss last ditch tactics, wrenching up the tension around the rink, but there was no further scoring and the game finished 4-5 to the Kingston Sharks.

The MVP awards were donated and presented by Mr Richard Beevers, CEO of Customer Plus - who are one of the Ducks' team sponsors for the season.

These went to Joe Gray for Kingston and Deeside netminder Callum Preston who managed to turn away an incredible 42 of the 47shots that he faced over the 60 minutes.

Speaking about the game afterwards, Head Coach Gary Shaw said:

"For the first competitive game for the newly formed Ducks, the team performed well together. They had to overcome not really knowing each other's game as they have been on the ice for less than 2 months and only 1 practice game. The experienced players in the team helped the junior players at this level."

"As the game progressed, they made a few mistakes, which we expected to happen, and we can see as a coaching team what we need to focus on to be able to build on this performance. We have a good base to build on, and as the team grows together from this strong performance, we should see that they will have a good competitive season."

The Ducks now have two away games – away to Coventry NIHL Blaze this Saturday 21st September in a combined league and cup game and then to Kingston in Hull the following Saturday.

They are next at home on Sunday 29th September when they take on the Sheffield Titans at Deeside Leisure Centre, 5pm face off.

Ducks Line-Up v Kingston Sharks: Paul Jones (NM), Charlie Spridgeon, Michael Speare, Louis Morgan, Gary Dixon, Stewart Cutting, Henry Phillips, Thomas Milnes, Kieran Clarkson, Heather Clarkson, Ben Roscoe, Louis Ellwood, Cody Ogden, Callum Preston (NM), Chris Jones, Joshua Jones, George Spofforth, Kenny Williams, Rory Sillery, Luke Wainwright, James Morgan, Jack Davies

LIKE US ON FACEBOOK facebook.com/Lead

MVP: Ducks' Callum Preston with Richard Beevers. Picture: Paul Breeze

Deeside Ducks put in a plucky performance in their first ever league game, only narrowly losing out 5-4 to the Kingston Sharks at Deeside Leisure Centre.

The Ducks' first ever league goal in Division Two came on 12 minutes and 32 seconds, and it was scored by Thomas Milnes, assisted by Charlie Spridgeon and the score stood at 1-1 at the first interval.

Two unanswered goals in the second period, plus a couple more early in the third, saw the Sharks leading 5-1 with a quarter-of-an-hour left to play.

A strike from team captain Chris Jones and two from Cody Ogden drew the home side to within one goal of their opponents, but there was no further scoring in the tense finale.

The MVP awards were donated and presented by Richard Beevers, CEO of Customer Plus - one of the Ducks' team sponsors for the season - and they went to Joe Gray (Kingston) and Deeside netminder Callum Preston.

The Ducks now have two away games to look forward to in the league and they are next at home on September 29 when they take on the Sheffield Titans.

Deeside Ducks In The Newspaper!

There is a short report in today's newspaper (Flintshire & Wrexham leader, 17th September p37) about the Ducks' league debut match against Kingston, along with a nice mention of team sponsor Richard Beevers of Customer Plus.

Deeside Ducks' First League Game

An excellent result for your first game Ducks, so three cheers
For all the Ducks Team, their coaches and those amazing volunteers.
The MVP awards were donated and presented by Mr Richard Beevers
CEO of Customer Plus - one of the Ducks team sponsors for the season.

Lucy London, 15.09.2024

Deeside Ducks 4-5 Kingston Sharks

North 2 Regular Season, Saturday 14th September
Game 004

Deeside Ducks (0-0-0-1)   (1-1-0-0) Kingston Sharks

SCORING SUMMARY

G	Per	Time	Score	Team	Goal Scorer	Assist	Assist	Str
1	1	0:42	0-1	KIN	Cain Taylor (1)	Chris Hogarth (1)		E
2	1	12:41	1-1	DEE	Thomas Milnes (1)	Charlie Spridgeon (1)		DP
3	2	25:25	1-2	KIN	Chris Hogarth (2)	Cain Taylor (1)	Tom Humphries (1)	E
4	2	35:20	1-3	KIN	Tom Humphries (2)	Chris Hogarth (2)	Cain Taylor (2)	E
5	3	42:23	1-4	KIN	Joe Gray (1)	Ethan Whitham (1)		E
6	3	46:12	1-5	KIN	Ellis Martin (1)	Chris Hogarth (3)		E
7	3	50:53	2-5	DEE	Chris Jones (1)	Stewart Cutting (1)	Ben Roscoe (1)	SH
8	3	54:32	3-5	DEE	Louis Ellwood (1)	Thomas Milnes (1)	Chris Jones (1)	PP
9	3	57:32	4-5	DEE	Louis Ellwood (2)	Henry Phillips (1)	Louis Morgan (1)	E

PENALTY SUMMARY

DEESIDE DUCKS							KINGSTON SHARKS					
#	Per	Time	Player	PIM	Penalty		#	Per	Time	Player	PIM	Penalty
1	1	3:07	Ben Roscoe	2	Cross Checking		1	1	3:07	Chirs Hogarth	2	High Sticks
2	1	8:34	Thomas Milnes	2	Cross Checking		2	1	12:41	Ellis Martin	0	Tripping
3	1	12:26	Gary Dixon	2	Slashing		3	2	40:00	Joe Gray	2	Cross Checking
4	3	50:44	Kenneth Williams	2	Cross Checking		4	3	53:39	Eden Cooper	2	Charging
5	3	57:43	Chris Jones	2	Cross Checking		5	3	57:39	Cain Taylor	2	Elbowing

TOT (PN-PIM) 5-10	TOT (PN-PIM) 4-8
Power Plays (Goals-Opp) 1-3	Power Plays (Goals-Opp) 0-4

TEAM SUMMARY

		DEESIDE DUCKS	G	A	P	PN	PIM
1	NM	Callum Preston					
2	NM	Paul Jones					
3	D	Keiron Clarkson					
4	F	Charlie Spridgeon		1	1		
5	F	Michael Speare					
7	D	Kenneth Williams				1	2
8	D	Louis Morgan		1	1		
9	F	Gary Dixon				1	2
10	F	Stewart Cutting		1	1		
11	F	Josh Jones					
12	D	Henry Phillips		1	1		
13	F	Louis Ellwood	2		2		
14	F	Thomas Milnes	1	1	2	1	2
16	D	Chris Jones	1	1	2	1	2
17	D	Goerge Spofforth					
20	D	Heather Clarkson					
29	F	Ben Roscoe		1	1	1	2
40	F	Cody Ogden					
62	F	Jack Davies					
91	D	Rory Sillery					
98	D	Luke Wainwright					
	D	James Morgan					
		Team Penalty					
		TEAM TOTALS	4	7	11	5	10

		KINGSTON SHARKS	G	A	P	PN	PIM
1	NM	Evan Byron-Bates					
2	D	Eden Cooper				1	2
5	F	Gavin Tidy					
6	F	Jack Hayward					
11	D	Lewis Fenwick					
20	F	Cain Taylor	1	2	3	1	2
25	F	Tom Humphries	1	1	2		
33	D	Jenson Hardy					
57	D	Ellis Martin	1		1		
65	D	Ethan Whitham		1	1		
75	F	MacKenzie Barker					
84	F	Joe Gray	1		1	1	2
91	F	Chris Hogarth	1	3	4	1	2
92	F	Liam Archer					
93	F	Kyle Mitchell-Quinn					
96	NM	Tim Lyons					
		Team Penalty					
		TEAM TOTALS	5	7	12	4	8

GOALTENDER SUMMARY

DEESIDE DUCKS		TOI	1	2	3	OT	TOT
			Goals-Shots Against				
1	Callum Preston	60:00	1-15	2-20	2-9		5-44
2	Paul Jones						
	Empty Net						

KINGSTON SHARKS		TOI	1	2	3	OT	TOT
			Goals - Shots Against				
1	Evan Byron-Bates	60:00	1-5	0-8	3-12		4-25
96	Tim Lyons						
	Empty Net						

Source: NIHLStats.wordpress.com (Box Scores)
Note: the stats here incorrectly credit Louis Ellwood with two goals
which were actually scored by #40 Cody Ogden

Deeside Ducks warming up for their first away game at Coventry
(Photo by Maxine Roscoe)

Saturday 21st September – NIHL Laidler Division
Coventry NIHL Blaze 13 – Deeside Ducks 1

The Deeside Ducks had a difficult time on their first ever away trip – losing 13-1 to a highly organised Coventry Blaze side on Saturday.

Continuing their policy of encouraging young talent and providing a stepping stone into senior league hockey, the Ducks gave NIHL debuts to three more promising players – Mackenzie Wilkes, Liam Yarwood and 16-year old Deacon Wilkes.

Deeside found themselves up against it right from the start and were 3-0 down by the end of the first period. It was 8-0 after two periods and they were 12-0 down by the time Michael Speare scored their first ever away goal in the third period.

The netminding partnership of Callum Preston and Paul Jones were kept busy all night but managed to keep out 55 of the 68 shots that they faced between them. Deacon Wilkes was named the Ducks' Most Valuable Player (MVP) for the match.

After the game, lead coach Peter Bleackley said:

"I'm not going to make any excuses. We just didn't gel as a team last night. We've lots of areas to work on in training and I am putting this down to a bad day at the office. Coventry were a well organised team and played good simple hockey from the start. They outworked us and took every opportunity and capitalised on it."

"We will dust ourselves off and the team are looking forward to this weekend. It is early days for us all as a new development team and we just need to bring to the games the energy and competitive levels that we have at training."

The Ducks have another away game this Saturday 28th September when they go to Hull and back to face the Kingston Sharks, who they lost very narrowly to 4-5 in their first game of the season. They are then at home on Sunday to Sheffield Titans at Deeside Leisure Centre, 5pm face off.

Coventry NIHL Blaze 13-1 Deeside Ducks

North 2 League and Cup, Saturday 21st September
Game 011

Coventry NIHL Blaze (2-0-0-0) (0-0-0-2) Deeside Ducks

SCORING SUMMARY

G	Per	Time	Score	Team	Goal Scorer	Assist	Assist	Str
1	1	8:29	1-0	COV	Charles Coney (1)	Jordan Stokes (1)	Arthur Brookes (1)	PP
2	1	9:23	2-0	COV	Oliver Dixon (1)	Harrison Sumner (1)		E
3	1	19:32	3-0	COV	Jamie Lewis (1)	Daniel Upton (1)	Ethan Wheeldon (2)	E
4	2	20:41	4-0	COV	Jordan Stokes (1)	Tom Brooke-Smith (1)		E
5	2	27:03	5-0	COV	Oliver Harris (2)	Charles Coney (1)	Daniel Kent (1)	E
6	2	35:28	6-0	COV	Charles Coney (2)			E
7	2	38:46	7-0	COV	Kyle Nash (2)	Oliver Harris (2)	Daniel Kent (2)	E
8	2	39:12	8-0	COV	Kyle Nash (3)	Oliver Harris (3)	Daniel Kent (3)	E
9	3	40:32	9-0	COV	Connor Mellett (2)	Harrison Sumner (2)	Oliver Harris (4)	E
10	3	40:45	10-0	COV	Ethan Wheeldon (1)			E
11	3	42:29	11-0	COV	Kyle Nash (4)	Oliver Harris (5)		E
12	3	53:17	11-1	DEE	Michael Speare (1)	Keiron Clarkson (1)		E
13	3	57:08	12-1	COV	Jordan Stokes (2)	Ryan James (1)	Jamie Lewis (1)	E
14	3	58:45	13-1	COV	Oliver Dixon (2)	Connor Mellett (2)		E

PENALTY SUMMARY

COVENTRY NIHL BLAZE						DEESIDE DUCKS				
#	Per	Time	Player	PIM	Penalty	#	Per	Time	Player	PIM	Penalty
1	1	14:32	Ashton Rudkin	2	Interference	1	1	8:16	Josh Jones	2	Tripping
2	2	31:20	Joel Gavigan	2	Cross Checking	2	2	22:15	Keiron Clarkson	2	Holding
3						3	3	45:34	James Morgan	2	Elbowing
			TOT (PN-PIM) 2-4						TOT (PN-PIM) 3-6		
			Power Plays (Goals-Opp) 1-3						Power Plays (Goals-Opp) 0-2		

TEAM SUMMARY

COVENTRY NIHL BLAZE			G	A	P	PN	PIM
5	D	Jordan Stokes	2	1	3		
8	F	Ryan James		1	1		
9	F	Jamie Lewis	1	1	2		
12	F	Harrison Sumner		2	2		
15	D	Reuben Sweenie-Fuller					
18	D	Max Parham					
19	F	Tom Brooke-Smith		1	1		
20	F	Oliver Dixon	2		2		
24	F	Ethan Wheeldon	1	1	2		
25	F	Daniel Kent		3	3		
34	NM	Hayden Laverick					
37	F	Connor Mellett	1	1	2		
39	NM	Joel Bearman					
49	D	Will Kibkalo					
50	F	Ashton Rudkin				1	2
57	F	Daniel Upton		1	1		
59	F	Oliver Harris	1	4	5		
70	F	Kyle Nash	3		3		
87	F	Arthur Brookes		1	1		
88	D	Charles Coney	2	1	3		
93	F	Sam Prosser					
95	D	Joel Gavigan				1	2
		Team Penalty					
		TEAM TOTALS	13	18	31	2	4

DEESIDE DUCKS			G	A	P	PN	PIM
2	NM	Paul Jones					
4	F	Charlie Spridgeon					
5	F	Michael Speare	1		1		
10	F	Stewart Cutting					
18	D	George Spofforth					
19	F	Mackenzie Wilkes					
20	F	Thomas Milnes					
21	D	Keiron Clarkson		1	1	1	2
25	F	Liam Yarwood					
27	D	Heather Clarkson					
29	F	Ben Roscoe					
31	D	James Morgan				1	2
34	F	Louis Ellwood					
40	F	Cody Ogden					
47	NM	Callum Preston					
51	D	Deacon Wilkes					
52	F	Gary Dixon					
62	F	Jack Davies					
73	F	Josh Jones				1	2
81	F	Daniels Fadejevs					
91	D	Rory Sillery					
98	D	Luke Wainwright					
		Team Penalty					
		TEAM TOTALS	1	1	2	3	6

GOALTENDER SUMMARY

COVENTRY NIHL BLAZE		TOI	Goals-Shots Against				
			1	2	3	OT	TOT
34	Hayden Laverick	30:13	0-9	0-3			0-12
39	Joel Bearman	29:47		0-2	1-3		1-5
	Empty Net						

DEESIDE DUCKS		TOI	Goals - Shots Against				
			1	2	3	OT	TOT
2	Paul Jones	20:00			5-30		5-30
47	Callum Preston	40:00	3-18	5-20			8-38
	Empty Net						

Source: NIHLStats.wordpress.com (Box Scores)

Continuing their policy of encouraging young talent and providing a stepping stone into senior league hockey, the Ducks gave NIHL debuts to three more promising players – Mackenzie Wilkes, Liam Yarwood and 16-year old Deacon Wilkes.

Deeside found themselves up against it right from the start and were 3-0 down by the end of the first period. It was 8-0 after two periods and they were 12-0 down by the time Michael Speare scored their first ever away goal in the third period.

The netminding partnership of Callum Preston and Paul Jones were kept busy all night but managed to keep out 55 of the 68 shots that they faced between them.

Deacon Wilkes was named the Ducks' MVP for the match.

Lead coach Peter Bleackley said: "I'm not going to make any excuses. We just didn't gel as a team last night.

"We've lots of areas to work on in training and I am putting this down to a bad day at the office.

"Coventry were a well organised team and played good simple hockey from the start. They outworked us and took every opportunity and capitalised on it.

"We will dust ourselves off and the team are looking forward to this weekend."

Deeside Ducks In The Newspaper!

Report about the Deeside Ducks' away game at Coventry in today's newspaper (Flintshire & Wrexham leader, 24th September - p35)

You can also the match report here: https://www.icehockeyreview.co.uk/2024/09/match-report-coventry-nihl-blaze-13.html

#Keepquacking #fowlnotfoul

Coventry 13 – Deeside 1

Quack on regardless of the score Ducks
Keep on icing and pushing those pucks
Above all don't forget the reason
The team was created this season.

Lucy London - 22nd September 2024

Players discuss the damaged ice surface at Hull
(Photo by Maxine Roscoe)

Saturday 28th September – NIHL Laidler Division
Kingston Sharks 5 – Deeside Ducks 0
(Abandoned after 20 mins)

The Deeside Ducks Laidler Division game away to Kingston Sharks was abandoned after a single 20 minute period had been played on Saturday evening at Hull Arena.

The home side had taken the lead 1m17 into the game and led 5-0 by the first period break. However, the surface of the ice was damaged during the routine ice cleaning operation between periods and it took over an hour for the rink staff to plug up the resulting hole and get the ice to freeze properly again.

With the amount of time lost - and concerns about player safety - the match was called off at that point and the remaining two periods were not played.

Ducks' Lead Coach Peter Bleackley commented:

"We expressed concerns regarding player safety - but rules apparently state that both coaches have to agree that the surface is unsafe. Their coach would not as they don't have any available dates to replay and they didn't want to forfeit. I decided player safety was more important after the team sitting for more than an hour. The ref agreed."

The sport's governing body – England Ice Hockey - will now have to decide what to do next.

The Rules Of Competition for the NIHL for the 2024/25 season - as displayed on the Englandicehockey.com website - state:

12.23. A game in-progress may be abandoned if it is determined that it cannot continue. All referees and team representatives accept the moral and ethical responsibility to implement procedures to provide a duty of care to all participants and spectators.

A game may be abandoned for the following reasons where no team is at fault:

- *Ice facility failure as determined only by rink management*
- *Unsafe rink conditions as determined only by rink management •*
- *If teams and officials deem the rink unsafe, but rink management do not, teams should submit supporting evidence to EIH to decide the outcome*

of the fixture. Teams will still be responsible for costs. •

- *The behaviour of anyone involved puts the welfare of a participant or spectator at risk as determined by rink management. Where this is a team member, the abandoned match will be treated under section 6.10 Failure to fulfil a fixture by the offending team or teams. •*
- *Medical emergency at venue / fixture as determined by rink management or by the officials in consultation with the team representatives.*

12.25. Where no team is at fault for the abandonment of the fixture, the following will apply when declaring a result: •

- *Where less than 2 periods of the match have elapsed has been played, a 0-0 draw will be declared with each team being awarded one point. •*
- *Where more than 2 periods of the match have been played, the result at the point of abandonment will stand.*

No abandoned games will be rearranged, unless exceptional circumstances are evidenced in writing with the agreement from both teams

Post Season Note:

It later emerged that this game was awarded as a 5-0 win to Kingston based on the score at the time of the abandonment, although no official decision was ever formally announced.

Kingston Sharks 5-0 Deeside Ducks

North 2 Regular Season, Saturday 28th September
Game 017

Kingston Sharks (2-1-0-1)   (0-0-0-3) Deeside Ducks

SCORING SUMMARY

G	Per	Time	Score	Team	Goal Scorer	Assist	Assist	Str
1	1	1:16	1-0	KIN	Cain Taylor (2)	Nathan Sutcliffe (2)		E
2	1	8:33	2-0	KIN	Tom Humphries (3)	Ellis Martin (2)		E
3	1	8:51	3-0	KIN	Scott Howells (3)	Tom Humphries (2)	Nathan Sutcliffe (3)	E
4	1	10:24	4-0	KIN	Chris Hogarth (3)	Cain Taylor (4)		E
5	1	18:33	5-0	KIN	Tom Humphries (4)	Scott Howells (1)	Nathan Sutcliffe (4)	E

KINGSTON SHARKS	DEESIDE DUCKS

PENALTY SUMMARY

#	Per	Time	Player	PIM	Penalty	#	Per	Time	Player	PIM	Penalty
1	1	13:55	Cain Taylor	2	Clipping	1	1	17:31	Rory Sillery	2	Delay of Game
			TOT (PN-PIM) 1-2						TOT (PN-PIM) 1-2		
			Power Plays (Goals-Opp) 0-1						Power Plays (Goals-Opp) 0-1		

TEAM SUMMARY

		KINGSTON SHARKS	G	A	P	PN	PIM			DEESIDE DUCKS	G	A	P	PN	PIM
1	NM	Evan Byron-Bates						2	NM	Paul Jones					
5	F	Gavin Tidy						4	F	Charlie Spridgeon					
6	D	Jack Hayward						5	F	Michael Speare					
11	F	Ethan Daintith						18	D	George Spofforth					
13	D	Joe Anson						19	F	Mackenzie Wilkes					
15	F	Lewis Rogers						20	F	Tom Milnes					
18	D	Chris Lister						21	D	Kieran Clarkson					
20	F	Cain Taylor	1	1	2	1	2	25	F	Liam Yarwood					
23	F	Liam Grant						27	D	Heather Clarkson					
24	D	Nathan Sutcliffe		3	3			29	F	Ben Roscoe					
25	F	Tom Humphries	2	1	3			40	F	Cody Ogden					
33	D	Jenson Hardy						47	NM	Callum Preston					
35	NM	Dominic Smith						52	F	Gary Dixon					
57	D	Ellis Martin		1	1			62	F	Jack Davies					
65	D	Ethan Witham						70	D	Alfie Kelly					
66	F	Grant Cook						72	D	Chris Jones					
77	F	Scott Howells	1	1	2			73	F	Josh Jones					
91	F	Chris Hogarth	1		1			81	F	Daniels Fadejevs					
92	F	Liam Archer						91	D	Rory Sillery				1	2
93	F	Kyle Mitchell-Quinn													
		Team Penalty								Team Penalty					
		TEAM TOTALS	5	7	12	1	2			TEAM TOTALS				1	2

GOALTENDER SUMMARY

KINGSTON SHARKS		Goals-Shots Against						DEESIDE DUCKS		Goals - Shots Against				
	TOI	1	2	3	OT	TOT			TOI	1	2	3	OT	TOT
1 Evan Byron-Bates								2 Paul Jones						
35 Dominic Smith	20:00	0-7				0-7		47 Callum Preston	20:00	5-23				5-23
Empty Net								Empty Net						

Source: NIHLStats.wordpress.com (Box Scores)

Ducks' MVP against Sheffield, Rory Sillery
(Photo by Chris Jones).

Sunday 29th September – NIHL Laidler Division
Deeside Ducks 4 – Sheffield Titans 3

The Deeside Ducks picked up their first ever win with a 4-3 victory over Sheffield Titans at Deeside Leisure Centre on Sunday

Two goals from Kieran Clarkson, one from Cody Ogden and a short-handed winner from captain Chris Jones with 14 minutes left to play secured the historic first league win for the Ducks.

Ducks' Head Coach Gary Shaw said of the game:

"The team went into this game with a line less then we have playing to see if it would benefit the players as we had run 4 lines before to get everyone ice time."

"The game was a very close affair and Sheffield went 2 goals up capitalising on mistakes made by our players. The team rallied and pulled a goal back before the end of the period."

"With a tight second period and end to end plays the period ended goal less. So the first goal in the 3rd period was a big factor and we instructed the team to compete in Sheffield's zones and to keep the puck low and only shoot if a good opportunity arose."

"And doing this Kieran Clarkson came around the net and banked the puck in off the goalie into the roof of the net to tie the game short-handed."

"A few minutes later, another short-handed goal from Cody Ogden put us in front."

"Having spoken to Chris Jones in-between the periods about shooting more, he took a speculative shot from our on blue line and, with the netminder not ready, the puck ended in the net. Sheffield scored again to draw it to a one goal advantage but we managed to hold out for the first win for the Ducks."

The Deeside Ducks are next in action this Saturday 5th October when they take on the Bradford Bulldogs at Deeside Leisure Centre – 5pm face off.

Deeside Ducks 4-3 Sheffield Titans

North 2 Regular Season, Sunday 29th September
Game 020

Deeside Ducks	(0-0-1-4) Sheffield Titans

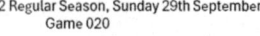

SCORING SUMMARY

G	Per	Time	Score	Team	Goal Scorer	Assist	Assist	Str
1	1	5:52	0-1	SHE	Jacob Sheahan (1)	Mark Illingworth (2)		E
2	1	7:45	0-2	SHE	Joe Matthewman (3)			E
3	1	18:08	1-2	DEE	Kieran Clarkson (1)	Cody Ogden (1)		E
4	3	40:51	2-2	DEE	Kieran Clarkson (2)	Cody Ogden (2)	Chris Jones (2)	E
5	3	44:47	3-2	DEE	Cody Ogden (1)			SH
6	3	45:34	4-2	DEE	Chris Jones (2)			SH
7	3	48:57	4-3	SHE	Jacob Sheahan (2)	Rory Ross-Docherty (2)	George Hallam (1)	E

PENALTY SUMMARY

DEESIDE DUCKS						SHEFFIELD TITANS				
#	Per	Time	Player	PIM	Penalty	#	Per	Time	Player	PIM	Penalty
1	2	27:37	Tom Milnes	2	Roughing	1	2	27:37	George Hallam	2	Roughing
2	2	27:37	Tom Milnes	2	Roughing	2	2	27:37	George Hallam	2	Roughing
3	2	33:24	Daniels Fadejevs	2	Holding	3	2	33:24	Oliver Keeling	2	Hooking
4	3	43:48	Louis Ellwood	2	Interference	4					
5	3	45:55	Tom Milnes	2	Misconduct	5					

TOT (PN-PIM) 5-10	TOT (PN-PIM) 3-6
Power Plays (Goals-Opp) 0-0	Power Plays (Goals-Opp) 0-2

TEAM SUMMARY

		DEESIDE DUCKS	G	A	P	PN	PIM				SHEFFIELD TITANS	G	A	P	PN	PIM
2	NM	Paul Jones							2	D	Jacob Sheahan	2		2		
4	F	Charlie Spridgeon							7	F	Joe Matthewman	1		1		
5	F	Michael Speare							8	F	Mark Illingworth		1	1		
19	F	Mackenzie Wilkes							9	F	Simon Williams					
20	F	Tom Milnes				3	6		15	D	Sam Burrows					
21	D	Kieran Clarkson	2		2				36	F	Lewis Swaffield					
25	F	Liam Yarwood							37	NM	Elliott Russan					
29	F	Ben Roscoe							46	F	George Hallam		1	1	2	4
31	D	James Morgan							52	D	Aaron Larner					
34	F	Louis Ellwood				1	2		63	F	Rory Ross-Docherty		1	1		
40	F	Cody Ogden	1	2	3				68	NM	Nathaniel Bell					
47	NM	Callum Preston							81	F	Oliver Keeling				1	2
51	F	Gary Dixon														
70	D	Alfie Kelly														
72	D	Chris Jones	1	1	2											
73	F	Josh Jones														
81	F	Daniels Fadejevs				1	2									
88	D	Kenny Williams														
91	D	Rory Sillery														
		Team Penalty									Team Penalty					
		TEAM TOTALS	4	3	7	5	10				TEAM TOTALS	3	3	6	3	6

GOALTENDER SUMMARY

DEESIDE DUCKS		TOI	Goals-Shots Against					SHEFFIELD TITANS		TOI	Goals - Shots Against				
			1	2	3	OT	TOT				1	2	3	OT	TOT
2	Paul Jones							37	Elliott Russan						
47	Callum Preston	60:00	2-9	0-8	1-11		3-28	68	Nathaniel Bell	60:00	1-17	0-9	3-13		4-39
	Empty Net								Empty Net						

Source: NIHLStats.wordpress.com (Box Scores)

Deeside Ducks had a rollercoaster weekend, seeing their away game against the Kingston Sharks abandoned after the first period on Saturday but then picking up their first ever win with a 4-3 victory at home to Sheffield Titans on Sunday at Deeside Leisure Centre.

At Hull, the home side had taken the lead in the second minute and led 5-0 by the interval.

However, the surface of the ice was damaged during the routine ice cleaning operation between periods and it took over an hour for the rink staff to plug up the resulting hole and get the ice to freeze properly again.

With the amount of time lost - and concerns about player safety - the match was called off.

Two goals from Kieran Clarkson, one from Cody Ogden and a short-handed winner from captain Chris Jones with 14 minutes left to play secured the historic first ever league win for the Ducks on Sunday.

Division One North results: Sheffield 1

Deeside Ducks In The Newspaper!

There's a brief round-up of the Ducks' eventful weekend in today's Flintshire & Wrexham Leader (1st October 2024 - Page 35)

You can read fuller versions of the two match reports - along with coaches' comments on www.icehockeyreview.co.uk.

An Eventful Weekend.

Bravo Ducks – you've quacked it!
You've even got a little bit
In the paper. I hope Lady Luck
Will favour every Deeside Duck.

Lucy London, 1st October 2024

Ducks MVP Josh Jones with mascots (Photo by Paul Breeze)

Saturday 5th October 2024 – NIHL Laidler Division
Deeside Ducks 3 – Bradford Bulldogs 4

The Deeside Ducks narrowly lost out in a highly entertaining and closely fought 3-4 defeat to the Bradford Bulldogs at Deeside Leisure Centre on Saturday.

The game started well for Deeside as Michael Speare fired them into the lead after just 36 seconds but Bradford struck back and were level 4 minutes later.

Deeside edged ahead once again on 15 minutes with a goal from Josh Jones but the visitors again had an answer and equalised just 24 seconds later to leave the score standing at 2-2 at the first period break.

The second period was very close - with chances for both teams - but produced no goals, and the score remained at a finely balanced 2-2 with just 20 minutes left to play.

The Bulldogs were fastest out of the traps for the third period and finally got their snouts in front with a goal 31 seconds in.

Despite having outshot the visitors by some margin over the course of the game, the Ducks were finding it difficult to break down the stubborn Bradford defence – but they got a helping hand with just over 6 minutes left to play.

A Bulldogs player was banished from the ice for a dangerous cross check, for which he was handed a 5 plus game penalty by the match officials.

This meant that the Ducks would have a man advantage for pretty much the rest of the third period.

Charlie Spridgeon pulled Deeside back level with a powerplay goal two minutes later and the Ducks pushed forward to try and force a late winner.

Unfortunately, they got caught out at the back and Bradford fired in a shorthanded goal to retake the lead with just 3 minutes left to play.

Deeside were unable to bounce back from this – even with their continued man advantage - and they even withdrew their netminder in favour of an extra attacker for the last 30 seconds, but the game finished 3-4 to Bradford.

The Ducks are without a game this weekend and then have three away trips in a row – away to Sheffield on 20th October, Telford on 26th October and Bradford on 3rd November – before their next home match, which will be against Telford Tigers on Sunday 17th November at Deeside Leisure Centre.

Coach's Comments – From Head Coach Gary Shaw

The team went into the game open minded as both clubs are building, with Bradford a little ahead of us because they have had a more stable junior setup.

With a bit more confidence after the first win of the season, the team started well, bringing some of the work we had done in training. We moved the puck well and broke out of our own defensive zone easily, but our offensive play still needs work gaining the zone to make different decisions and gain better possession.

Once we got into the zone, we made some good progress and we went ahead - only for Bradford to come back and take advantage of our indecision in the defensive zone.

So, the conversation between the periods was to make the right decisions and play the puck low in the zone and take the opportunity to shoot in good areas.

The game was back and forth with both netminders making some good saves. We applied some good pressure but came up empty handed for most of our efforts.

We focused on telling the team to be patient and do the right things, at the start of the period Bradford had stepped up their game and for the first five minutes we struggled to get into our game.

The game was still to and fro and we scored to equalise as the game progressed it was down to who would make the fewer mistakes that would take the spoils.

So Bradford took the lead with us making a mistake on the half wall, they chipped the puck out and then went on to score.

Then Bradford took a five minute penalty in the last six minutes of the game and we had a lot of chances but shot the puck high and wide, with three minutes of the game left we scored the equaliser, still having the advantage of the penalty we pushed for the winner.

But, as before we lost the puck on the half wall and they went on to score the winning goal.

After the final whistle, we spoke about the mistakes that had lost us the game – and also about shot variety, because we had shot the puck high a lot and quite a lot missed the net and ended up with an easy exit from the zone for the opponents.

Although we had lost right and fair, we had a lot of positives to take out of the game, and as a coaching team, have again identified where we need to work on to improve their game and hopefully make us stronger and harder to beat.

As we move on, the players can hold their heads up high as they are getting better with each game and their bond with each other is growing.

Deeside Ducks 3-4 Bradford Bulldogs

North 2 League and Cup, Saturday 5th October
Game 024

Deeside Ducks (1-0-0-4)   (1-0-0-3) Bradford Bulldogs

SCORING SUMMARY

G	Per	Time	Score	Team	Goal Scorer	Assist	Assist	Str
1	1	0:36	1-0	DEE	Michael Speare (2)	Charlie Spridgeon (2)	Tom Milnes (2)	E
2	1	4:30	1-1	BRA	Kacper Andrukianiec (2)	Tom Mardell (3)	Lucas Vince (3)	E
3	1	15:53	2-1	DEE	Josh Jones (1)	Ben Roscoe (2)		E
4	1	16:19	2-2	BRA	Tom Mardell (3)	Lucas Vince (4)		PP
5	3	40:31	2-3	BRA	Tom Mardell (4)	Lucas Vince (5)		E
6	3	54:46	3-3	DEE	Charlie Spridgeon (1)	Keiron Clarkson (2)		PP
7	3	56:42	3-4	BRA	Jacob Brownlie (1)	Tom Mardell (4)	Ben Fox (1)	SH

PENALTY SUMMARY

DEESIDE DUCKS						BRADFORD BULLDOGS				
#	Per	Time	Player	PIM	Penalty	#	Per	Time	Player	PIM	Penalty
1	1	9:42	Louis Morgan	2	Tripping	1	2	29:01	David Williams	2	Slashing
2	1	12:02	Louis Morgan	2	Roughing	2	3	53:41	David Williams	25	Cross Checking
3	2	23:43	Alfie Kelly	2	Roughing	3	3	59:09	Kieron Furlong	2	Tripping
4	2	35:35	Alfie Kelly	2	Interference	4					
5	3	41:47	James Morgan	2	Slashing	5					
6	3	47:21	Chris Jones	2	Interference	6					
			TOT (PN-PIM) 6-12						TOT (PN-PIM) 3-29		
			Power Plays (Goals-Opp) 1-4						Power Plays (Goals-Opp) 1-6		

TEAM SUMMARY

		DEESIDE DUCKS	G	A	P	PN	PIM			BRADFORD BULLDOGS	G	A	P	PN	PIM
2	NM	Paul Jones						4	D	David Williams				2	27
4	F	Charlie Spridgeon	1	1	2			11	F	Lucas Vince		3	3		
5	F	Michael Speare	1		1			15	F	Oliver Massey					
18	D	George Spofforth						16	D	Ben Darbyshire					
20	F	Tom Milnes		1	1			18	F	Tyler Hall					
21	D	Keiron Clarkson		1	1			22	D	Jacob Brownlie	1		1		
25	F	Liam Yarwood						26	F	Kacper Andrukianiec	1		1		
29	F	Ben Roscoe		1	1			28	F	Thomas Chong					
31	D	James Morgan				1	2	29	F	Tom Mardell	2	2	4		
34	F	Louis Ellwood						33	NM	Jacob Lowndes					
40	F	Cody Ogden						74	F	Ben Fox		1	1		
47	NM	Callum Preston						84	D	Joel Bark					
52	F	Gary Dixon						86	D	Kieron Furlong				1	2
62	F	Jack Davies													
70	D	Alfie Kelly				2	4								
72	D	Chris Jones				1	2								
73	F	Josh Jones	1		1										
85	D	Louis Morgan				2	4								
88	D	Kenny Williams													
91	D	Rory Sillery													
		Team Penalty								Team Penalty					
		TEAM TOTALS	3	4	7	6	12			TEAM TOTALS	4	6	10	3	29

GOALTENDER SUMMARY

DEESIDE DUCKS	TOI	Goals-Shots Against					BRADFORD BULLDOGS	TOI	Goals - Shots Against				
		1	2	3	OT	TOT			1	2	3	OT	TOT
2 Paul Jones							33 Jacob Lowndes	60:00	2-9	0-17	1-10		3-36
47 Callum Preston	59:35	2-8	0-9	2-7		4-24							
Empty Net	0:25			0-0		0-0	Empty Net						

Source: NIHLStats.wordpress.com (Box Scores)

ICE HOCKEY: DEESIDE IN TOP FORM

Goal-den spell for Dragons

DEESIDE DRAGONS have managed to maintain that winning habit.

It's now four triumphs on the bounce for the Dragons, who eased to a pair of victories in their double-header versus Sheffield Scimitars.

The opening contest in Sheffield witnessed an 8-2 success for Deeside.

Jake Witkowski grabbed four of the goals and he was joined on the scoresheet by James Parsons, Ross Kennedy, Jayson Burgess and Alex Parry.

Fast forward to the following day and Dragons impressed once more courtesy of a 9-1 outcome at home.

James Shaw, Ryan Broster Jones, Burgess, Matt Wainwright, Parry, Jakub Hajek and Oli Howells were amongst the scores to make sure Dragons made it three consecutive triumphs in the league.

It was important that the Dragons were focused ahead of the encounters.

Assistant head coach Matt Compton said: "That's what I said on Saturday, don't take these for granted.

"Don't think because where they are in the table you can go through the motions.

"That could be the attitude why we went 4-0 down in Cardiff.

"But we got off to a decent start. It could have and should have been more."

Other results: Hull 3 Billingham 7; Leeds 5 Widnes 2; Nottingham 0 Blackburn 4; Billingham 8 Solihull 3; Nottingham 4 Hull 9; Whitley 9 Widnes 2.

Deeside Ducks narrowly lost out 4-3 in a highly entertaining and closely fought contest at home to the Bradford Bulldogs.

The game started well for Deeside as Michael Speare fired them into the lead after just 36 seconds but Bradford struck back and were level four minutes later.

Deeside edged ahead once

IMPRESSIVE: Deeside Ducks MVP Josh Jones with mascots.
Picture: PAUL BREEZE

again on 15 minutes with a goal from Josh Jones but the visitors again had an answer and equalised just 24 seconds later to leave the score standing at 2-2 at the first period break.

The second period was very close - with chances for both teams - but it produced no goals.

The Bulldogs were fastest out of the traps for the third period and they finally got their snouts in front with a goal 31 seconds in.

Deeside continued to press and, with six minutes left to play, a Bulldogs player was banished from the ice for a dangerous cross check, for which he was handed a five-plus game penalty, giving the Ducks a man advantage for pretty much the rest of the game.

Charlie Spridgeon pulled Deeside back level with a powerplay goal two minutes later and the Ducks pushed forward to try and force a late winner.

Unfortunately, they got caught out at the back and Bradford fired in a shorthanded winner themselves instead with just three minutes left to play.

Ducks head coach Gary Shaw said: "Although we had lost right and fair, we had a lot of positives to take out of the game, and as a coaching team have again identified where we need to work on to improve their game and hopefully make us stronger and harder to beat.

"As we move on, the players can hold their heads up high as they are getting better with each game and their bond with each other is growing."

Ducks are without a game this weekend and then have three away trips in a row before their next home match, which will be against Telford Tigers on November 17.

Jess grabs England try treble

JESS BREACH scored a hat-trick as England swept past New Zealand 49-31 in a convincing nine-try win in their second Women World Rugby WXV1 match in Canada.

The Red Roses, ranked the world's number one side, recovered from a slow start to ruthlessly dispatch the Black Ferns and lay down another marker ahead of next year's home World Cup.

Kevin Sinfield is to remain part of Steve Borthwick's England coaching team after agreeing revised terms for his role.

In a lift for the national set-up following the sudden departures of Aled Walters and Felix Jones, who served as head of strength and conditioning and as defence coach respectively, Sinfield will continue working with England on an ongoing basis.

The rugby league great was due to step down after the recent tour to Japan and New Zealand but has chosen to stay on in his post as skills and kicking coach, as well as a providing mentorship to the squad.

"Working with Steve and the team has been an immensely rewarding experience and I am excited to continue my involvement with the team," Sinfield said.

A few short verses about the Deeside Ducks home game against Bradford on Saturday and the coverage in the local paper (Flintshire & Wrexham Leader, 8th October 2024 - Page 35)

Ducks v Bradford Bulldogs 05.10.2024:

Although the final score
Was 3 – 4
You played really well Ducks
Just keep pushing those pucks

Lucy London - 6.10.2024

Don't forget to 'play the puck low in the zone'
As your Ducks technique you hone
Well done Ducks MVP Josh Jones …

Lucy London - 7.10.2024

Look who's
In the news -
Deeside Ducks MVP -
Thanks to sports writer PB

Lucy London - 8.10.2024

Widnes v Blackburn.

Deeside Ducks were without a game at the weekend and they now face three tough trips on the road.

The Ducks, competing in their first season in Division Two North, are away to Sheffield this Sunday, while they will then travel to face last season's league and cup champions Telford Tigers the following Saturday, October 26.

They cross the Pennines to take on the Bradford Bulldogs on Sunday, November 3 prior to the next home game - against Telford - at Deeside Leisure Centre on November 17 (5pm face-off).

These early season games against Bradford and Telford all count towards both the league standings and the cup qualification group, so the Ducks will be keen to get some more points on the board as they continue with their exciting debut season.

Deeside Ducks In The Newspaper!

A short preview of the Ducks' forthcoming fixtures in today's Flintshire & Wrexham Leader (18th October 2024 - Page 33)

Ducks in action at Sheffield (Photo by Jake Renzi @renzimedia)

Sunday 20th October 2024 – NIHL Laidler Division
Sheffield Titans 6 – Deeside Ducks 0

The Deeside Ducks suffered a 6-0 defeat to the Sheffield Titans away in the Steel City on Sunday.

The game was very close in its early stages – with numerous chances for both sides – but remained goal-less until the Titans finally broke the deadlock on 17 minutes.

The hosts took a narrow 1-0 lead into the first interval but 4 more unanswered goals in the second period left the Ducks trailing 5-0 with 20 minutes left to play.

Deeside have struggled to score on their away trips so far this season and the only goal of the third period fell to Sheffield, handing them a 6-0 victory.

Despite the defeat, netminder Paul Jones put in a creditable display in goal and was named Most Valuable Player for the Ducks.

The Ducks travel to face last season's league and cup champions Telford Tigers this Saturday 26th October, 5.30pm face off.

Paul Jones was the Ducks' MVP away at Sheffield
(Photo by Jake Renzi @renzimedia)

Sheffield Titans 6-0 Deeside Ducks
North 2 Regular Season, Sunday 20th October
Game 035

Sheffield Titans (2-0-1-5)  (1-0-0-5) Deeside Ducks

SCORING SUMMARY

G	Per	Time	Score	Team	Goal Scorer	Assist	Assist	Str
1	1	16:24	1-0	SHE	Simon Williams (2)			E
2	2	23:26	2-0	SHE	Rory Ross-Docherty (1)			E
3	2	29:05	3-0	SHE	Mark Illingworth (1)	Harry Roebuck (2)	Lewis Swaffield (3)	E
4	2	37:22	4-0	SHE	Harry Roebuck (1)	Joe Matthewman (4)	Lewis Swaffield (4)	E
5	2	37:52	5-0	SHE	Aiden Dancer (1)			E
6	3	43:46	6-0	SHE	Finlay Heraghty (1)			E

PENALTY SUMMARY

SHEFFIELD TITANS						DEESIDE DUCKS				
#	Per	Time	Player	PIM	Penalty	#	Per	Time	Player	PIM	Penalty
1	1	10:56	Finlay Heraghty	2	Interference	1	2	34:01	Josh Jones	2	Misconduct
2	2	32:28	Miles Jones	2	High Sticking	2	2	39:39	Liam Yarwood	2	Cross Checking
3	2	34:01	Joe Matthewman	2	Interference	3	3	42:08	Josh Jones	2	Slashing
4	2	39:39	Rory Ross-Docherty	2	Roughing	4	3	46:16	Tom Milnes	2	Cross Checking
5	3	46:44	Finlay Heraghty	2	Tripping	5	3	51:14	Mackenzie Wilkes	2	Misconduct
6	3	56:30	Finlay Heraghty	2	Tripping	6	3	51:52	Charlie Spridgeon	2	Delay of Game
7	3	59:33	Miles Jones	2	Cross Checking	7	3	53:10	Alfie Kelly	10	Misconduct
8						8	3	55:07	Gary Dixon	2	Slashing

TOT (PN-PIM) 7-14 | TOT (PN-PIM) 8-24
Power Plays (Goals-Opp) 0-5 | Power Plays (Goals-Opp) 0-5

TEAM SUMMARY

	SHEFFIELD TITANS	G	A	P	PN	PIM
7	F	Joe Matthewman		1	1	1	2
8	F	Mark Illingworth	1		1		
9	F	Simon Williams	1		1		
14	F	Will Weaver					
15	D	Sam Burrows					
16	D	Finlay Heraghty	1		1	3	6
28	F	Harry Roebuck	1	1	2		
36	F	Lewis Swaffield		2	2		
39	NM	Hayden Oates					
44	D	Jacob Sheahan					
46	F	George Hallam					
52	D	Aaron Larner					
63	F	Rory Ross-Docherty	1		1	1	2
68	NM	Nathaniel Bell					
77	F	Oliver Keeling					
91	F	Miles Jones				2	4
96	F	Leland Walker					
98	F	Aiden Dancer	1		1		
		Team Penalty					
		TEAM TOTALS	6	4	10	7	14

	DEESIDE DUCKS	G	A	P	PN	PIM
2	NM	Paul Jones					
4	F	Charlie Spridgeon				1	2
5	F	Michael Speare					
10	F	Stewart Cutting					
12	D	Henry Phillips					
18	D	George Spofforth					
19	F	Mackenzie Wilkes				1	2
20	F	Tom Milnes				1	2
21	D	Keiron Clarkson					
25	F	Liam Yarwood				1	2
29	F	Ben Roscoe					
31	D	James Morgan					
34	F	Louis Ellwood					
40	F	Cody Ogden					
47	NM	Callum Preston					
51	F	Deacon Wilkes					
52	D	Gary Dixon				1	2
70	D	Alfie Kelly				1	10
73	D	Josh Jones				2	4
98	D	Luke Wainwright					
		Team Penalty					
		TEAM TOTALS				8	24

GOALTENDER SUMMARY

SHEFFIELD TITANS		Goals-Shots Against				
	TOI	1	2	3	OT	TOT
39 Hayden Oates						
68 Nathaniel Bell	60:00	0-10	0-8	0-5		0-23
Empty Net						

DEESIDE DUCKS		Goals - Shots Against				
	TOI	1	2	3	OT	TOT
2 Paul Jones	60:00	1-8	4-14	1-20		6-42
47 Callum Preston						
Empty Net						

Source: NIHLStats.wordpress.com (Box Scores)

Deeside Ducks suffered a 6-0 Division Two North defeat to the Sheffield Titans away in the Steel City on Sunday.

The game was very close in its early stages, with numerous chances for both sides.

It remained goalless until the Titans finally broke the deadlock on 17 minutes.

The hosts took a narrow 1-0 lead into the first interval, but four more unanswered goals in the second period left the Ducks trailing 5-0 with 20 minutes left to play.

Deeside have struggled to score on their away trips so far this season and the only goal of the third period fell to Sheffield, handing them a 6-0 victory.

Despite the defeat, netminder Paul Jones put in a creditable display in goal and he was named the Ducks' MVP.

Things don't get any easier for Deeside.

The Ducks travel to face last season's league and cup champions Telford Tigers on Saturday (5.30pm).

Flintshire & Wrexham Leader, 22nd October 2024 - p35

Ducks In The Newspaper!

There's a brief report about Sunday's Ducks' game away to Sheffield in today's Flintshire & Wrexham Leader (22nd October 2024 - Page 35)

You can also see the match report - along with some photos - here: http://www.icehockeyreview.co.uk/2024/10/match-report-sheffield-titans-6-deeside.html

#keepquacking   #fowlnotfoul

Ducks battle away at Telford (Photo by Karen Booth)

Saturday 26th October 2024 – NIHL Laidler Division
Telford Tigers2 24 – Deeside Ducks 4

The Deeside Ducks played their part in a 28-goal thriller but most of the goals went in at the wrong end as they lost 24-4 away to Telford Tigers on Saturday.

This away trip to face the reigning league champions - who have a strong line-up, including former Deeside import Filip Supa and also Dragons title winner Paul Davies - was always likely to be a difficult one and so it turned out.

The Ducks actually took the lead with a goal from Cody Ogden after just 57 seconds of the match but Telford went on to hit 12 goals in the first period. A second Ogden strike just before the break narrowed the score to 12-2 but Telford were well in control by that stage.

The second period continued in similar vein and the score was 19-3 at the second interval, with the only real plus point for the Ducks being a first ever league goal for Jack Davies in the 35th minute.

Early in the third period, Ogden scored his hat trick goal to bring the score to 19-4 but 5 more unanswered goals sealed an emphatic win for the Tigers.

After the game, Ducks Head Coach Gary Shaw said:

"We always knew this was going to be a tough game in Telford, as they are the favourites to take the title again this year, with the depth and calibre of their squad."

"Going into the game we really wanted to show what team we wanted to be, and felt we achieved this by playing for the whole game and never gave up, and created some good opportunities to score."

"The boys played with heart and earned the chances they took."

"We were happy with the players' attitude. They didn't give up and never let their heads drop. We have big things that went right and a lot of things we can improve - and it is all baby steps towards our goal."

The Ducks are away again - to the Bradford Bulldogs - this Saturday 3rd November and are next at home on Sunday 17th November when they take on Telford Tigers at Deeside Leisure Centre, 5pm face off.

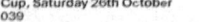

Telford Tigers NIHL 2 24-4 Deeside Ducks
North 2 League and Cup, Saturday 26th October
Game 039
Telford Tigers NIHL 2 (8-0-0-0)   (1-0-0-6) Deeside Ducks

SCORING SUMMARY

G	Per	Time	Score	Team	Goal Scorer	Assist	Assist	Str
1	1	0:28	0-1	DEE	Cody Ogden (2)	Michael Speare (1)	Josh Jones (1)	E
2	1	3:47	1-1	TEL	Taylor Stanton (5)			E
3	1	5:00	2-1	TEL	Ben Washburn (2)	Oliver Hunt (9)		E
4	1	9:01	3-1	TEL	Taylor Stanton (6)	Filip Supa (4)	Oliver Hunt (10)	E
5	1	9:12	4-1	TEL	Filip Supa (13)	Oliver Hunt (11)	Josh Hustwick (10)	E
6	1	10:22	5-1	TEL	Connor McNaughton (5)	Karol Jets (9)		E
7	1	11:49	6-1	TEL	Dan Mitchell (3)	Stephen Crowe (1)		E
8	1	13:33	7-1	TEL	Daniel Retter (2)	Lewis Smith (2)		E
9	1	13:44	8-1	TEL	Taylor Stanton (7)	Oliver Hunt (12)	Filip Supa (5)	E
10	1	14:31	9-1	TEL	Oliver Hunt (8)	Josh Hustwick (11)	Filip Supa (6)	E
11	1	15:50	10-1	TEL	Kyle Watt (2)	Callum Griffin (4)	Dan Mitchell (1)	E
12	1	17:03	11-1	TEL	Robert Oxley (1)	Callum Griffin (5)		E
13	1	17:55	12-1	TEL	Filip Supa (14)	Taylor Stanton (7)	Oliver Hunt (13)	E
14	1	18:28	12-2	DEE	Cody Ogden (3)	Josh Jones (2)		E
15	2	20:49	13-2	TEL	Karol Jets (4)	Ben Washburn (9)		E
16	2	22:41	14-2	TEL	Connor McNaughton (6)	Callum Griffin (6)	Robert Oxley (5)	E
17	2	26:46	15-2	TEL	Filip Supa (15)	Taylor Stanton (8)	Oliver Hunt (14)	E
18	2	30:26	16-2	TEL	Karol Jets (5)	Paul Davies (6)	Ben Washburn (10)	E
19	2	30:51	17-2	TEL	Taylor Stanton (8)	Josef Lauder (7)		E
20	2	32:33	18-2	TEL	Oliver Hunt (9)	Filip Supa (7)	Daniel Retter (8)	SH
21	2	34:34	18-3	DEE	Jack Davies (1)			E
22	2	38:03	19-3	TEL	Oliver Hunt (10)	Taylor Stanton (9)	Josef Lauder (8)	E
23	3	40:42	19-4	DEE	Cody Ogden (4)			E
24	3	41:10	20-4	TEL	Oliver Hunt (11)	Taylor Stanton (10)	Robert Oxley (6)	E
25	3	50:54	21-4	TEL	Josh Hustwick (3)	Callum Griffin (7)	Connor McNaughton (7)	E
26	3	52:03	22-4	TEL	Ben Washburn (2)	Karol Jets (10)	Paul Davies (7)	E
27	3	52:12	23-4	TEL	Karol Jets (6)	Paul Davies (8)	Robert Oxley (7)	E
28	3	56:23	24-4	TEL	Filip Supa (16)	Connor McNaughton (8)	Callum Griffin (8)	PP

PENALTY SUMMARY

			TELFORD TIGERS NIHL 2						DEESIDE DUCKS		
#	Per	Time	Player	PIM	Penalty	#	Per	Time	Player	PIM	Penalty
1	2	31:39	Connor Keyes	2	Misconduct	1	2	39:05	Jack Davies	2	Roughing
2	2	39:05	Stephen Crowe	2	Roughing	2	3	47:24	Cody Ogden	2	Roughing
3	3	58:05	Liam Bartholomew	2	Roughing	3	3	55:05	Alfie Kelly	2	Delay of Game
4	3	58:05	Liam Bartholomew	2	Roughing	9	3	58:05	Alfie Kelly	2	Roughing
			TOT (PN-PIM) 4-8						TOT (PN-PIM) 4-8		
			Power Plays (Goals-Opp) 1-4						Power Plays (Goals-Opp) 0-3		

TEAM SUMMARY

		TELFORD TIGERS NIHL 2	G	A	P	PN	PIM			DEESIDE DUCKS	G	A	P	PN	PIM
4	F	Karol Jets	3	2	5			2	NM	Paul Jones					
5	D	Robert Oxley	1	3	4			5	F	Michael Speare		1	1		
13	F	Lewis Smith		1	1			12	D	Henry Phillips					
15	F	Daniel Retter	1	1	2			18	D	George Spofforth					
18	D	Josh Hustwick		3	3			19	F	Mackenzie Wilkes					
25	D	Stephen Crowe		1	1	1	2	20	F	Tom Milnes					
26	F	Paul Davies		3	3			29	F	Ben Roscoe					
27	F	Callum Griffin		5	5			31	D	James Morgan					
29	D	Connor Keyes				1	2	34	F	Louis Ellwood					
31	NM	Matthew Byrne						40	F	Cody Ogden	3		3	1	2
36	D	Josef Lauder		2	2			47	NM	Callum Preston					
40	F	Ben Washburn	2	2	4			51	F	Deacon Wilkes					
50	NM	Hal Griffiths						62	F	Jack Davies	1		1	1	2
51	F	Liam Bartholomew				2	4	70	D	Alfie Kelly				2	4
53	F	Oliver Hunt	4	6	10			73	D	Josh Jones		2	2		
59	D	Connor Bennett						88	D	Kenny Williams					
61	F	Kyle Watt	1		1			96	D	Luke Wainwright					
71	F	Taylor Stanton	4	4	8										
81	F	Filip Supa	4	4	8										
88	F	Daniel Mitchell	1	1	2										
95	F	Connor McNaughton	2	2	4										
		Team Penalty								Team Penalty					
		TEAM TOTALS	24	39	63	4	8			TEAM TOTALS	4	3	7	4	8

GOALTENDER SUMMARY

	TELFORD TIGERS		Goals-Shots Against						DEESIDE DUCKS		Goals - Shots Against				
		TOI	1	2	3	OT	TOT			TOI	1	2	3	OT	TOT
31	Matthew Byrne	30:36	2-8	0-2			2-10	2	Paul Jones	29:09		2-14	5-24		7-38
50	Hal Griffiths	29:24		1-4	1-9		2-13	47	Callum Preston	30:51	12-31	5-9			17-40
	Empty Net								Empty Net						

Source: NIHLStats.wordpress.com (Box Scores)

100

setting the tone, with recent acquisition Gary Simpson opening the scoring, while Jared Dickinson and Jakub Hajek added to the tally.

Although Callum Queenan got Whitley on the board, the Dragons ended the period 3-1 ahead.

There was a real back-and-to in the second period, which ended up 2-2.

Charles Phillips and Hajek made sure Deeside remained clear, but Warriors' interest was maintained by efforts from Dean Holland and Kyle Hindmarsh-Ross.

The final period saw both teams battle for control.

Hindmarsh-Ross grabbed his second goal for the Warriors to cut the gap to just one, but Deeside put the game to bed when MVP Hajek completed his hat-trick with less than a minute left.

Dragons' assistant head coach Matt Compton said: "We did win at Whitley last year, but this year was so much more controlled.

"We didn't back down from anything. We got away from our game plan when they got physical, but we got on with it."

The sides met once more 24 hours later and home advantage was Deeside's on this occasion.

Making it a perfect couple of days, the Dragons roared to a 7-2 outcome for their eighth consecutive triumph.

Following a goalless first period, goals from Ross Kennedy and Jared Dickinson (2) made sure Dragons were 3-0 to the good by the next break.

Further efforts from Hajek (2), Jake Witkowski and MJ Clancy would seal the deal.

"Saturday was a long day and everyone did so well to recover and go again on Sunday," added Compton.
Other results: Hull 1 Billingham 4; Sheffield 2 Blackburn 12; Billingham 9 Nottingham 2; Blackburn 4 Leeds 0; Solihull 7 Sheffield 2; Widnes 1 Hull 3.

Deeside Ducks played their part in a 28-goal thriller, but most of the

goals went in at the wrong end from their point of view as they lost 24-4 at Telford Tigers.

The Ducks actually took the lead with a goal from Cody Ogden after just 57 seconds, but Telford went on to hit 12 goals in the first period.

A second Ogden strike just before the break narrowed the score to 12-2 but Telford were well in control by that stage.

The second period continued in similar vein and the score was 19-3 at the second interval, with the only real plus point for the Ducks being a first ever league goal for Jack Davies in the 35th minute.

Early in the third period, Ogden scored his hat-trick goal to bring the score to 19-4 but five more unanswered goals sealed an emphatic win for the Tigers.

TOP DISPLAY: Cody Ogden scored a hat-trick for Deeside Ducks at Telford. Picture: Andrea Petrie

After the game, Ducks' head coach Gary Shaw said: "The boys played with heart and earned the chances they took.

"We were happy with the players' attitude. They didn't give up and never let their heads drop.

"We have big things that went right and a lot of things we can improve - and it is all baby steps towards our goal."

Ducks In The Newspaper!

There's a brief report about Saturday's Ducks' game away to Telford in today's Flintshire & Wrexham Leader (29th October 2024 - Page 37)

You can read a fuller version of the match report - along with the complete coach's comments - here: https://www.icehockeyreview.co.uk/2024/10/match-report-telford-tigers2-24-deeside.html

#keepquacking   #fowlnotfoul

Michael Speare (Photo by Paul Breeze)

Sunday 3rd November 2024 – NIHL Laidler Division
Bradford Bulldogs 5 – Deeside Ducks 6 (PS)

The Deeside Ducks picked up their second Laidler Division win of the season with a 5-6 penalty shot victory away to Bradford Bulldogs on Sunday.

Bradford opened the scoring just one minute into the game but goals from Stewart Cutting and Daniel Fadejevs saw Deeside leading 1-2 at the first break.

The Bulldogs pulled a goal back early in the second period but goals from Kieran Clarkson and Thomas Milnes helped the Ducks soar into a 2-4 lead. However, Bradford had the better of the chances after this and three unanswered goals gave them a 5-4 lead at the second interval.

The only goal in a closely fought third period fell to the Ducks' Michael Speare, tying the scores at 5-5 and sending the match into an extra 5 minute period of sudden death over time.

With no deciding goal in the extra 5 minutes of play, the game had to be decided on a penalty shoot-out and strikes from Speare, Clarkson and Josh Jones sealed a first ever away win for the Ducks.

Under new regulations introduced for this season, Deeside receive 2 league points for the penalty shot win while Bradford get 1 point for drawing at the end of regulation time.

After the game, Ducks' Lead Coach Peter Bleackley said:

"Following last week's heavy defeat at Telford, we decided to re-set mentally and really dig in. The whole team bought into a totally different positive mindset and the lads worked hard for the win."

"It was a very close game but silly penalties made it harder than it needed to be. We have the next couple of weeks to work on some things before we face Telford at home."

The Ducks are without a game this coming weekend but are back in action on Sunday 17th November when they face title favourites Telford Tigers 2 at Deeside Leisure Centre, 5pm face off.

on the night were power play efforts and Compton felt the visitors were on the wrong side of a few decisions.

"We just couldn't get momentum," he added.

Other results: Leeds 0 Whitley 2; Sheffield 2 Widnes 3 (overtime); Billingham 7 Widnes 0; Blackburn 6 Hull 0; Whitley 1 Solihull 3.

to a decider

losing the opening frame to take control of the contest with breaks of 73, 87, 83 and 70.

Chinese player He edged a tight sixth frame to reduce his deficit before two further half-century breaks from world number five O'Sullivan set up a last-32 meeting with Pang Junxu.

"I get very good support wherever I go all over the world," O'Sullivan, who is playing a tournament for the first time since losing to He at the English Open in September, told the World Snooker Tour following his win.

"As well as my style of play, I've managed to entertain the fans."

World champion Kyren Wilson sealed a 6-3 win over Liu Hongyu with a break of 143, while world number one Judd Trump also ended with a century in his 6-0 defeat of Sanderson Lam.

Stuart Bingham, the 2015 world champion, was whitewashed 6-0 by Thepchaiya Un-Nooh. Mark Williams awaits the Thai player following his walkover victory against Mark Davis.

Shaun Murphy also advanced with a walkover win, while defending champion Zhang Anda overcame David Grace 6-3.

Ducks' delight

DEESIDE DUCKS picked up their second Laidler Division win of the season with a 6-5 penalty shot victory away to Bradford Bulldogs.

Bradford opened the scoring just one minute into the game but goals from Stewart Cutting and Daniel Fadejevs saw Deeside leading 2-1 at the first break.

Bulldogs tied things up early in the second period, but goals from Kieran Clarkson and Thomas Milnes helped the Ducks soar into a 4-2 advantage.

However, Bradford had the better of the chances after this and three unanswered goals gave them a 5-4 lead at the second interval.

The only goal in a closely fought third period fell to the Ducks' Michael Speare (pictured above), tying the scoreline at 5-5 and sending the match into an extra five-minute period of sudden death overtime.

With no deciding goal in the extra five minutes of play, the game had to be decided on a penalty shoot-out and strikes from Speare, Clarkson and Josh Jones sealed a first ever away win for the Ducks.

Under new regulations introduced for this season, Deeside receive two league points for the penalty shot win while Bradford get one point for drawing at the end of regulation time.

Ducks In The Newspaper!

There's a report about Sunday's Ducks' sensational penalty shot victory away to Bradford in today's Flintshire & Wrexham Leader (5th November 2024 - Page 35)

You also read the match report - along with coach's comments - here: https://www.icehockeyreview.co.uk/2024/11/match-report-bradford-bulldogs-5.html

Bradford Bulldogs 5-6 Deeside Ducks

North 2 League and Cup, Sunday 3rd November
Game 048

Bradford Bulldogs (2-0-1-6)   (1-1-0-6) Deeside Ducks

SCORING SUMMARY

G	Per	Time	Score	Team	Goal Scorer	Assist	Assist	Str
1	1	1:04	1-0	BRA	Keiron Furlong (2)			E
2	1	7:18	1-1	DEE	Stewart Cutting (1)			E
3	1	8:06	1-2	DEE	Daniels Fadejevs (1)	Kieran Clarkson (3)	Charlie Spridgeon (3)	E
4	2	25:42	2-2	BRA	Lucas Vince (4)			E
5	2	25:55	2-3	DEE	Kieran Clarkson (3)	Charlie Spridgeon (4)		PP
6	2	26:15	2-4	DEE	Tom Milnes (2)	Daniels Fadejevs (1)	Michael Speare (2)	E
7	2	31:04	3-4	BRA	Kai Hathaway (9)			SH
8	2	35:22	4-4	BRA	Lucas Vince (5)	Kacper Andrukianiec (5)		E
9	2	36:49	5-4	BRA	Tom Carroll (1)	Kacper Andrukianiec (6)	Keiron Furlong (3)	E
10	3	41:59	5-5	DEE	Michael Speare (3)	Tom Milnes (3)		E
11	4	PS	5-6	DEE	Michael Speare			GWG

PENALTY SUMMARY

BRADFORD BULLDOGS							DEESIDE DUCKS					
#	Per	Time	Player	PIM	Penalty		#	Per	Time	Player	PIM	Penalty
1	1	8:06	Cameron Williams	2	Slashing		1	2	35:07	Charlie Spridgeon	5	Boarding
2	2	25:36	Keiron Furlong	2	Slashing		2	2	39:16	Mackenzie Wilkes	2	Slashing
3	2	30:23	Keiron Furlong	2	Slashing		3	2	39:16	Mackenzie Wilkes	2	Interference
4	2	34:59	Kai Hathaway	2	Boarding		4	3	54:13	Tom Milnes	25	Kicking
5	3	45:26	Ben Fox	2	Slashing		5	4	63:40	Daniels Fadejevs	2	Hooking
6	3	54:03	Keiron Furlong	2	Slashing		6					
7	3	59:52	Bench	2	Too Many Men		7					
			TOT (PN-PIM) 7-14							TOT (PN-PIM) 5-36		
			Power Plays (Goals-Opp) 0-4							Power Plays (Goals-Opp) 1-7		

TEAM SUMMARY

		BRADFORD BULLDOGS	G	A	P	PN	PIM				DEESIDE DUCKS	G	A	P	PN	PIM
1	NM	Jack Mickevicius							2	NM	Paul Jones					
11	F	Lucas Vince	2		2				4	D	Charlie Spridgeon		2	2	1	5
11	F	Archie Grayson							5	F	Michael Speare	1	1	2		
15	F	Oliver Massey							10	F	Stewart Cutting	1		1		
16	D	Ben Darbyshire							12	D	Henry Phillips					
18	F	Tyler Hall							19	F	Mackenzie Wilkes				2	4
20	D	Cameron Williams				1	2		20	F	Tom Milnes	1	1	2	1	25
22	D	Jacob Brownlie							21	D	Kieran Clarkson	1	1	2		
26	F	Kacper Andrukianiec		2	2				25	F	Liam Yarwood					
29	D	Tom Carroll	1		1				29	F	Ben Roscoe					
30	D	Lewis Sinclair							31	D	James Morgan					
33	NM	Jacob Lowndes							34	F	Louis Ellwood					
66	F	Thomas Chong							40	F	Cody Ogden					
74	F	Ben Fox				1	2		47	NM	Callum Preston					
77	F	Kai Hathaway	1		1	1	2		51	F	Deacon Wilkes					
84	D	Joel Bark							62	F	Jack Davies					
86	D	Keiron Furlong	1	1	2	3	6		70	D	Alfie Kelly					
98	F	Abigail Culshaw							73	D	Josh Jones					
									81	F	Daniels Fadejevs	1	1	2	1	2
									91	D	Rory Sillery					
		Team Penalty				1	2				Team Penalty					
		TEAM TOTALS	5	3	8	7	14				TEAM TOTALS	5	6	11	5	36

GOALTENDER SUMMARY

BRADFORD BULLDOGS		Goals-Shots Against						DEESIDE DUCKS		Goals - Shots Against				
		TOI	1	2	3	OT	TOT			TOI	1	2	3	OT	TOT
1	Jack Mickevicius	65:00	2-16	2-16	1-11	0-4	5-47	2	Paul Jones	65:00	1-14	4-15	0-10	0-2	5-41
33	Jacob Lowndes							47	Callum Preston						
	Empty Net								Empty Net						

Source: NIHLStats.wordpress.com (Box Scores)

*Cody Ogden is the Ducks' top goal-scorer so far this season with 6
(Photo by Paul Breeze)*

Deeside Ducks Season So Far

The Deeside Ducks team were without a game at the weekend and are preparing for a big home game against title favourites Telford Tigers this Sunday.

They are now one third of the way through their debut competitive season in the NIHL's Laidler Division and certainly seem to be heading in the right direction.

From their eight league games to date, the Ducks have two wins and five defeats – with a question mark over the away game at Kingston in September that was abandoned due to safety concerns after a problem with the ice surface. A decision regarding the outcome of that game is still awaited from the sport's governing body.

Cody Ogden is the Ducks' leading goalscorer so far this season with 6 strikes – including an impressive hat-trick away to league leaders Telford Tigers – while Michael Speare, scorer of the winning penalty shot away to Bradford in the last game – is a close second with 4.

Looking back over the season so far, Ducks Head Coach Gary Shaw said:

"The season for the Ducks so far has been a big learning curve from a group of players that we have put together from all different levels."

"They are still trying to figure out each other's skills and the best way of playing, the biggest problem that we have as a coaching team is trying to get them to communicate with each other, they are very quiet when on the ice. If they would talk to each other giving information of what was happening, this would give the players the opportunity to make the right decision and not throw the puck away to the other team."

"The players have a good base to work from and we just need them to play as a unit on the ice and play as a group of five and not individually."

"We give them the opportunity to express themselves and make decisions, some they get right and others wrong but as a coaching team we need them to make mistakes so they can learn from their wrong decisions. We just need them to make fewer mistakes - the less they make the better for the team and the more chance they have to win the game."

"For the next few weeks we will be trying to get the players to be more aggressive in the plays that they are doing, to get the opponents to turn the puck over and create more scoring chances for us."

"Overall we as a coaching team are happy with the progression of the players, we just need more intensity on what they are doing in all areas of the ice and try not to over complicate what they do."

"With two wins this season already we have over-achieved, as some new teams that joined the league took two seasons to get the win."

"I was not expecting to win any games this season and focus on keeping the score as low as possible but, looking on what is happening in the league, I am expecting to win a few more, and hopefully with the big defeats we have suffered against the top teams in this league we can try and cut the score by half - with the first one coming up this weekend against Telford."

"We the coaches believe that they can do it, they themselves have to believe it and put it into practice and it will come right."

After three consecutive away games - and an absence of almost 6 weeks – the Ducks are finally at home this Sunday 17th November when they take on defending champions and cup holders Telford Tigers at Deeside Leisure Centre, 5pm face off.

Deeside Ducks' team were without a game at the weekend and are now preparing for a big home match against title favourites Telford Tigers on Sunday.

Looking back over the season so far, Ducks' head coach Gary Shaw said: "The players have a good base to work from and we just need them to play as a unit on the ice and play as a group of five and not individually.

"For the next few weeks we will be trying to get the players to be more aggressive in the plays that they are doing, to get the opponents to turn the puck over and create more scoring chances for us."

Results: Sutton 10 Bradford 2; Telford 8 Sheffield 2; Billingham 3 Altrincham 2; Bradford 7 Nottingham 3.

Ducks In The Newspaper! (#1)

There's a rather short piece about the Ducks in today's Flintshire & Wrexham Leader (12th November 2024 - Page 35).

You can read the full version of the "Season So Far" report - along with extended comments from Head Coach Gary Shaw - here:

https://www.icehockeyreview.co.uk/2024/11/deeside-ducks-season-so-far.html

#keepquacking   #fowlnotfoul

SPORT

ICE HOCKEY: DRAGONS AWAY DAY

Deeside face Warriors' test

DEESIDE DRAGONS will be hoping to make it a terrific treble when they come up against Whitley Warriors this weekend.

The Dragons make the long trip up to the North East on Sunday, having already demonstrated the requisite Warrior spirit to defeat Whitley twice so far this season.

Those results came during a weekend double-header between the teams, with Deeside winning 6-4 in Whitley, before returning home the following day to record a 7-2 outcome.

"We worked so hard for both of those wins," admitted Dragons' assistant head coach Matt Compton.

"They are a good, physical side. We know what to expect going up there on Sunday."

Results have been somewhat mixed of late for Deeside, who had sparked their season with eight triumphs on the bounce in all competitions.

Dragons managed to make the most of home comforts with a 4-0 triumph versus Solihull Barons on Sunday, but this followed a 9-6 defeat away to Hull Jets.

If there were defensive issues during the Hull match, that cannot be said of the Solihull contest and goaltender Matt Croyle was named MVP as Deeside managed to shut out their opponents.

Dragons had the lead with five minutes of the first period remaining via Jared Dickinson's goal, before James Shaw doubled the tally close to the midway point of the match.

There was no final period fightback from the Barons and goals from Jakub Hajek and Marc Lovell marked a welcome return to winning ways for Deeside.

"We need to be better for another team this week," added Compton. "We have proven we can go there and get a result.

"Stay disciplined. Momentum in sport is a big thing. Try and build more momentum and confidence."

Tomorrow: Billingham v Widnes; Hull v Nottingham; Sheffield v Solihull. **Sunday:** Billingham v Hull; Leeds v Nottingham; Solihull v Blackburn, Widnes v Sheffield.

Deeside Ducks have a home game against Division Two North title favourites Telford Tigers on Sunday.

Ducks are now a third of the

IMPRESSIVE: Cody Ogden. Picture: Ducks Media

way through their debut competitive season in the NIHL's Laidler Division and certainly seem to be heading in the right direction.

From their eight league games to date, the Ducks have two wins and five defeats – with a question mark over the away game at Kingston in September that was abandoned due to safety concerns after a problem with the ice surface.

A decision regarding the outcome of that game is still awaited from the sport's governing body.

Cody Ogden is the Ducks' leading goalscorer so far this season with six strikes, including an impressive hat-trick at league leaders Telford Tigers.

Ducks' head coach Gary Shaw said: "The players have a good base to work from and we just need them to play as a unit on the ice and play as a group of five and not individually.

"For the next few weeks we will be trying to get the players to be more aggressive in the plays that they are doing, to get the opponents to turn the puck over and create more scoring chances for us.

"With two wins this season already we have over-achieved, as some new teams that joined the league took two seasons to get the win. I was not expecting to win any games this season and focus on keeping the score as low as possible but, looking on what is happening in the league, I am expecting to win a few more."

Tomorrow: Coventry v Kingston, Sutton v Billingham; Telford v Altrincham. **Sunday:** Altrincham v Bradford; Nottingham v Sutton; Sheffield v Billingham.

LEFT: Action from Deeside Dragons' home win over Whitley in October. Picture: Dragons Media

Tyson's tense

BOXING: A weary-looking Mike Tyson uttered only 135 words during a bizarre press conference before tonight's fight with Jake Paul, but insisted he was ready for the YouTuber-turned-boxer.

Former world heavyweight champion Tyson (50-6, 44KOs) will step back into the ring for a first professional bout in 19 years at AT&T Stadium in a fight which will be streamed on Netflix.

Tyson took part in an exhibition with Roy Jones Jr in 2020, but will be up against an opponent 31 years his junior.

Host Ariel Helwani attempted to broach a number of topics with Tyson but the 58-year-old was not ready to bite.

"Are you talking to me? Yes I am back. I am just happy to be here. I love you too," said Tyson. "I'm just looking forward to fighting."

Rob's big win

DARTS: Rob Cross made safe progress into the Grand Slam of Darts quarter-finals after a 10-4 win over Ritchie Edhouse in Wolverhampton.

Cross will now face Martin Lukeman, who defeated Ross Smith 10-5 in their last-16 clash.

Three-time beaten finalist James Wade bowed out with a dramatic 10-9 loss to Scotland's Cameron Menzies, who came back from 6-4 down to move into his maiden televised quarter-final.

He will vie for a place in the semis with Northern Irishman Mickey Mansell, a 10-7 victor over Danny Noppert.

110

Ducks In The Newspaper!

(#2)

Twice in the same week! We have the Deeside Ducks in the newspaper once again.

This is same article that was originally covered in Tuesday's paper but is fleshed out more in today's edition of the Flintshire & Wrexham Leader (15th November 2024 - Page 33).

Interim Tables as at 11th November 2024

Laidler Division	GP	W	OTW	OTL	L	GF	GA	Pts
Sutton Sting	14	14	0	0	0	83	17	42
Telford Tigers 2	11	11	0	0	0	104	27	33
Billingham Bucc'rs	10	7	0	0	3	45	28	21
Kingston Sharks	12	4	1	1	6	43	54	15
Coventry Blaze	9	4	1	0	4	32	19	14
Altrincham Aces	12	4	0	0	8	39	54	12
Sheffield Titans	11	3	0	1	7	25	58	10
Bradford Bulldogs	11	3	0	1	7	38	63	10
Deeside Ducks	8	1	1	0	6	22	65	5
Nottingham Lions	12	1	0	0	11	39	85	3

Laidler Cup	GP	W	OTW	OTL	L	GF	GA	Pts
Telford Tigers 2	5	5	0	0	0	55	13	15
Coventry Blaze	6	4	0	0	2	28	14	12
Altrincham Aces	5	2	0	0	3	15	23	6
Bradford Bulldogs	6	1	0	1	4	19	35	4
Deeside Ducks	4	0	1	0	3	14	46	2

Based on information provided by NIHLstats.wordpress.com.

NIHL Stats have recorded the abandoned game away at Kingston Sharks as a 5-0 win for Kingston, with the result after 1 period being allowed to stand. At the time of writing (11th November) that decision hadn't been confirmed by the EIHA.

Netminder Statistics – up to 11th November 2024

Netminder	GPI	Mins	SA	GA	GAA	SV%	SO
Callum Preston	6	270:26	197	42	9.32	78.68	0
Paul Jones	4	174:09	151	23	7.89	84.77	0
Empty Net	1	00:25					
Totals		445:00	348	65	8.76	81.32	0

Deeside Ducks Player Statistics Up To 10th Nov 2024

Player	GP	G	A	Pts	PIM
Cody Ogden	8	6	2	8	2
Keiron Clarkson	7	3	3	6	2
Michael Speare	7	4	2	6	0
Thomas Milnes	8	2	3	5	39
Charlie Spridgeon	7	1	4	5	7
Chris Jones	4	2	2	4	4
Josh Jones	8	1	2	3	2
Stewart Cutting	4	1	1	2	0
Daniels Fadejevs	4	1	1	2	4
Ben Roscoe	8	0	2	2	2
Jack Davies	6	1	0	1	2
Louis Morgan	2	0	1	1	4
Henry Phillips	4	0	1	1	0
Paul Jones	8	0	0	0	0
Louis Ellwood	7	0	0	0	2
Gary Dixon	6	0	0	0	4
George Spofforth	6	0	0	0	0
Heather Clarkson	3	0	0	0	0
James Morgan	7	0	0	0	4
Callum Preston	8	0	0	0	0
Kenny Williams	4	0	0	0	2
Rory Sillery	6	0	0	0	2
Luke Wainwright	4	0	0	0	0
Deacon Wilkes	4	0	0	0	0
Mackenzie Wilkes	6	0	0	0	6
Alfie Kelly	6	0	0	0	18
Liam Yarwood	6	0	0	0	2

Based on information provided by NIHLstats.wordpress.com

Note: NIHL Stats have incorrectly recorded 2 goals for Louis Ellwood which were actually scored by Cody Ogden. Michael Speare also has an extra goal for the Penalty Shot win away at Bradford. The above table shows the corrected figures for all three players.

Player appearances include the abandoned away game at Kingston

Ducks match night merchandise table (Photo by Paul Breeze)

Ducks Merchandise!

The Ducks are at home for the first time in ages this Sunday when they take on the Telford Tigers at Deeside Leisure Centre, so make sure you check out the goodies for sale on the merchandise table.

Homemade cakes	Order Ducks replica shirts
Cookies	Try your luck in the raffle
Candies	Have a go at the Duck's
Ducks pucks	"Guess The" game
Light sticks	
Duck whistles	Cash and card payments
Wristbands	accepted.

All funds raised on the merchandise table go to help the Ducks club – which, in turn, benefits the whole of Deeside junior ice hockey.

See you on Sunday!

More Ducks Merchandise (Photos by Paul Breeze)

The Deeside Ducks MVP against Telford was Stewart Cutting
(Photo by Paul Breeze)

Sunday 17th November 2024 – NIHL Laidler Division
Deeside Ducks 1 – Telford Tigers2 11

The Deeside Ducks put in a spirited performance but lost out 1-11 to Laidler Division title favourites Telford Tigers at Deeside Leisure Centre on Sunday.

While this might sound like a heavy defeat, the Tigers won the away game in Shropshire 24-4 just two weeks ago so, in comparison, this was actually quite an improvement.

Telford took the lead after just 16 seconds and never really looked like losing. They were 0-4 up at the end of the first period and 0-6 ahead by the second interval.

Deeside were outshot by some 4 to 1 over the course of the game and, were it not for spells of staunch defending and an impressive performance by Paul Jones in goal, the score would undoubtedly have been much higher.

The Tigers hit three quick-fire goals within 50 seconds of each other early in the third period to further extend their lead but the Ducks finally broke their duck at 49.13 when Luke Wainwright fired in a rocket shot from outside the blueline that beat the Telford netminder to record his first senior goal.

Two late goals put Telford past double figures and the game ended up as a 1-11 win for the visitors.

The Ducks are away to Coventry Blaze this Saturday 23rd November and then at home to the same opposition the following Saturday 30th November at Deeside Leisure Centre, 5pm face off.

Talking after the game, Head Coach Gary Shaw said: "I was away but going on what we have been doing over the last couple of weeks in training and the request for the players to interact more and force errors from our opponents, the team has taken this on board. I wanted to cut the goals against by half and we achieved that. Plus we were missing a few good players on Sunday, so the result could have been better for us."

"We obviously are still making mistakes in poor areas, but once we have things done better in our zone, we can improve the score again."

"The team are away this weekend at Coventry and it will be another tough encounter, but we need to keep progressing and I'm confident that we will improve again."

Deeside Ducks 1-11 Telford Tigers NIHL 2

North 2 League and Cup, Sunday 17th November

Game 057

Deeside Ducks (1-1-0-7) (12-0-0-0) Telford Tigers NIHL 2

SCORING SUMMARY

G	Per	Time	Score	Team	Goal Scorer	Assist	Assist	Str
1	1	0:16	0-1	TEL	Taylor Stanton (14)	Liam Bartholomew (4)	Dan Mitchell (2)	E
2	1	14:57	0-2	TEL	Filip Supa (21)	Taylor Stanton (14)		E
3	1	16:54	0-3	TEL	Karol Jets (10)	Connor McNaughton (16)		E
4	1	17:16	0-4	TEL	Lewis Smith (7)	Connor Bennett (3)	Kyle Watt (10)	E
5	2	24:10	0-5	TEL	Josh Hustwick (4)	Filip Supa (13)	Oliver Hunt (17)	E
6	2	31:50	0-6	TEL	Ben Washburn (5)	Oliver Hunt (18)		PP
7	3	44:04	0-7	TEL	Ben Washburn (6)	Connor Keyes (1)	Taylor Stanton (15)	PP
8	3	44:43	0-8	TEL	Karol Jets (11)	Connor McNaughton (17)	Oliver Hunt (19)	E
9	3	44:54	0-9	TEL	Oliver Hunt (16)	Karol Jets (13)	Connor McNaughton (18)	E
10	3	49:13	1-9	DEE	Luke Wainwright (1)			E
11	3	53:55	1-10	TEL	Karol Jets (12)	Connor McNaughton (19)		PP
12	3	55:35	1-11	TEL	Lewis Smith (8)	Oliver Hunt (20)		PP

PENALTY SUMMARY

DEESIDE DUCKS						TELFORD TIGERS NIHL 2				
#	Per	Time	Player	PIM	Penalty	#	Per	Time	Player	PIM	Penalty
1	2	29:56	Kenny Williams	2	Tripping	1	3	50:10	Connor McNaughton	2	Interference
2	3	43:03	Ben Roscoe	2	Kneeing	2	3	54:36	Connor Keyes	2	Holding Stick
3	3	45:54	Charlie Spridgeon	2	Holding	3					
4	3	52:38	Ben Roscoe	25	Check to Head	4					

TOT (PN-PIM) 4-31 TOT (PN-PIM) 2-4

Power Plays (Goals-Opp) 0-2 Power Plays (Goals-Opp) 4-6

TEAM SUMMARY

	DEESIDE DUCKS	G	A	P	PN	PIM			TELFORD TIGERS NIHL 2	G	A	P	PN	PIM
2	NM Paul Jones							4	F Karol Jets	3	1	4		
4	D Charlie Spridgeon				1	2		5	D Robert Oxley					
5	F Michael Speare							11	F Callum O'Reilly					
9	F Gary Dixon							13	F Lewis Smith	2		2		
10	F Stewart Cutting							15	F Daniel Retter					
13	D Deacon Wilkes							18	D Josh Hustwick	1		1		
19	F Mackenzie Wilkes							29	D Connor Keyes		1	1	1	2
21	D Keiron Clarkson							31	NM Joshua Minns					
25	F Liam Yarwood							36	D Josef Lauder					
29	F Ben Roscoe				2	27		40	F Ben Washburn	2		2		
34	F Louis Ellwood							50	NM Hal Griffiths					
40	F Cody Ogden							51	F Liam Bartholomew		1	1		
47	NM Callum Preston							53	F Oliver Hunt	1	4	5		
70	D Alfie Kelly							59	D Connor Bennett		1	1		
73	F Josh Jones							61	F Kyle Watt		1	1		
88	F Kenny Williams				1	2		71	F Taylor Stanton	1	2	3		
91	D Rory Sillery							81	F Filip Supa	1	1	2		
98	D Luke Wainwright	1		1				88	F Dan Mitchell		1	1		
								95	F Connor McNaughton		4	4	1	2
	Team Penalty								Team Penalty					
	TEAM TOTALS	1		1	4	31			TEAM TOTALS	11	17	28	2	4

GOALTENDER SUMMARY

DEESIDE DUCKS	TOI	Goals-Shots Against					TELFORD TIGERS	TOI	Goals - Shots Against				
		1	2	3	OT	TOT			1	2	3	OT	TOT
2 Paul Jones	60:00	4-22	2-20	5-30		11-72	31 Joshua Minns	20:00			1-10		1-10
47 Callum Preston							50 Hal Griffiths	40:00	0-8	0-5			0-13
Empty Net							Empty Net						

Source: NIHL Stats.wordpress.com (Box Scores)

STAR: Stewart Cutting was Ducks' MVP. Picture: Paul Breeze

Ducks this season, grabbed his first ever goal for the Dragons with just under eight minutes left to play.

Simpson was brought in by the Dragons last month and he has proved to be an excellent acquisition, signing from NIHL side Bristol Pitbulls.

Other results: Billingham 15 Widnes 2; Hull 5 Nottingham 1; Sheffield 3 Solihull 4; Billingham 6 Hull 1; Leeds 1 Nottingham 7; Solihull 3 Blackburn 8; Widnes 2 Sheffield 5.

for Littler

there just doing what they do, but he's actually had a curry, a Boost, and them little sweets half pink, half white... squashies.

"He even had them in the break, while I'm having a fag, and a water.

"I can't compete with that, it was like Godly. He was relentless, he is so good, it's ridiculous."

Littler is now favourite for the forthcoming World Championship, one year on from his breakthrough tournament at Alexandra Palace.

Lukeman has tipped him to break the records set by Phil Taylor and Michael van Gerwen, but Littler said: "If I want it then I should get it, but it is going to take some years that not only Michael has got, but also Phil Taylor.

"We will have to see, it has been a very long week and a bit, I can't wait to go home and chill out."

Lukeman added: "If he gets his head on, forget Michael's records, he is going to beat Phil Taylor's records. If he gets his head right, stays away from drink, girls, whatever, that boy is going to go very far. He will break records ridiculously."

Deeside Ducks put in a spirited performance, but they lost out 11-1 in their encounter against Laidler Division title favourites Telford Tigers.

While this might sound like a heavy defeat, the Tigers won the away game in Shropshire 24-4 just two weeks ago so, in comparison, this was actually quite an improvement.

Telford took the lead after just 16 seconds and never really looked like losing.

They were 4-0 up at the end of the first period and leading 6-0 by the second interval.

Deeside were outshot by some four-to-one over the course of the game and, were it not for spells of staunch team defending and an impressive performance by Paul Jones in goal, the score would undoubtedly have been much higher.

The Tigers hit three quickfire goals within 50 seconds early in the third period to further extend their lead but the Ducks finally broke their duck at 49.13 when Luke Wainwright fired in a rocket shot from outside the blueline that beat the Telford netminder to record his first senior goal.

Two late goals put Telford past double figures.

Deeside Ducks are away to Coventry Blaze this Saturday and they will then conclude the month at home to the same opposition the following Saturday, November 30.

Other results: Coventry 3 Kingston 2 (overtime); Sutton 6 Billingham 2; Telford 8 Altrincham 2; Altrincham 6 Bradford 0; Nottingham 1 Sutton 3; Sheffield 1 Billingham 3.

Ducks In The Newspaper!

The report from Sunday's Ducks v Telford Tigers2 game appears in today's Flintshire & Wrexham Leader (19th November 2024 - Page 35).

You can read the same report - along with lots of other interesting stuff - on the highly informative grass roots ice hockey website www.icehockeyreview.co.uk

Ducks face off away at Coventry (Photo by Maxine Roscoe)

Saturday 23rd November 2024 – NIHL Laidler Division
Coventry NIHL Blaze 17 – Deeside Ducks 2

The Deeside Ducks suffered a heavy 17-2 defeat on the road away to the Coventry NIHL Blaze on Saturday.

Coventry led 5-0 after the first period and 12-0 at the second break. Third period goals from Charlie Spridgeon and Luke Wainwright – his second in two games - finally gave the travelling fans something to cheer about but 5 more for the Blaze handed them a convincing victory.

The Ducks are in action again this Saturday when they face the Blaze at home at Deeside Leisure Centre, 5pm face off.

*****

Ducks player Ben Roscoe has been handed a 2-game suspension by the governing body's Department of Player Safety (DOPS) after being banished from last Sunday's home game against Telford for an illegal check to the head.

The disciplinary panel observed: "The player recklessly endangered his opponent. This was an unnecessary check on a player who was in a vulnerable position and unaware of the impending hit."

Another Ducks player, Thomas Milnes, previously received a 1-game ban for kicking out at an opponent who had legally checked him in the away game at Telford two weeks earlier.

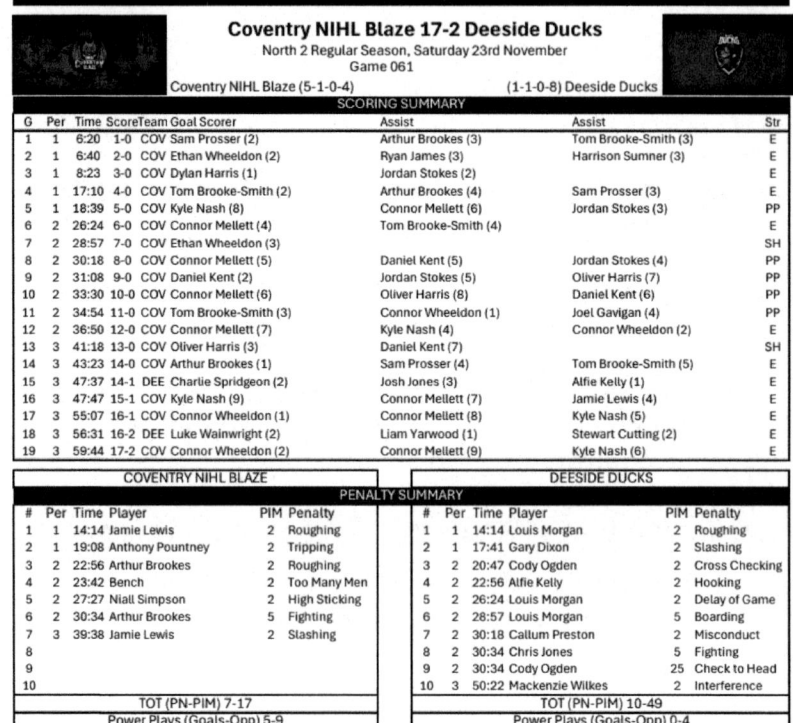

Coventry NIHL Blaze 17-2 Deeside Ducks
North 2 Regular Season, Saturday 23rd November
Game 061

Coventry NIHL Blaze (5-1-0-4) (1-1-0-8) Deeside Ducks

SCORING SUMMARY

G	Per	Time	Score	Team	Goal Scorer	Assist	Assist	Str
1	1	6:20	1-0	COV	Sam Prosser (2)	Arthur Brookes (3)	Tom Brooke-Smith (3)	E
2	1	6:40	2-0	COV	Ethan Wheeldon (2)	Ryan James (3)	Harrison Sumner (3)	E
3	1	8:23	3-0	COV	Dylan Harris (1)	Jordan Stokes (2)		E
4	1	17:10	4-0	COV	Tom Brooke-Smith (2)	Arthur Brookes (4)	Sam Prosser (3)	E
5	1	18:39	5-0	COV	Kyle Nash (8)	Connor Mellett (6)	Jordan Stokes (3)	PP
6	2	26:24	6-0	COV	Connor Mellett (4)	Tom Brooke-Smith (4)		E
7	2	28:57	7-0	COV	Ethan Wheeldon (3)			SH
8	2	30:18	8-0	COV	Connor Mellett (5)	Daniel Kent (5)	Jordan Stokes (4)	PP
9	2	31:08	9-0	COV	Daniel Kent (2)	Jordan Stokes (5)	Oliver Harris (7)	PP
10	2	33:30	10-0	COV	Connor Mellett (6)	Oliver Harris (8)	Daniel Kent (6)	PP
11	2	34:54	11-0	COV	Tom Brooke-Smith (3)	Connor Wheeldon (1)	Joel Gavigan (4)	PP
12	2	36:50	12-0	COV	Connor Mellett (7)	Kyle Nash (4)	Connor Wheeldon (2)	E
13	3	41:18	13-0	COV	Oliver Harris (3)	Daniel Kent (7)		SH
14	3	43:23	14-0	COV	Arthur Brookes (1)	Sam Prosser (4)	Tom Brooke-Smith (5)	E
15	3	47:37	14-1	DEE	Charlie Spridgeon (2)	Josh Jones (3)	Alfie Kelly (1)	E
16	3	47:47	15-1	COV	Kyle Nash (9)	Connor Mellett (7)	Jamie Lewis (4)	E
17	3	55:07	16-1	COV	Connor Wheeldon (1)	Connor Mellett (8)	Kyle Nash (5)	E
18	3	56:31	16-2	DEE	Luke Wainwright (2)	Liam Yarwood (1)	Stewart Cutting (2)	E
19	3	59:44	17-2	COV	Connor Wheeldon (2)	Connor Mellett (9)	Kyle Nash (6)	E

PENALTY SUMMARY

COVENTRY NIHL BLAZE						DEESIDE DUCKS				
#	Per	Time	Player	PIM	Penalty	#	Per	Time	Player	PIM	Penalty
1	1	14:14	Jamie Lewis	2	Roughing	1	1	14:14	Louis Morgan	2	Roughing
2	1	19:08	Anthony Pountney	2	Tripping	2	1	17:41	Gary Dixon	2	Slashing
3	2	22:56	Arthur Brookes	2	Roughing	3	2	20:47	Cody Ogden	2	Cross Checking
4	2	23:42	Bench	2	Too Many Men	4	2	22:56	Alfie Kelly	2	Hooking
5	2	27:27	Niall Simpson	2	High Sticking	5	2	26:24	Louis Morgan	2	Delay of Game
6	2	30:34	Arthur Brookes	5	Fighting	6	2	28:57	Louis Morgan	5	Boarding
7	3	39:38	Jamie Lewis	2	Slashing	7	2	30:18	Callum Preston	2	Misconduct
8						8	2	30:34	Chris Jones	5	Fighting
9						9	2	30:34	Cody Ogden	25	Check to Head
10						10	3	50:22	Mackenzie Wilkes	2	Interference
		TOT (PN-PIM) 7-17						TOT (PN-PIM) 10-49		
		Power Plays (Goals-Opp) 5-9						Power Plays (Goals-Opp) 0-4		

TEAM SUMMARY

COVENTRY NIHL BLAZE			G	A	P	PN	PIM
5	D	Jordan Stokes		4	4		
8	D	Ryan James		1	1		
9	F	Jamie Lewis		1	1	2	4
10	D	Jodie Alderson-Smith					
12	F	Harrison Sumner		1	1		
15	D	Reuben Sweenie-Fuller					
19	F	Tom Brooke-Smith	2	3	5		
21	F	Connor Wheeldon	2	2	4		
24	F	Ethan Wheeldon	2		2		
25	F	Daniel Kent	1	3	4		
27	F	Dylan Harris	1		1		
28	D	Antony Pountney				1	2
34	NM	Hayden Laverick					
37	F	Connor Mellett	4	4	8		
39	NM	Joel Bearman					
40	D	Niall Simpson				1	2
49	D	Will Kibkalo					
59	F	Oliver Harris	1	2	3		
60	F	Kyle Nash	2	3	5		
87	F	Arthur Brookes	1	2	3	2	7
93	F	Sam Prosser	1	2	3		
95	F	Joel Gavigan		1	1		
		Team Penalty				1	2
		TEAM TOTALS	17	27	44	7	17

DEESIDE DUCKS			G	A	P	PN	PIM
2	NM	Paul Jones					
4	D	Charlie Spridgeon	1		1		
9	F	Gary Dixon				1	2
10	F	Stewart Cutting		1	1		
19	F	Mackenzie Wilkes				1	2
25	F	Liam Yarwood		1	1		
31	D	Louis Morgan				3	9
40	F	Cody Ogden				2	27
47	NM	Callum Preston				1	2
52	F	Harry Shearman					
62	F	Jack Davies					
70	D	Alfie Kelly		1	1	1	2
72	D	Chris Jones				1	5
73	F	Josh Jones		1	1		
91	D	Rory Sillery					
98	D	Luke Wainwright	1		1		
		Team Penalty					
		TEAM TOTALS	2	4	6	10	49

GOALTENDER SUMMARY

COVENTRY NIHL BLAZE		TOI	Goals-Shots Against				
			1	2	3	OT	TOT
34	Hayden Laverick	26;24	0-10	0-2			0-12
39	Joel Bearman	33:36		0-1	2-7		2-8
	Empty Net						

DEESIDE DUCKS		TOI	Goals - Shots Against				
			1	2	3	OT	TOT
2	Paul Jones	29:42		4-18	5-30		9-48
47	Callum Preston	30:18	5-28	3-11			8-39
	Empty Net						

Source: NIHLStats.wordpress.com (Box Scores)

ON TARGET: Deeside Ducks' Luke Wainwright. Picture: Mark Ray

"On Sunday, we had a really, really good crowd in." added Compton.
"It was so disappointing we couldn't win.
"We didn't get ourselves going to win on Sunday.
"We didn't put ourselves in a position to win the game. It didn't look right."
Reflecting on the defeat, Witkowski told the Puck 'N' Dragon podcast: "It's disappointing at home to not get the three points.
"It's just, I think we're better than that. So, just regroup, have a good week of practice and then try to forget about it."
Other results: Hull 1 Solihull 5; Nottingham 4 Whitley 5; Blackburn 1 Billingham 3; Nottingham 3 Solihull 7; Sheffield 1 Hull 7; Whitley 3 Leeds 8

Heavy away defeat for Ducks

THINGS didn't go the way of the Deeside Ducks in their most recent piece of Division Two North action.
The Ducks found themselves on the wrong end of a 17-2 defeat during their trip to Coventry Blaze.
Coventry hit the ground running and they led 5-0 after the first period and 12-0 at the second break.
Third period goals from Charlie Spridgeon and Luke Wainwright - his second in two games - finally gave the travelling fans something to cheer about but five more successful efforts from the Blaze handed them a convincing victory.
Ducks' Ben Roscoe has been handed a two-game suspension by the governing body's Department of Player Safety (DOPS) after being banished from the home game against Telford for an illegal check to the head.
The disciplinary panel observed: "The player recklessly endangered his opponent. This was an unnecessary check on a player who was in a vulnerable position and unaware of the impending hit."
Thomas Milnes previously received a one-game ban for kicking out at an opponent who had legally checked him in the away game at Telford two weeks earlier.
Other results: Billingham 4 Hoffingham 2; Bradford 0 Altrincham 9

Ducks In The Newspaper!

The report from Saturday's Deeside Ducks game away at Coventry appears in today's Flintshire & Wrexham Leader (26th November 2024 - Page 35).

You can read the same report - along with lots of other interesting stuff - on the highly informative grass roots ice hockey review website: www.icehockeyreview.co.uk

The Ducks debut season wristband, modelled by Olivia
(Photo by Paul Breeze)

More Ducks Merchandise!

The Ducks are at home this Saturday 30th November when they take on the Coventry NIHL Blaze at Deeside Leisure Centre (5pm face off), so make sure you check out the goodies for sale on the merchandise table.

Homemade cakes	Debut Season Wristbands
Cookies	Order Ducks replica shirts
Candy cones	
Ducks pucks	Try your luck in the raffle
Light sticks	Have a go at the Duck's
Duck whistles	"Guess The" game

All funds raised on the merchandise table go to help the Ducks club – which, in turn, benefits the whole of Deeside junior ice hockey.

Charlie Spridgeon was the Ducks' MVP against Coventry
(Photo by Paul Breeze)

Saturday 30th November – NIHL Laidler Division
Deeside Ducks 2 – Coventry NIHL Blaze 3

The Deeside Ducks put in a battling performance but narrowly lost out 2-3 to Coventry NIHL Blaze at Deeside Leisure Centre on Saturday.

When the two teams met a week earlier in Coventry, the Blaze had come out easy 17-2 winners, so this was certainly a great improvement, but will probably still be viewed as a disappointing result.

The first period was goal-less and it took until the 27th minute for the deadlock to be broken when Chris Jones raced straight out of the penalty box to slot the puck home for a Ducks' powerplay goal.

The lead lasted just 2½ minutes, however, as Coventry went on to equalise, but a Stewart Cutting goal on 36 minutes edged the Ducks back in front.

This game was littered with niggly penalties for both sides and the Blaze took advantage of a powerplay to equalise again with 90 seconds left in the second period.

The score was finely balanced at 2-2 with one period left to play but a major slashing penalty for the Ducks on 47 minutes left them shorthanded for an extended 5 minute spell and the Blaze managed to fire in what would turn out to be the winning goal.

The final minutes were played at a furious pace with the Ducks pushing forward trying to force a late equaliser and Jace Gledhill performing heroics in the Deeside net to keep Coventry at bay – but there was no further scoring and the game finished in a 2-3 win for the Blaze.

The Ducks are next in action this Sunday 8th December away to Altrincham Aces and are next at home on Saturday 14th December when they face Bradford Bulldogs at Deeside Leisure Centre, 5pm face off.

Commenting on Facebook afterwards, Ducks Assistant Coach Simon Hughes said:

The team worked hard all game and showed great heart and determination. They worked on a new D-zone system and it paid off, forcing long range shots all night that any of the keepers would stop all night. Jace in his

Ducks debut played a blinder and made several crucial saves from the house to keep us in contention.

The forecheck and centre ice coverage worked well, created the pressure to break them down and force errors and turnovers.

A massive improvement and another demonstration that the Deeside Ducks can compete at this level.

A huge "well done" from the bench and just a shame not to take something away with a little more discipline other than immense pride at a solid performance.

Special thanks to James Parson (Deeside Juniors Head Coach) this week and well done to U19 Charlie Nicholson on his senior hockey debut.

The game against Coventry on Saturday saw home debuts for 17 year old netminder Jace Gledhill, former Blackpool and Deeside junior Harry Shearman and current Dragons U19 player Charlie Nicholson.

Before the game, there was a minute's applause in memory of Peter Sheffield – long term Deeside photographer and media man - who tragically died last weekend after an accident two weeks earlier.

Ducks player Cody Ogden has been handed a 2-game suspension by the governing body's Department of Player Safety (DOPS) after being banished from the away game at Coventry for an illegal check to the head.

The disciplinary panel observed: "The player recklessly endangered his opponent with the check, with primary contact to the neck/head area."

Deeside Ducks Poem from Lucy

Deeside Ducks are quacking on strong –
What they need now is their own specially written song -
But it does seem clear, Ducks, that if you want to win
Your players need to steer clear of that Sin Bin.

Lucy London,- 1st December 2024

Deeside Ducks 2-3 Coventry NIHL Blaze
North 2 Regular Season, Sunday 24th November
Game 062

Deeside Ducks (1-1-0-9)   (6-1-0-4) Coventry NIHL Blaze

SCORING SUMMARY

G	Per	Time	Score	Team	Goal Scorer	Assist	Assist	Str
1	2	25:32	1-0	DEE	Chris Jones (3)	Gary Dixon (1)	Daniels Fadejevs (2)	PP
2	2	28:07	1-1	COV	Daniel Kent (3)	Dylan Harris (1)	Oliver Harris (9)	E
3	2	35:48	2-1	DEE	Stewart Cutting (2)	Chris Jones (3)		E
4	2	38:16	2-2	COV	Arthur Brookes (2)	Daniel Kent (8)		PP
5	3	47:51	2-3	COV	Tom Brooke-Smith (4)	Ryan James (4)		PP

PENALTY SUMMARY

DEESIDE DUCKS

#	Per	Time	Player	PIM	Penalty
1	1	5:02	Louis Morgan	2	Tripping
2	1	12:13	Chris Jones	2	Roughing
3	1	13:34	Gary Dixon	2	Hooking
4	1	15:24	Rory Sillery	2	Roughing
5	1	18:50	Daniels Fadejevs	2	High Sticking
6	1	18:50	Charlie Spridgeon	2	Cross Checking
7	2	23:24	Chris Jones	2	Tripping
8	2	30:34	Daniels Fadejevs	2	Roughing
9	2	34:12	Gary Dixon	2	Slashing
10	2	37:14	Gary Dixon	2	Hooking
11	3	46:47	Alfie Kelly	25	Slashing
12	3	48:55	Harry Shearman	2	Slashing
13	3	56:37	Chris Jones	2	Cross Checking
14	3	57:13	Gary Dixon	2	Misconduct

TOT (PN-PIM) 14-51
Power Plays (Goals-Opp) 1-4

COVENTRY NIHL BLAZE

#	Per	Time	Player	PIM	Penalty
1	1	15:24	Connor Mellett	2	Roughing
2	1	18:50	Charles Coney	2	Cross Checking
3	2	25:24	Oliver Harris	2	Slashing
4	2	32:00	Tom Brooke-Smith	2	Interference
5	2	34:24	Charles Coney	2	Tripping
6	2	39:28	Connor Wheeldon	2	Cross Checking
7	3	48:55	Arthur Brookes	2	Cross Checking
8	3	57:13	Sam Prosser	2	Hooking
9					
10					
11					
12					
13					
14					

TOT (PN-PIM) 8-16
Power Plays (Goals-Opp) 2-11

TEAM SUMMARY

		DEESIDE DUCKS	G	A	P	PN	PIM
1	NM	Jace Gledhill					
4	D	Charlie Spridgeon				1	2
9	F	Gary Dixon		1	1	4	8
10	F	Stewart Cutting	1		1		
13		Deacon Wilkes					
18	F	George Spofforth					
19	F	Mackenzie Wilkes					
21		Kieran Clarkson					
31	D	James Morgan				1	2
34		Louis Ellwood					
47	NM	Callum Preston					
51	F	Harry Shearman				1	2
52		Charles Nicholson				1	25
70	D	Alfie Kelly				3	6
72	D	Chris Jones	1	1	2	2	4
81	F	Daniels Fadejevs		1	1	1	2
91	D	Rory Sillery					
98	D	Luke Wainwright					
		Team Penalty					
		TEAM TOTALS	**2**	**3**	**5**	**14**	**51**

		COVENTRY NIHL BLAZE	G	A	P	PN	PIM
8	D	Ryan James		1	1		
9	F	Jamie Lewis					
12	F	Harrison Sumner					
15	D	Reuben Sweenie-Fuller					
18	D	Max Parham					
19	F	Tom Brooke-Smith	1		1	1	2
21	F	Connor Wheeldon				1	2
24	F	Ethan Wheeldon					
25	F	Daniel Kent	1	1	2		
27	F	Dylan Harris		1	1		
34	NM	Hayden Laverick					
37	F	Connor Mellett				1	2
39	NM	Joel Bearman					
40	D	Niall Simpson					
49	D	Will Kibkalo					
57	F	Daniel Upton					
59	F	Oliver Harris		1	1	1	2
60	F	Kyle Nash					
87	F	Arthur Brookes	1		1	1	2
88	D	Charles Coney				2	4
93	F	Sam Prosser				1	2
		Team Penalty					
		TEAM TOTALS	**3**	**4**	**7**	**8**	**16**

GOALTENDER SUMMARY

	DEESIDE DUCKS	TOI	Goals-Shots Against 1	2	3	OT	TOT
1	Jace Gledhill	60:00	0-15	2-33	1-14		3-62
47	Callum Preston						
	Empty Net						

	COVENTRY BLAZE	TOI	Goals - Shots Against 1	2	3	OT	TOT
34	Hayden Laverick	60:00	0-4	2-7	0-5		2-16
39	Joel Bearman						
	Empty Net						

Source: NIHLStats.wordpress.com (Box Scores)

wanted to do it. He was such a nice guy and we'll miss him."

Deeside were in control of proceedings from the off and they managed to build-up a two-goal advantage prior to the first break.

Charlie Phillips broke the deadlock and this was followed by a goal from Jakub Hajek.

Dragons continued to control the match in the second period and Jake Witkowski was on the mark to make it 3-0.

James Parsons duly added a fourth goal, before Scimitars pulled one back late in the second period.

No further goals would arrive as Deeside comfortably saw the game out.

Other results: Hull 2 Nottingham 4; Leeds 5 Blackburn 7; Nottingham 2 Hull 3; Widnes 1 Whitley 4.

What a difference a week makes. Deeside Ducks put in a battling performance as they narrowly lost out 3-2 to Coventry Blaze at Deeside Leisure Centre.

When the two teams met a week earlier in Coventry, the Blaze had come out easy 17-2 winners, so this was certainly a great improvement, but it will probably still be viewed as a disappointing result.

The first period was goal-less and it took until the 27th minute for the deadlock to be broken when Chris Jones raced straight out of the penalty box to slot the puck home for a Ducks' powerplay goal.

The lead lasted just two-and-a-half minutes, however, as Coventry went on to equalise, but a Stewart Cutting goal on 36 minutes edged the Ducks back in front.

This game was littered with niggly penalties for both sides and the Blaze took advantage of a powerplay to equalise again with 90 seconds left in the second period.

The score was finely balanced at 2-2 with one period left to play but a major slashing penalty for the Ducks on 47 minutes left them shorthanded for an extended five-minute spell and the Blaze managed to fire in what would turn out to be the winning goal.

The final minutes were played at a furious pace with the Ducks pushing forward trying to force a late equaliser and Jace Gledhill performing heroics in the Deeside net to keep Coventry at bay - but there was no further scoring and the game finished in a win for the Blaze.

Ducks are next in action this Sunday when they travel away to Altrincham Aces.

Deeside are next at home on Saturday, December 14 when they come up against Bradford Bulldogs.

Other results: Billingham 7 Sheffield 1; Kingston 6 Nottingham 2; Telford 5 Bradford 3.

MVP: Charlie Spridgeon impressed for Deeside Ducks versus Coventry. Picture: Paul Breeze

Five titles in a row for Bills

AMERICAN FOOTBALL: Buffalo Bills clinched a fifth straight AFC East title as they swept aside San Francisco 49ers 35-10 in the snow.

A 30-yard field goal from Chase McLaughlin helped Tampa Bay Buccaneers beat Carolina Panthers 26-23 in overtime to move to a tie at the top of the NFC South.

Philadelphia Eagles recovered from a two-score deficit against the Baltimore Ravens in the first quarter to win 24-19, their tenth of the season.

Los Angeles Rams clinched a 21-14 win over New Orleans Saints and Houston Texans kept their play-off hopes on track with a 23-20 win over Jacksonville Jaguars.

Pittsburgh Steelers beat Cincinnati Bengals 44-38 and Minnesota Vikings needed a late comeback to win their fifth straight game as they edged out Arizona Cardinals 23-22.

Washington Commanders scored three touchdowns in the first quarter as they got back on track with a 42-19 rout of Tennessee Titans while Atlanta Falcons went down 17-13 to Los Angeles Chargers.

Indianapolis Colts stunned New England Patriots with a late touchdown and a two-point conversion to win 25-24 while Seattle Seahawks beat New York Jets 26-21.

Ducks In The Newspaper!

The report from Saturday's Deeside Ducks home game against Coventry appears in today's Flintshire & Wrexham Leader (3rd December 2024 - Page 34).

You can read the same report - along with some other interesting bits and pieces - on the highly informative grass roots ice hockey review website

www.icehockeyreview.co.uk

*Harry Shearman in action for the Ducks away at Altrincham
(Photo by Gary Shearman)*

Sunday 8th December – NIHL Laidler Division
Altrincham Aces 16 – Deeside Ducks 4

The Deeside Ducks made the relatively short trip up the M56 to face the Altrincham Aces for a combined Laidler Division league and cup game on Sunday but came home on the back of a heavy 16-4 defeat.

The Aces took a modest 3-0 lead into the first break and ran riot in the latter stages with the Ducks never really looking in contention - and Deeside goals from Josh Jones, Kieran Clarkson, Daniels Fadejevs and Gary Dixon only served to give the score-line a bit of respectability.

The Ducks have a busy weekend coming up as they are at home to Bradford Bulldogs this Saturday 14th December at Deeside Leisure Centre – 5pm face off

- and then make the long journey up to the North East on Sunday to face Billingham Buccaneers for the first time.

****

Ducks player Alfie Kelly has been handed a 2-game suspension by the governing body's Department of Player Safety (DOPS) after being banished from last week's home game against Coventry for slashing.

The panel observed that the offence was an "aggressive slashing motion to the groin area of an opponent, recklessly endangering them."

Fellow Duck Cody Ogden has just completed a 2-game suspension for an illegal check to the head in the away game at Coventry the week before.

Oh dear Ducks but what the deuce
Whether you win or lose
Just keep quacking on Ducks
Keep on icing those pucks

Lucy Poet in Residence, 9th December 2024

PENALTY SUMMARY

ALTRINCHAM ACES					
#	Per	Time	Player	PIM	Penalty
1	1	19:19	Sam Daintith	2	Kneeing
2	3	51:24	Sam Hockey	2	Tripping
3	3	52:50	Kane Morin	2	Cross Checking
4	3	55:02	C.J Ashton	2	Hooking
5					
6					
7					
TOT (PN-PIM) 4-8					
Power Plays (Goals-Opp) 2-6					

DEESIDE DUCKS					
#	Per	Time	Player	PIM	Penalty
1	2	24:56	Mackenzie Wilkes	2	Tripping
2	2	26:43	Charlie Spridgeon	2	High Sticking
3	2	30:23	Gary Dixon	2	Slashing
4	2	32:09	Mackenzie Wilkes	2	Holding Stick
5	2	36:38	Rory Sillery	2	Holding
6	3	47:28	Charlie Spridgeon	2	Hooking
7	3	52:50	Mackenzie Wilkes	2	Roughing
TOT (PN-PIM) 7-14					
Power Plays (Goals-Opp) 0-3					

Altrincham Aces 16-4 Deeside Ducks
North 2 League and Cup, Sunday 8th December
Game 071

Altrincham Aces (7-0-0-8)   (1-1-0-10) Deeside Ducks

				SCORING SUMMARY			
G	Per	Time	ScoreTeam Goal Scorer	Assist	Assist		Str
1	1	0:38	1-0 ALT Sam Dunford (4)				E
2	1	1:07	2-0 ALT Carl Price (10)	Kane Morin (11)			E
3	1	18:34	3-0 ALT Jake Frost (6)				E
4	2	21:36	4-0 ALT Josh Milnes (6)	Ollie Gotts (6)			E
5	2	21:59	5-0 ALT Ollie Gotts (8)	Malachi Budd (9)	Sam Daintith (1)		E
6	2	23:04	6-0 ALT David Kamenicek (5)	Kane Morin (12)	Sam Dunford (4)		E
7	2	23:53	7-0 ALT James Best (1)	Billy King (5)			E
8	2	29:51	8-0 ALT C.J Ashton (1)	Carl Price (3)			E
9	2	32:57	9-0 ALT David Kamenicek (6)	Max Sullivan (4)	Kane Morin (13)		PP
10	2	34:25	9-1 DEE Josh Jones (2)	Ben Roscoe (3)			E
11	2	35:39	10-1 ALT Josh Milnes (7)	Malachi Budd (10)	Ollie Gotts (7)		E
12	2	37:12	10-2 DEE Gary Dixon (1)	Daniels Fadejevs (3)			SH
13	2	39:26	10-3 DEE Keiron Clarkson (4)	Stewart Cutting (3)	Charlie Spridgeon (5)		E
14	3	40:16	10-4 DEE Daniels Fadejevs (2)	Louis Morgan (2)	Gary Dixon (2)		E
15	3	42:57	11-4 ALT Jake Frost (7)	Billy King (6)			E
16	3	46:50	12-4 ALT Billy King (4)				E
17	3	48:51	13-4 ALT Max Sullivan (3)	Kane Morin (14)	Carl Price (4)		PP
18	3	54:47	14-4 ALT Billy King (5)	Jake Frost (7)	Elliot Hunt (4)		E
19	3	58:08	15-4 ALT Carl Price (11)	Malachi Budd (11)			E
20	3	58:32	16-4 ALT Josh Milnes (8)	Malachi Budd (12)	Ollie Gotts (8)		E

		TEAM SUMMARY															
	ALTRINCHAM ACES		G	A	P	PN	PIM			DEESIDE DUCKS		G	A	P	PN	PIM
1	NM	Cameron Valentine-Higgs							4	D	Charlie Spridgeon		1	1	2	4
5	F	Sam Dunford	1	1	2				9	F	Gary Dixon	1	1	2	1	2
8	F	Kane Morin		4	4	1	2		10	F	Stewart Cutting		1	1		
14	F	Brad Chapman							13	D	Deacon Wilkes					
15	F	Jake Forst	2	1	3				19	F	Mackenzie Wilkes				3	6
16	D	Max Sullivan	1	1	2				21	D	Keiron Clarkson	1		1		
21	F	Josh Milnes	3		3				25	F	Liam Yarwood					
23	F	C.J Ashton	1		1	1	2		29	F	Ben Roscoe		1	1		
35	NM	Mike Rogers							31	D	James Morgan					
36	F	Elliot Hunt		1	1				33	NM	Jace Gledhill					
45	D	James Best	1		1				34	F	Louis Ellwood					
46	D	Sam Daintith		1	1	1	2		47	NM	Callum Preston					
55	D	David Kovacs							51	F	Harry Shearman					
62	F	Sam Hockey				1	2		52	D	Louis Morgan		1	1		
69	D	David Kamenicek	2		2				73	F	Josh Jones	1		1		
90	F	Malachi Budd		4	4				81	F	Daniels Fadejevs	1	1	2		
95	F	Ollie Gotts	1	3	4				88	D	Kenny Williams					
96	F	Cark Price	2	2	4				91	F	Rory Sillery				1	2
98	F	Billy King	2	2	4											
		Team Penalty									Team Penalty					
		TEAM TOTALS	16	20	36	4	8				TEAM TOTALS	4	6	10	7	14

		GOALTENDER SUMMARY															
ALTRINCHAM ACES				Goals-Shots Against					DEESIDE DUCKS				Goals - Shots Against			
			TOI	1	2	3	OT	TOT				TOI	1	2	3	OT	TOT
1	Cameron Valetine-Higgs		60:00	0-12	3-8	1-15		4-35	33	Jace Gledhill		24:56	3-12	4-7			7-19
35	Mike Rogers								47	Callum Preston		35:04		3-18	6-21		9-39
	Empty Net									Empty Net							

Source: NIHLStats.wordpress.com (Box Scores)

"The fifth goal came from a turnover, but we stuck to it and it shows we go to the end of games.

"We conceded with a bit of time left, but we didn't let it affect us."

Other results: Blackburn 6 Billingham 4; Leeds 3 Sheffield 2; Solihull 8 Widnes 2; Billingham 9 Blackburn 0; Hull 6 Whitley 1; Nottingham 4 Solihull 8.

Deeside Ducks made the relatively short trip up the M56 to face Altrincham Aces for a combined Laidler Division league and cup game on Sunday, but they came home on the back of a heavy 16-4 defeat.

The Aces took a modest 3-0 advantage into the first break and they ran riot in the latter stages, with the Ducks never really looking in contention.

Deeside goals from Josh Jones, Kieran Clarkson, Daniel Fadejevs and Gary Dixon only served to give the scoreline a bit of respectability.

Ducks' player Alfie Kelly has been handed a two-game suspension by the governing body's Department of Player Safety (DOPS) after being banished from last week's home game against Coventry for slashing.

The panel observed that the offence was an "aggressive slashing motion to the groin area of an opponent, recklessly endangering them".

Fellow Deeside player Cody Ogden has just completed a two-match suspension for an illegal check to the head in the away game at Coventry the week before.

Other results: Coventry 2 Telford 3; Kingston 2 Sutton 5; Sheffield 2 Billingham 5.

Ducks In The Newspaper!

There's a short piece about the Deeside Ducks' away trip to Altrincham - along with some other interesting bits and pieces - in today's Flintshire & Wrexham Leader (10th December 2024 - Page 34).

You can read the same report on the highly informative grass roots ice hockey review website:

https://www.icehockeyreview.co.uk/2024/12/match-report-altrincham-aces-16-deeside.html

#keepquacking   #fowlnotfoul

Andy Brown showing off the hot drinks now available at Ducks home games (Photo by Paul Breeze)

Yet More Ducks Merchandise!

The Ducks are at home this Saturday 14th December when they take on the Bradford Bulldogs at Deeside Leisure Centre (5pm face off),

And, with Christmas just around the corner, make sure you check out the goodies for sale on the merchandise table.

We are now also able to offer hot and cold drinks (depending on rink cafe opening times).

Chris Jones was the Ducks' MVP against Bradford
(Photo by Chris Jones – a different one...)

Saturday 14th December 2020 – NIHL Laidler Division Deeside Ducks 5 – Bradford Bulldogs 6

The Deeside Ducks put in a battling performance before narrowly losing out 5-6 to Bradford Bulldogs at Deeside Leisure Centre on Saturday

This game was played between two very closely matched teams and there was never more than one goal in it. It was entertaining end to end hockey throughout with plenty of chances for both sides.

Continuing with the Ducks' policy of encouraging young talent, the game saw senior league debuts for Dragons Under 19 players Callum Garwell and Rafferty Smith.

After a tense opening phase, the Ducks took the lead on 6 minutes with a debut goal from Rafferty Smith.

Bradford equalised on 12 minutes but Deeside edged back into the lead with a Stewart Cutting goal just 14 seconds later. The Bulldogs equalised on 14 minutes and the score remained 2-2 at the first period break.

The second period was just as close and Gary Dixon fired the Ducks back in front just 90 seconds in. Bradford equalised again and Chris Jones re-established the Deeside lead on 26 minutes.

Cue another equaliser from the visitors before Rory Sillery scored his first ever league goal to hand the Ducks a narrow 5-4 lead at the second interval.

Unfortunately, the game slipped away from Deeside in the third period as two quick goals within 90 seconds of each other saw Bradford draw level again and then take the lead for the first time.

A spate of late penalties hampered the Ducks attempts to salvage something from the match and it finished up as a 5-6 win to the Bulldogs.

The MVP (Most Valuable Player) awards went to Liam Hine for Bradford and Chris Jones for Deeside.

Deeside Ducks 5-6 Bradford Bulldogs
North 2 Regular Season, Saturday 14th December
Game 072

Deeside Ducks (1-1-0-11) (4-0-1-10) Bradford Bulldogs

SCORING SUMMARY

G	Per	Time	Score	Team	Goal Scorer	Assist	Assist	Str
1	1	6:02	1-0	DEE	Rafferty Smith (1)	James Morgan (1)	Gary Dixon (3)	E
2	1	12:07	1-1	BRA	Kai Hathaway (10)	Cameron Williams (1)	Abigail Culshaw (1)	E
3	1	12:21	2-1	DEE	Stewart Cutting (3)	Charlie Spridgeon (6)		E
4	1	13:57	2-2	BRA	Daragh Spawforth (3)	Kacper Andrukianiec (7)	Jared Knowles (2)	E
5	2	21:34	3-2	DEE	Gary Dixon (2)	Chris Jones (4)		E
6	2	24:35	3-3	BRA	Kai Hathaway (11)	Jared Knowles (2)		E
7	2	26:02	4-3	DEE	Chris Jones (4)	Cody Ogden (3)	Charlie Spridgeon (7)	PP
8	2	31:08	4-4	BRA	Jared Knowles (1)	David Williams (1)		E
9	2	34:10	5-4	DEE	Rory Sillery (1)	Stewart Cutting (4)	Kieran Clarkson (4)	E
10	3	50:59	5-5	BRA	Liam Hine (1)			SH
11	3	52:22	5-6	BRA	Daragh Spawforth (4)	Kacper Andrukianiec (8)	Keiron Furlong (7)	E

PENALTY SUMMARY

DEESIDE DUCKS

#	Per	Time	Player	PIM	Penalty
1	2	37:13	Mackenzie Wilkes	2	Hooking
2	2	38:46	Cody Ogden	2	Slashing
3	3	42:23	Cody Ogden	2	Roughing
4	3	46:05	Josh Jones	2	Slashing
5	3	57:10	Cody Ogden	2	Interference
6	3	58:16	Charlie Spridgeon	2	Slashing
7	3	59:03	Louis Morgan	2	Interference

TOT (PN-PIM) 7-14
Power Plays (Goals-Opp) 1-5

BRADFORD BULLDOGS

#	Per	Time	Player	PIM	Penalty
1	1	19:22	Kacper Andrukianiec	2	Boarding
2	2	24:53	Cameron Williams	2	Tripping
3	2	28:28	David Williams	2	Hooking
4	3	49:13	Daragh Spawforth	2	Tripping
5	3	54:39	Abigail Culshaw	2	Tripping
6					
7					

TOT (PN-PIM) 5-10
Power Plays (Goals-Opp) 0-7

TEAM SUMMARY

DEESIDE DUCKS

#		Player	G	A	P	PN	PIM
4	D	Charlie Spridgeon		2	2	1	2
5	F	Michael Speare					
9	F	Gary Dixon	1	1	2		
10	F	Stewart Cutting	1	1	2		
11	F	Rafferty Smith	1		1		
13	D	Deacon Wilkes					
18	D	George Spofforth					
19	F	Mackenzie Wilkes				1	2
21	D	Kieran Clarkson		1	1		
25	F	Liam Yarwood					
29	F	Ben Roscoe					
31	D	James Morgan		1	1		
40	F	Cody Ogden		1	1	3	6
45	D	Charlie Nicholson					
47	NM	Callum Preston					
52	D	Louis Morgan				1	2
72	D	Chris Jones	1	1	2		
73	F	Josh Jones				1	2
85	F	Callum Garwell					
91	F	Rory Sillery	1		1		
		Team Penalty					
		TEAM TOTALS	5	8	13	7	14

BRADFORD BULLDOGS

#		Player	G	A	P	PN	PIM
1	NM	Jack Mickevicius					
4	D	David Williams		1	1	1	2
11	F	Lucas Vince					
13	F	Archie Grayson					
15	F	Oliver Massey					
18	F	Tyler Hall					
20	D	Cameron Williams		1	1	1	2
21	F	Daragh Spawforth	2		2	1	2
22	D	Jacob Brownlie					
26	F	Kacper Andrukianiec		2	2	1	2
27	D	Liam Hine	1		1		
33	NM	Jake Lowndes					
72	F	Kai Hathaway	2		2		
74	F	Ben Fox					
75	F	Thomas Chong					
78	F	Jared Knowles	1	2	3		
86	F	Keiron Furlong		1	1		
98	F	Abigail Culshaw		1	1	1	2
		Team Penalty					
		TEAM TOTALS	6	8	14	5	10

GOALTENDER SUMMARY

DEESIDE DUCKS

		TOI	1	2	3	OT	TOT
47	Callum Preston	60:00	2-9	2-16	2-16		6-41
	Empty Net						

Goals-Shots Against

BRADFORD BULLDOGS

		TOI	1	2	3	OT	TOT
1	Jack Mickevicius						
33	Jake Lowndes	60:00	2-10	3-14	0-10		5-34
	Empty Net						

Goals - Shots Against

Source: NIHLStats.wordpress.com (Box Scores)

Rafferty Smith was the Ducks' MVP away at Billingham
(Photo by Paul Ali Photography)

Sunday 15th December 2020 – NIHL Laidler Division
Billingham Buccaneers 12 - Deeside Ducks 0

The Ducks' first ever trip to the north east to face high flying Billingham was always going to be a tough one, and that is exactly how it turned out.

The hosts led 3-0 after the first period and 8-0 after the second. Four more goals in the final 20 minutes handed them a comprehensive 12-0 victory and saw the Ducks making the long journey home on the back of their second shut-out of the season.

The Deeside Ducks play their last game of the calendar year this Saturday 21st December when they entertain the Altrincham Aces at Deeside Leisure Centre, 5pm face off.

Billingham Buccaneers 12-0 Deeside Ducks
North 2 Regular Season, Sunday 15th December
Game 075

Billingham Buccaneers (12-0-0-3)   (1-1-0-12) Deeside Ducks

SCORING SUMMARY

G	Per	Time	Score	Team	Goal Scorer	Assist	Assist	Str
1	1	16:49	1-0	BIL	James McCabe (4)	Sam Dowd (8)	Connor Stoves (1)	E
2	1	17:38	2-0	BIL	Sam Dowd (12)	James McCabe (13)	Stuart Jackson (5)	E
3	1	18:07	3-0	BIL	Kyle Black (2)	Michael Plant (1)		E
4	2	25:31	4-0	BIL	Michael Plant (1)	Matt Keeley (2)		E
5	2	32:41	5-0	BIL	Connor Stoves (1)	Sam Dowd (9)	Abi McCourt (2)	E
6	2	33:49	6-0	BIL	Ben Greenhalgh (5)	Lucas Dowdle (3)		E
7	2	34:51	7-0	BIL	Abi McCourt (1)	Kieran Wrench (4)	James McCabe (14)	E
8	2	38:56	8-0	BIL	Michael Plant (2)	Lewis Hall (3)		E
9	3	51:34	9-0	BIL	Daniel Hughes (1)	Ben Greenhalgh (3)	Lucas Dowdle (4)	E
10	3	57:30	10-0	BIL	Ethan McLaughlin (1)	James McCabe (15)		E
11	3	58:01	11-0	BIL	Stephen Wallace (9)	James McCabe (16)	Ethan McLaughlin (2)	E
12	3	59:55	12-0	BIL	Kyle Black (3)	Matt Keeley (2)	Simon Geldart (5)	E

PENALTY SUMMARY

BILLINGHAM BUCCANEERS						DEESIDE DUCKS					
#	Per	Time	Player	PIM	Penalty	#	Per	Time	Player	PIM	Penalty
1	1	12:51	Ben Greenhalgh	2	Cross Checking	1	2	29:40	Bench	2	Too Many Men
2	1	19:15	Lewis Hall	2	Delay of Game	2	3	46:21	Michael Speare	2	Boarding
3	1	20:00	Tom Wakefield	2	Abuse	3					
4	2	35:54	Matt Keeley	2	Interference	4					
5	3	45:01	Ethan McLaughlin	2	Tripping	5					
6	3	46:21	Daniel Hughes	2	Roughing	6					
		TOT (PN-PIM) 6-12						**TOT (PN-PIM) 2-4**			
		Power Plays (Goals-Opp) 0-1						**Power Plays (Goals-Opp) 0-5**			

TEAM SUMMARY

BILLINGHAM BUCCANEERS			G	A	P	PN	PIM		DEESIDE DUCKS			G	A	P	PN	PIM
4	F	Josh Nertney						5	F	Michael Speare				1	2
7	D	James McCabe	1	4	5			9	F	Rafferty Smith					
8	F	Lucas Dowdle		2	2			10	F	Stewart Cutting					
14	F	Stephen Wallace	1		1			12	D	Henry Phillips					
16	F	Michael Plant	2	1	3			13	D	Deacon Wilkes					
17	F	Kieran Wrench		1	1			19	F	Mackenzie Wilkes					
18	D	Ben Greenhalgh	1	1	2	1	2	25	F	Liam Yarwood					
21	D	Daniel Hughes	1		1	1	2	29	F	Ben Roscoe					
22	F	Sam Dowd	1	2	3			45	D	Charlie Nicholson					
25	F	Tom Cummings						47	NM	Callum Preston					
30	NM	Ronald Pierce						81	F	Daniels Fadejevs					
35	F	Tom Wakefield				1	2	91	F	Rory Sillery					
36	F	Kyle Black	2		2										
38	D	Stuart Jackson		1	1										
40	D	Ethan McLaughlin	1	1	2	1	2								
45	F	Simon Geldart		1	1										
48	F	Abi McCourt	1	1	2										
50	F	Connor Stoves	1	1	2										
77	F	Lewis Hall		1	1	1	2								
81	D	Matt Keeley		2	2	1	2								
		Team Penalty								Team Penalty				1	2
		TEAM TOTALS	12	19	31	6	12			**TEAM TOTALS**				2	4

GOALTENDER SUMMARY

BILLINGHAM BUCCANEERS		Goals-Shots Against						DEESIDE DUCKS		Goals - Shots Against				
	TOI	1	2	3	OT	TOT			TOI	1	2	3	OT	TOT
30 Ronald Pierce	60:00	0-11	0-4	0-6		0-21		47 Callum Preston	60:00	3-16	5-27	4-21		12-64
Empty Net								Empty Net						

Source: NIHLStats.wordpress.com (Box Scores)

IMPRESSIVE: Rafferty Smith was Deeside Ducks' MVP away at Billingham. Picture: Paul Ali Photography

Tough spell of action for Ducks

goaltender Matt Croyle face 45 shots over the course of the encounter.

"It was such a good performance," added Compton.

"We only had five defencemen.

"I just didn't feel at any point we were in trouble.

"Matt Croyle was solid and our defence was solid. Everybody played so well."

It was a far from unlucky 13th win of the season for the Dragons and it moves them up to third in the league standings, just three points behind second-placed Blackburn Hawks.

Billingham Stars, who have lost just three times this season, are leading the way.

Other results: Nottingham 2 Billingham 3; Sheffield 1 Widnes 4; Blackburn 7 Widnes 1; Nottingham 8 Sheffield 1; Solihull 15 Leeds 3.

DEESIDE DUCKS had a frustrating weekend in two contests.

They narrowly lost out 6-5 at home to Bradford Bulldogs and this was followed by getting shut out 12-0 away defeat to Billingham Buccaneers.

Continuing with the Ducks' policy of encouraging young talent, the game on Saturday saw senior league debuts for Dragons' U19 players Callum Garwell and Rafferty Smith and, after a tense opening phase, Smith opened the scoring on six minutes.

Bradford equalised on 12 minutes but Deeside edged back into the lead with a Stewart Cutting goal

14 seconds later. The Bulldogs equalised on 14 minutes and it was 2-2 at the first break.

The second period was just as close, with Gary Dixon, Chris Jones and Rory Sillery handing Ducks a 5-4 lead at the second interval.

The game slipped away from Deeside in the third period as two quick goals within 90 seconds of each other saw Bradford draw level again and then take the lead for the first time.

A spate of late penalties hampered the Ducks' attempts to salvage something.

Other results: Altrincham 5 Kingston 4; Telford 1 Sutton 3.

Ducks In The Newspaper!

There's a short piece about the Deeside Ducks' home game against Bradford in today's Flintshire & Wrexham Leader (17th December 2024 - Page 36).

You can read a longer report about the Ducks' two weekend matches on the highly informative grass roots ice hockey review website:

http://www.icehockeyreview.co.uk/2024/12/deeside-ducks-weekend-report-14th-15th.html

Callum Preston receives the MVP award (Photo by Maxine Roscoe)

Saturday 21st December – NIHL Laidler Division
Deeside Ducks 1 – Altrincham Aces 6

The Deeside Ducks put in another spirited performance but ultimately lost out 1-6 to near neighbours Altrincham Aces at Deeside Leisure Centre on Saturday.

The game saw two new faces in Ducks shirts with debuts for former Deeside junior Corey Swift and ex-Telford forward Rhys Howells, who played for the Dragons in the Moralee Division last season.

The Ducks had been trounced 16-4 in the away game in Altrincham a few weeks ago so this was a much better performance all round and it remained very close until the latter stages.

The first period ended 0-1 to the Aces and they only managed to score their second goal with just 7 seconds left to play in the second period.

The score was 0-3 to the visitors by the time Deeside managed to find the net themselves with a strike from Rhys Howells – scoring on his Ducks debut - on 53 minutes.

This breakthrough did not spark a late Deeside rally, unfortunately, and 3 late goals for the Aces gave the final score a slightly more one-sided look than the Ducks' performance necessarily deserved.

As well as taking the 3 league points back up the M56, the 5-goal margin means that Altrincham leapfrog Coventry in the group table for the parallel Laidler Cup competition and qualify for the semi finals in second place behind Telford.

Deeside finish bottom of the cup group with just 1 win from their 8 qualifying games.

Following on from the festive break, the Ducks will be away to unbeaten league leaders Sutton Sting on Saturday 4th January and are then at home again to Altrincham Aces on Sunday 5th at Deeside Leisure Centre – 5pm face off.

Deeside Ducks 1-6 Altrincham Aces

North 2 League and Cup, Saturday 21st December
Game 077

Deeside Ducks (1-1-0-13)   (8-1-0-8) Altrincham Aces

SCORING SUMMARY

G	Per	Time	Score	Team	Goal Scorer	Assist	Assist	Str
1	1	15:59	0-1	ALT	Jake Frost (8)	Kane Morin (16)		E
2	2	39:53	0-2	ALT	Jake Frost (9)	Carl Price (6)		PP
3	3	45:49	0-3	ALT	Kane Morin (3)	Max Sullivan (5)		PP
4	3	52:27	1-3	DEE	Rhys Howells (1)	Ben Roscoe (4)	Cody Ogden (4)	E
5	3	52:46	1-4	ALT	Billy King (6)	Carl Price (7)	Sam Daintith (2)	E
6	3	59:25	1-5	ALT	Josh Milnes (9)	Carl Price (8)	Sam Dunford (6)	E
7	3	59:33	1-6	ALT	Ronnie Grimes (4)	Carl Price (9)	Sam Dunford (7)	E

PENALTY SUMMARY

DEESIDE DUCKS

#	Per	Time	Player	PIM	Penalty
1	1	10:16	Josh Jones	2	Tripping
2	1	13:52	Cody Ogden	2	Elbowing
3	2	28:38	Rhys Howells	2	Roughing
4	2	39:50	Luke Wainwright	2	Holding
5	3	43:55	James Morgan	2	Cross Checking
6	3	49:27	Rhys Howells	2	Misconduct
7	3	53:33	Daniels Fadejevs	2	Holding
8	3	58:52	Cody Ogden	2	Roughing

TOT (PN-PIM) 8-16
Power Plays (Goals-Opp) 0-1

ALTRINCHAM ACES

#	Per	Time	Player	PIM	Penalty
1	2	28:38	Elliot Hunt	2	Roughing
2	3	53:33	Sam Daintith	2	Hooking
3	3	58:29	Max Sullivan	2	Cross Checking
4					
5					
6					
7					
8					

TOT (PN-PIM) 3-6
Power Plays (Goals-Opp) 2-5

TEAM SUMMARY

DEESIDE DUCKS

#		Player	G	A	P	PN	PIM
2	NM	Paul Jones					
4	D	Charlie Spridgeon					
5	F	Michael Speare					
10	F	Stewart Cutting					
11	F	Rafferty Smith					
12	D	Henry Phillips					
13	D	Deacon Wilkes					
19	F	Mackenzie Wilkes					
29	F	Ben Roscoe		1	1		
31	D	James Morgan				1	2
34	F	Louis Ellwood					
40	F	Cody Ogden		1	1	2	4
45	D	Charlie Nicholson					
47	NM	Callum Preston					
52	F	Corey Swift					
73	F	Josh Jones				1	2
81	F	Daniels Fadejevs				1	2
85	F	Rhys Howells	1		1	2	4
88	D	Kenny Williams					
98	D	Luke Wainwright				1	2
		Team Penalty					
		TEAM TOTALS	1	2	3	8	16

ALTRINCHAM ACES

#		Player	G	A	P	PN	PIM
1	NM	Cameron Valentine-Higgs					
5	F	Sam Dunford		2	2		
8	F	Kane Morin	1	1	2		
14	F	Brad Chapman					
15	F	Jake Frost	2		2		
16	D	Max Sullivan		1	1	1	2
21	F	Josh Milnes	1		1		
23	F	C.J Ashton					
31	NM	Bayley Hodkinson					
36	F	Elliot Hunt				1	2
45	D	James Best					
46	D	Sam Daintith		1	1	1	2
55	D	David Kovacs					
62	F	Sam Hockey					
69	D	David Kamenicek					
75	F	Alfie Kelly					
77	F	Ronnie Grimes	1		1		
90	F	Malachi Budd					
95	F	Ollie Gotts					
96	F	Carl Price		4	4		
98	F	Billy King	1		1		
		Team Penalty					
		TEAM TOTALS	6	9	15	3	6

GOALTENDER SUMMARY

DEESIDE DUCKS

		TOI	1	2	3	OT	TOT
				Goals-Shots Against			
2	Paul Jones						
47	Callum Preston	60:00	1-19	1-21	4-15		6-55
	Empty Net						

ALTRINCHAM ACES

		TOI	1	2	3	OT	TOT
				Goals - Shots Against			
1	Cameron Valentine-Higgs						
31	Bayley Hodkinson	60:00	0-11	0-4	1-11		1-26
	Empty Net						

Source: NIHLStats.wordpress.com (Box Scores)

142

Jakub Hajek, who grabbed one of the goals.

There was a hat-trick from Jake Witkowski, while MJ Clancy netted twice and they were joined on the scoresheet by James Parsons, Will Harper, Garry Simpson (pictured bottom right) and Jared Dickinson.

"We didn't really get going until the last period. It was close," said assistant head coach Matt Compton.

"We did out-shoot them a bit, but we didn't get into our stride until the third period.

"But 10-4 is 10-4. We came away with the win."

Then came an epic Sunday showdown with leaders Billingham Stars, who had defeated the Dragons 11-4 earlier in the campaign.

It was much closer on this occasion and Billingham ended the first period holding a slender 2-1 advantage.

James Parsons slotted in Deeside's opening goal, while Dragons fought back to make sure it was tied at 3-3 at the next break.

Jake Witkowski levelled things up less than a minute into the second period, while Ross Kennedy struck the home side's third goal.

Deeside had the lead for the first time on the evening when Will Harper found the target in the third period.

However, Billingham responded with three goals in the closing 10 minutes to confirm their triumph. Cade King was Deeside's MVP.

"We know how good Billingham are," added Compton. "They're a good side and we matched them."

Other results: Hull 5 Blackburn 10; Solihull 11 Nottingham 3; Widnes 12 Sheffield 4.
Saturday fixture: Billingham v Whitby.
Sunday: Blackburn v Sheffield, Whitby v Billingham.

Deeside Ducks put in another spirited performance but ultimately lost out 6-1 at home to Altrincham Aces.

The game saw two new faces in Ducks' shirts, with debuts for former Deeside junior Corey Swift and ex-Telford forward Rhys Howells, who played for the Dragons in the Moralee Division last season.

The Ducks had been trounced 16-1 in the game at Altrincham a few weeks ago so this was a much better performance all round and it

STAR MAN: Deeside Ducks' MVP Callum Preston. Picture: Maxine Roscoe

remained very close until the latter stages.

Aces had a 1-0 advantage at the end of the first period and they only managed to score their second goal with seven seconds left to play in the second period.

It was 3-0 by the time Deeside managed to find the net themselves with a strike from Howells on 55 minutes.

This breakthrough did not spark a late Deeside rally and three late goals for the Aces gave the final score a slightly more one-sided look than the Ducks' performance deserved.

Other results: Billingham 2 Coventry 4, Kingston 4 Sutton 12, Bradford 3 Telford 9, Sutton 9 Nottingham 2

Eagles' 10-game

PHILADELPHIA EAGLES lost quarterback Jalen Hurts to concussion and saw their franchise-record 10-game winning streak come to an end with a dramatic 36-33 loss to Washington Commanders.

The injury-hit Detroit Lions enjoyed a 34-17 victory over Chicago Bears while Indianapolis Colts also remain in the play-off hunt following a 38-30 win over Tennessee Titans.

Arizona Cardinals cannot qualify for the post-season after suffering a 36-30 loss at Carolina Panthers. Atlanta Falcons picked up a 34-7

Ducks In The Newspaper!

There's a short piece about the Deeside Ducks' home game against Altrincham Aces in today's Flintshire & Wrexham Leader (24th December 2024 - Page 36).

You can read a longer version of the report on the highly informative grass roots ice hockey review website:

http://www.icehockeyreview.co.uk/2024/12/match-report-deeside-ducks-1-altrincham.html

#keepquacking   #fowlnotfoul

Long term Deeside favourite Chris Jones has brought a wealth of experience to the new Ducks team. (Photo by Paul Breeze)

Deeside Ducks New Year Round Up

Heading into the New Year, the Deeside Ducks can look back upon their first few months as a club with some satisfaction, having already achieved much of what they set out to do at the start of the season.

They have given over 20 promising young local players the chance to play regular competitive league hockey that they might never have managed otherwise – or only after weeks of bench warming in the hope of the odd shift with a higher league team.

And Deeside junior club players Cody Ogden, Henry Phillips, Daniels Fadejevs and Jace Gledhill have all made appearances for the Dragons senior team this season, as well as playing for the Ducks, showing that the development pathway from juniors to seniors is working well.

The team has won two of their 15 league games so far this season – two more than Head Coach Gary Shaw admitted that he expected for their debut league campaign.

Add to that the fact that they have lost 4 more matches by a single goal margin, any of which – on another day with the rub of the green, or better player discipline, in some cases - could easily have been a win instead.

So, things are looking good as the Ducks head towards the business end of the season in the battle for a top 8 /play-off slot.

Cody Ogden remains the Ducks' top goal scorer on 6 strikes, with Kieran Clarkson and Chris Jones just behind on 4 each. Charlie Spridgeon is the leading playmaker with 7 assists while Clarkson, Jones, Michael Speare and Player Coach Stewart Cutting all have 4.

Following on from the festive break, the Ducks are away to unbeaten league leaders Sutton Sting this Saturday 4th January and are then at home to north-west rivals Altrincham Aces on Sunday at Deeside Leisure Centre – 5pm face off.

Promising debut season for Ducks

IMPRESSIVE: Chris Jones

IT'S been an all-action start to life for the Deeside Ducks.

Heading into the new year, the Deeside Ducks can look back upon their first few months as a team with some satisfaction, having already achieved much of what they set out to do at the start of the season.

They have given over 20 promising young local players the chance to play regular competitive league hockey that they might never have managed otherwise - or only after weeks of bench warming in the hope of the odd shift with a higher league team.

Meanwhile, Deeside junior club players Cody Ogden, Henry Phillips, Daniels Federevs and Jace Gledhill have all made appearances for the Deeside Dragons' senior team this season, as well as playing for the Ducks.

showing that the development pathway from juniors to seniors is working well.

The team has won two of their 15 league games so far this season – two more than head coach Gary Shaw admitted that he expected for their debut league campaign.

Add to that the fact that they have lost four more matches by a single goal margin, any of which - on another day with the rub of the green, or better player discipline, in some cases - could easily have been a win instead.

So, things are looking good as the Ducks head towards the business end of the season in the battle for a top-eight play-off slot.

Cody Ogden remains the Ducks' top goalscorer on six strikes, with Kieran Clarkson and Chris Jones just behind on four apiece.

Charlie Spridgeon is the leading playmaker with seven assists,

while Clarkson, Jones and player-coach Stewart Cutting all have four.

Following on from the festive break, the Ducks are away to unbeaten league leaders Sutton Sting this Saturday.

Making it a busy weekend, the Ducks are then at home to north-west rivals Altrincham Aces on Sunday (5pm face-off).

Two tough away days will mark Deeside Dragons' return to action following their festive break.

On Saturday, the Dragons pay a visit to Blackburn Hawks and this is followed by Sunday's match-up versus Solihull Barons.

After a promising first portion to the season, Deeside find themselves situated in third place in the Division One North rankings.

Results: Billingham 4 Whitley 2; Blackburn 10 Sheffield 3; Whitley 1 Billingham 4.

Ducks In The Newspaper!

Our "year end" review of the Ducks in their exciting debut season can be seen in today's Flintshire & Wrexham Leader (31st December 2024 - Page 35).

146

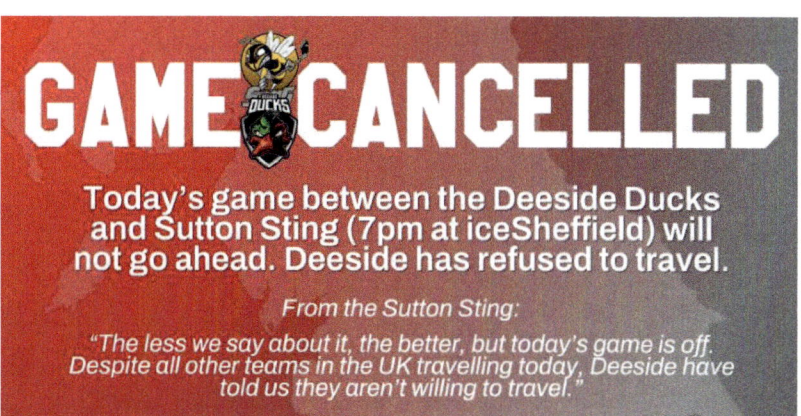

Saturday 4th January 2025 – NIHL Laidler Division
Sutton Sting P – Deeside Ducks P

The Deeside Ducks game away at Laidler Division
leaders Sutton Sting on Saturday was postponed after
Ducks officials decided not to travel amid concerns about
worsening weather conditions.

With the game not scheduled to face off until 7pm,
extreme weather warnings in place from the Met Office
and widespread snow forecast, it was felt that a late night
drive home from Sheffield across the Pennines would
represent potential safety risks to the travelling players.

Speaking of the decision, Ducks Head Coach Gary Shaw
said:

"The Ducks game against Sutton was called off by the
Ducks management for safety reasons, with the players
driving themselves to the game and with a lot of our
players inexperienced drivers in bad weather."

"The forecast for heavy snow on the high ground and the
late finish of the game, we decided that, with the risk of

the players' safety driving in these conditions, it was more important than fulfilling the game."

"As a person that has driven for a living, it was an easy decision to make for the protection of the players. I understand the frustration from Sutton as it is a nightmare trying to rearrange a game at the Sheffield Rink due to the amount of teams playing there, but the decision was not made lightly."

"Looking after our players is paramount and, if the decision was reversed, I would support and respect it."

Attempts will now be made to try and reschedule the game for another date – although that might be difficult with the amount of teams that use the ice at the iceSheffield venue.

If that is not possible and the game can't be fitted in before the end of the season, the sport's governing body – England Ice Hockey – will have to decide whether to award it as a forfeit win or a non-fault draw in the league standings.

The Ducks MVP against Altrincham was Dan Fadejevs
(Photo by Maxine Roscoe)

Sunday 5th January 2025 – NIHL Laidler Division
Deeside Ducks 2 – Altrincham Aces 4

With widespread snowfall across the north of England overnight on Saturday – and severe weather warnings remaining in place from the Met Office for all day Sunday - a number of NIHL games were called off as teams decided not to risk travelling.

Luckily, Sunday's visitors to the "Pond" – the Altrincham Aces - had an easier journey than most and that game went ahead as scheduled.

After a very tense opening, the Aces eventually opened the scoring on 18 minutes and took a 0-1 lead into the first break - but a Cody Ogden goal in the 25th minute saw the Ducks draw level.

The Aces retook the lead 4 minutes later and then a penalty shot for a tripping call with just 80 seconds left on the clock made it 1-3 at the second interval.

Deeside hopes were raised, however, by a Dan Fadejevs strike 76 seconds into the third period that narrowed the deficit to just one goal to set up a barnstorming finale.

Unfortunately the Ducks were unable to build on this and an Altrincham powerplay goal on 51 minutes saw the Aces end up with a 2-4 victory.

The Ducks now have two away games – at Bradford Bulldogs this Sunday 12th January and then at Telford on 26th January. They are next at home on Saturday 1st February when they take on Sutton Sting at Deeside Leisure Centre, 5pm face off.

Sunday 5th January 2025 – NIHL Laidler Division
Deeside Ducks 2 – Altrincham Aces 4

Scoring Summary

G	Per	Time	Team	Scorer	Assist 1	Assist 2	Str
1	1	18.01	ALT	Jacob Frost			E
2	2	24.22	DEE	Cody Ogden	Charlie Spridgeon		E
3	2	28.57	ALT	David Kovacs	Malachi Budd		E
4	2	38.40	ALT	Oliver Gotts			PS
5	3	41.15	DEE	Dan Fadejevs	Charlie Spridgeon	Rhys Howells	PP
6	3	51.08	ALT	Max Sullivan	Jacob Frost	Dylan Harcourt	PP

Penalty Summary

Deeside Ducks				Altrincham Aces			
Time	Player	PIM	Off	Time	Player	PIM	Off
30.04	Rhys Howells	2	X-CHE	30.04	David Kovacs	2	HOLD
30.04	Louis Morgan	5+Ga	X-CHE	30.04	Kane Morin	2	UNSP
38.40	Henry Phiilips	0	TRIP	32.59	Dylan Harcourt	2	HOOK
44.46	Rhys Howells	2	SLAS	39.50	???	2	TRIP
48.33	Luke Wainwright	2	TRIP	47.35	Billy King	2	INTF
50.12	Mackenzie Wilkes	2	INTF	58.48	Kane Morin	2	MISC
57.11	Cody Ogden	2	INTF				
Total		**35**		**Total**		**12**	

Team Summary

	Deeside Ducks	G	A	Pts	PIM		Altrincham Aces	G	A	Pts	PIM
4	C. Spridgeon		2	2		1	C. Val-Higgs				
5	M. Speare					5	S. Dunford				
8	L. Morgan				25	8	K. Morin				4
10	S. Cutting					14	B. Chapman				
12	H. Phillips					15	J. Frost	1	1	2	
13	D. Wilkes					16	M. Sullivan	1		1	
19	M. Wilkes				2	21	J. Milnes				
29	B. Roscoe					23	C. Ashton				
31	J. Morgan					24	R. Nixon				
40	C. Ogden	1		1	2	27	D. Harcourt		1	1	2
47	C. Preston					31	B. Hodkinson				
73	J. Jones					36	E. Hunt				
81	D. Fadejevs	1		1		55	D. Kovacs	1		1	2
85	R. Howells		1	1	4	62	S. Hockey				
91	R. Sillery					69	D. Kamenicek				
94	J. Gledhill					90	M. Budd		1	1	
98	L. Wainwright				2	95	O. Gotts	1		1	
						98	B. King				2
	Totals	**2**	**3**	**5**	**35**		**Totals**	**4**	**3**	**7**	**12**

Netminder Summary

Deeside Ducks	Mins	GA / SA				Altrincham Aces	Mins	GA / SA			
		1	2	3	Tot			1	2	3	Tot
Callum Preston						Valentine-Higgs					
Jace Gledhill						Hodkinson					

Match details and player stats transcribed into a readable format
from Gameday upload data by Paul Breeze

MVP: Dan Fadajevs impressed for both the Deeside Dragons and Ducks. Picture: Maxine Roscoe

Aces high in success over Ducks

outcome during their trip to Sheffield Scimitars.

Elsewhere, Hull Jets were able to get the better of visitors Whitley Warriors 6-1.

On the back of a two-game losing sequence, Elite League front-runners Cardiff Devils managed to battle their way from behind to defeat Nottingham Panthers 3-2.

After Reid Duke had given Cardiff the lead, goals from Samuel Herr and Tim Doherty turned things around to put the Panthers in the box seat heading into the closing period.

However, back came Cardiff through Tyler Busch's strike and Brett Perlini's goal confirmed their triumph.

This victory for the Devils followed a 3-2 loss to Dundee Stars and a 5-3 reverse to Guildford Flames.

THE cold snap meant Deeside Ducks had a belated start to their 2025 action.

Ducks' scheduled match at Laidler Division league leaders Sutton Sting on Saturday was postponed after Deeside officials decided not to travel amid concerns about worsening weather conditions.

With the game not scheduled to face off until 7pm, extreme weather warnings in place from the Met Office and widespread snow forecast, it was felt that a late night drive home from Sheffield across the Pennines would represent potential safety risks to the travelling players.

However, Sunday's visitors Altrincham Aces had an easier journey and that game went ahead as scheduled.

The Aces took a 1-0 lead into the first break but a Cody Ogden goal early in the second period saw

the Ducks draw level.

Two more Altrincham goals made it 3-1 at the second interval but a Rhys Howells strike narrowed the deficit to just one goal to set up a barnstorming finale.

Unfortunately for the Ducks, they were unable to build on this and another Altrincham goal saw the Aces end up with a 4-2 victory.

The Ducks now have two away games to look forward to as the month develops.

They will have a trip to Bradford Bulldogs this Sunday and this will be followed by the game at Telford on January 26.

They are next at home on Saturday, February 1 when they take on Sutton Sting at Deeside Leisure Centre (5pm face-off).

Other results: Coventry 4 Billingham 0; Kingston 7 Nottingham 8 (overtime); Nottingham 9 Sheffield 1; Telford 3 Coventry 1.

Ducks In The Newspaper!

There is a piece about the Ducks' eventful weekend in today's Flintshire & Wrexham Leader (7th January 2025 - Page 37).

Sunday 12th January 2025 – NIHL Laidler Division
Bradford Bulldogs 9 - Deeside Ducks 1

The Deeside Ducks slumped to their second defeat of the New Year with a 9-1 loss away to Bradford Bulldogs on Sunday.

Bradford took the lead on 3 minutes and the score was 2-0 by the time Chris Jones pulled a goal back for the Ducks on a tripping powerplay on 16 minutes.

Deeside still looked pretty much in contention at 2-1 down at the end of the first period and visibly upped their game in the second

Unfortunately, 4 unanswered goals in the period saw Bradford pull away and three more goals in the third handed the Bulldogs a convincing win.

Deeside have dropped to the bottom of the Laidler Division table after erstwhile wooden-spoon contenders Nottingham Lions put together a run of three straight wins to lift themselves into a play-off spot.

The Ducks still have an outside chance of catching them however, as they have two games to come against the Lions and two games in hand.

The Deeside Ducks are next in action away to Telford Tigers on 26th January and are then at home on Saturday 1st February when they take on Sutton Sting at Deeside Leisure Centre, 5pm face off.

Bradford Bulldogs 9-1 Deeside Ducks

North 2 Regular Season, Sunday 12th January
Game 089

Bradford Bulldogs (5-0-1-12)   (1-1-0-15) Deeside Ducks

SCORING SUMMARY

G	Per	Time	Score	Team	Goal Scorer	Assist	Assist	Str
1	1	3:23	1-0	BRA	Kacper Andrukianiec (12)	Ben Darbyshire (4)	Archie Grayson (1)	E
2	1	7:33	2-0	BRA	Kacper Andrukianiec (13)	Lucas Vince (6)	Kai Hathaway (4)	E
3	1	16:04	2-1	DEE	Chris Jones (5)	Gary Dixon (4)	Charlie Spridgeon (10)	PP
4	2	28:40	3-1	BRA	Kai Hathaway (12)	Kacper Andrukianiec (11)	Keiron Furlong (8)	PP
5	2	34:41	4-1	BRA	Kai Hathaway (13)	Keiron Furlong (9)		E
6	2	36:40	5-1	BRA	Oliver Massey (1)	Archie Grayson (2)	Keiron Furlong (10)	E
7	2	38:33	6-1	BRA	Kacper Andrukianiec (14)	Kai Hathaway (5)		E
8	3	43:40	7-1	BRA	Lucas Vince (9)	Ben Darbyshire (4)		PP
9	3	50:49	8-1	BRA	Ben Fox (2)	David Williams (3)		E
10	3	57:29	9-1	BRA	Kai Hathaway (12)	Kacper Andrukianiec (12)	Lucas Vince (7)	E

BRADFORD BULLDOGS	DEESIDE DUCKS

PENALTY SUMMARY

#	Per	Time	Player	PIM	Penalty	#	Per	Time	Player	PIM	Penalty
1	1	15:29	Keiron Furlong	2	Tripping	1	1	11:34	Harry Shearman	2	Boarding
2	2	25:49	Keiron Furlong	2	Tripping	2	2	27:59	Mackenzie Wilkes	2	Boarding
3	2	32:03	Keiron Furlong	2	Hooking	3	2	39:19	Josh Jones	2	Slashing
4	3	46:00	David Williams	2	Interference	4	2	39:19	Josh Jones	2	Misconduct
5						5	3	42:30	Mackenzie Wilkes	2	Hooking
		TOT (PN-PIM) 4-8						TOT (PN-PIM) 5-10			
		Power Plays (Goals-Opp) 2-4						Power Plays (Goals-Opp) 1-4			

TEAM SUMMARY

		BRADFORD BULLDOGS	G	A	P	PN	PIM			DEESIDE DUCKS	G	A	P	PN	PIM
1	NM	Jack Mickevicius						4	F	Charlie Spridgeon		1	1		
4	D	David Williams		1	1	1	2	5	F	Michael Speare					
11	F	Lucas Vince	1	2	3			9	F	Gary Dixon		1	1		
13	F	Archie Grayson		2	2			10	F	Stewart Cutting					
15	F	Oliver Massey	1		1			12	D	Henry Phillips					
16	D	Ben Darbyshire		2	2			13	D	Deacon Wilkes					
20	D	Cameron Williams						18	D	George Spofforth					
22	D	Jacob Brownlie						19	F	Mackenzie Wilkes				2	4
26	F	Kacper Andrukianiec	3	2	5			29	F	Ben Roscoe					
29	F	Tom Carroll						34	F	Louis Ellwood					
30	D	Lewis Sinclair						40	F	Cody Ogden					
33	NM	Jacob Lowndes						47	NM	Callum Preston					
66	F	Thomas Chong						50	F	Harry Shearman				1	2
72	F	Kai Hathaway	3	2	5			52	F	Corey Swift					
74	F	Ben Fox	1		1			72	D	Chris Jones	1		1		
86	D	Kieron Furlong		3	3	3	6	73	F	Josh Jones				2	4
								91	D	Rory Sillery					
		Team Penalty								Team Penalty					
		TEAM TOTALS	9	14	23	4	8			TEAM TOTALS	1	2	3	5	10

GOALTENDER SUMMARY

BRADFORD BULLDOGS		Goals-Shots Against						DEESIDE DUCKS		Goals - Shots Against				
	TOI	1	2	3	OT	TOT			TOI	1	2	3	OT	TOT
1 Jack Mickevicius	60:00	1-4	0-15	0-11		1-30		47 Callum Preston	60:00	2-11	4-14	3-16		9-41
33 Jacob Lowndes														
Empty Net								Empty Net						

Source: NIHLStats.wordpress.com (Box Scores)

Ducks still seek first 2025 win

DEESIDE DUCKS slumped to their second defeat of the new year with a 9-1 reverse away to Bradford Bulldogs.

A Chris Jones goal kept them in contention at 2-1 down at the end of the first period, but four unanswered goals in the second period then saw Bradford pull away.

Three more goals in the third period handed the Bulldogs a convincing win.

Deeside have dropped to the bottom of the Laidler Division table after erstwhile wooden-spoon contenders Nottingham Lions have managed to put together a run of three straight wins to lift themselves into a play-off spot.

The Ducks still have an outside chance of catching them, however, as they have two games to come against the Lions, in addition to two games in hand. There's now a break for Deeside, who return to the ice for their trip to Telford Tigers on January 26.

Other results: Coventry 7 Bradford 4; Sutton 9 Sheffield 1; Altrincham 2 Telford 16; Nottingham 6 Kingston 3; Sheffield 2 Coventry 3.

Ducks In The Newspaper!

There's a short piece about the Deeside Ducks' away game against Bradford Bulldogs in today's Flintshire & Wrexham Leader (14th January 2024 - Page 35).

You can read a longer version of the report – along with lots of other fascinating stuff - on the highly informative grass roots ice hockey review website:

https://www.icehockeyreview.co.uk/2025/01/match-report-bradford-bulldogs-9.html

#keepquacking   #fowlnotfoul

Dalton (DJ) Thompson scored within 22 seconds of his Deeside Ducks' debut away at Telford (Photo by Keith & Jenny Davies)

Sunday 26th January 2025 – NIHL Laidler Division
Telford Tigers 11 - Deeside Ducks 2

The Deeside Ducks slumped to an 11-2 defeat away to league title challengers Telford Tigers on Sunday.

The game saw a Ducks debut for Dalton (DJ) Thompson, a former Altrincham Aces and Deeside Dragons player who has spent the earlier part of this season playing Junior A hockey in the Greater Metro Hockey League (GMHL) in Ontario, Canada.

Thompson's arrival had an immediate effect as he fired the Ducks into an early lead with a goal after just 22 seconds of the first period.

The lead didn't last long, however, and two goals from Telford's new signing – experienced Czech forward Vladimir Luka - on 4 and 9 minutes put the Tigers ahead.

Deeside hit back again with goal from Stewart Cutting with 27 seconds left on the clock and the Ducks were able to go into the first interval on level terms at 2-2

That was as good as things got for the Deeside team, however, as Telford fired in 6 unanswered goals in the second period and 3 more in the third to cruise to a comprehensive 11-2 victory.

Much of the damage was done by Luka, who scored 5 goals overall in the game and also added 1 assist. His arrival in the Tigers 2 camp has raised a few eyebrows after he dropped down two divisions from the National Division to play in what many view as a development league.

So, in view of the strength of the opposition – and the fact that Deeside conceded 24 goals on their previous visit to Shropshire earlier in the season - Sunday's result would have to be viewed as an improvement.

The Ducks have another tough game this Saturday 1st February when they take on league leaders Sutton Sting at Deeside Leisure Centre, 5pm face off.

Telford Tigers NIHL 2 11-2 Deeside Ducks
North 2 Regular Season, Sunday 26th January
Game 097

Telford Tigers NIHL 2 (19-0-0-1)   (1-1-0-16) Deeside Ducks

SCORING SUMMARY

G	Per	Time	Score	Team	Goal Scorer	Assist	Assist	Str
1	1	0:22	0-1	DEE	Dalton Thompson (1)	Chris Jones (5)		E
2	1	3:43	1-1	TEL	Vladimir Luka (3)			E
3	1	8:47	2-1	TEL	Vladimir Luka (4)	Josef Lauder (14)	Ben Washburn (19)	E
4	1	19:33	2-2	DEE	Stewart Cutting (4)	Charlie Spridgeon (11)		E
5	2	20:13	3-2	TEL	Taylor Stanton (22)	Stephen Crowe (2)	Connor Keyes (2)	E
6	2	21:17	4-2	TEL	Ben Washburn (9)	Taylor Stanton (19)	Stephen Crowe (3)	E
7	2	25:14	5-2	TEL	Oliver Hunt (22)			E
8	2	31:06	6-2	TEL	Vladimir Luka (5)	Ben Washburn (20)	Taylor Stanton (20)	E
9	2	38:55	7-2	TEL	Vladimir Luka (6)	Taylor Stanton (21)	Connor McNaughton (25)	E
10	2	39:35	8-2	TEL	Taylor Stanton (23)	Vladimir Luka (1)	Ben Washburn (21)	E
11	3	43:41	9-2	TEL	Vladimir Luka (7)	Taylor Stanton (22)	Dan Mitchell (7)	E
12	3	48:31	10-2	TEL	Oliver Hunt (23)	Robert Oxley (9)	Dan Harrison (1)	E
13	3	56:05	11-2	TEL	Connor McNaughton (8)	Ben Washburn (22)		E

PENALTY SUMMARY

TELFORD TIGERS NIHL 2

#	Per	Time	Player	PIM	Penalty
1	1	14:56	Bench	2	Too Many Men
2	1	16:28	Liam Bartholomew	2	Slashing
3	2	26:00	Taylor Stanton	2	Tripping
4	3	44:34	Connor McNaughton	2	Slashing
5	3	58:56	Dan Mitchell	2	Misconduct

TOT (PN-PIM) 5-10
Power Plays (Goals-Opp) 0-1

DEESIDE DUCKS

#	Per	Time	Player	PIM	Penalty
1	1	31:20	Chris Jones	2	Delay of Game
2	3	58:56	Mackenzie Wilkes	2	Charging
3					
4					
5					

TOT (PN-PIM) 2-4
Power Plays (Goals-Opp) 0-4

TEAM SUMMARY

TELFORD TIGERS NIHL 2

		TELFORD TIGERS NIHL 2	G	A	P	PN	PIM
5	D	Robert Oxley		1	1		
8	D	Simon Harrison					
10	D	Dan Harrison		1	1		
13	F	Lewis Smith					
15	D	Daniel Retter					
18	D	Josh Hustwick					
25	D	Stephen Crowe		2	2		
27	F	Callum Griffin					
29	F	Connor Keyes		1	1		
31	NM	Matthew Byrne					
36	D	Josef Lauder		1	1		
39	F	Callum O'Reilly					
40	F	Ben Washburn	1	4	5		
50	NM	Hal Griffiths					
51	F	Liam Bartholomew				1	2
53	F	Oliver Hunt	2		2		
59	D	Connor Bennett					
61	F	Kyle Watt					
71	F	Taylor Stanton	2	4	6	1	2
88	F	Dan Mitchell	1	1	1	1	2
94	F	Vladimir Luka	5	1	6		
95	F	Connor McNaughton	1	1	2	1	2
		Team Penalty				1	2
		TEAM TOTALS	11	17	28	5	10

DEESIDE DUCKS

		DEESIDE DUCKS	G	A	P	PN	PIM
1	NM	Jace Gledhill					
4	F	Charlie Spridgeon		1	1		
10	F	Stewart Cutting	1		1		
11	F	Rafferty Smith					
13	D	Deacon Wilkes					
18	D	George Spofforth					
19	F	Mackenzie Wilkes				1	2
21	D	Kieran Clarkson					
29	F	Ben Roscoe					
44	F	Harry Shearman					
47	NM	Callum Preston					
52	F	Dalton Thompson	1		1		
72	D	Chris Jones		1	1	1	2
73	F	Josh Jones					
91	D	Rory Sillery					
		Team Penalty					
		TEAM TOTALS	2	2	4	2	4

GOALTENDER SUMMARY

TELFORD TIGERS NIHL 2

	TELFORD TIGERS NIHL 2	TOI	1	2	3	OT	TOT
							Goals-Shots Against
31	Matthew Byrne						
50	Hal Griffiths	60:00	2-9	0-8	0-3		2-20
	Empty Net						

DEESIDE DUCKS

	DEESIDE DUCKS	TOI	1	2	3	OT	TOT
							Goals - Shots Against
1	Jace Gledhill	40:00	2-12	6-18			8-30
47	Callum Preston	20:00			3-15		3-15
	Empty Net						

Source: NIHLStats.wordpress.com (Box Scores)

Ducks show their improvement

DEESIDE DUCKS slumped to an 11-2 defeat away to title challengers Telford Tigers on Sunday.

The score was actually 2-2 at the end of the first period, with goals from DJ Thompson – making his first appearance for the Ducks - and Stewart Cutting keeping the Deeside team in contention early on.

However, six unanswered goals in the second period and three more in the third saw the hosts cruise to an easy victory.

Much of the damage was done by Tigers' new signing, Czech forward Vladimir Luka, who scored five of the goals. His arrival in the Tigers 2 camp has raised a few eyebrows after he dropped down two divisions from the National Division to play in what many view as a development league.

So, in view of the strength of the opposition, and the fact that Deeside conceded 24 goals on their previous visit to Shropshire earlier in the season, Sunday's result would have to be viewed as an improvement.

Other results: Altrincham 8 Bradford 4; Kingston 3 Billingham 5; Sutton 4 Telford 6; Bradford 4 Kingston 5.

Ducks In The Newspaper!

There's a short piece about the Deeside Ducks' away game against Telford Tigers in today's Flintshire & Wrexham Leader (28th January 2025 - Page 34).

You can read a longer version of the report – along with lots of other fascinating stuff - on the highly informative grass roots Ice Hockey Review website:

http://www.icehockeyreview.co.uk/2025/01/match-report-telford-tigers-11-deeside.html

#keepquacking   #fowlnotfoul

Ducks MVP v Sutton Oli Booth (Photo by Maxine Roscoe)

Saturday 1st February 2025 – NIHL Laidler Division Deeside Ducks 1 – Sutton Sting 9

Sunday 2nd February 2025 – NIHL Laidler Division Altrincham Aces 5 – Deeside Ducks 3

The Deeside Ducks had an eventful weekend, losing 1-9 at home to league leaders Sutton Sting on Saturday and then having a much closer game, losing 5-3 away to Altrincham Aces on Sunday.

Sutton had won 20 of their 21 league games so far this season and, while Deeside put in a good showing, they never really looked like beating the title contenders. However, the game was very close in its earlier stages and it took Sutton until a good 9 minutes in to open the scoring.

It was 0-2 at the first period break and, with only a single goal scored in the second period, 0-3 at the second interval, leaving Deeside still in with a chance.

Sutton pulled away in the third period, however, with 6 more goals to lead 0-9 with 6 minutes left to play.

The Ducks continued to battle away and their perseverance eventually paid off with a consolation goal from Charlie Nicholson – his first senior goal - on 55 minutes, which also saw off the unwanted spectre of a first ever home shut-out.

Despite the scoreline, Oli Booth – playing his first game for the Ducks - put in a good performance in goal, keeping out 49 of the 58 shots that he faced, and was named MVP for Deeside.

The away game at Altricham on Sunday was a lot closer and Deeside were very much in conetation right up until the dying moments.

The Ducks scored first with a goal from Rhys Howells on 4 minutes but the lead didn't last long as the Aces equalised just 68 seconds later. A Chris Jones goal 76 seconds after that put the Ducks back in front but Altrincham fought back to equalise again and two more goals late in the period saw them leading 4-2 at the first break.

The second period was just as closely contested and remained goalless until Andrew Chappell – making his first Ducks appearance - scored with just 34 seconds left on the clock – to reduce the deficit to just one goal heading into the final 20 minutes.

Deeside weren't able to build on this in the third period, however, and an Aces strike with 7 minutes left to go rounded off the scoring for the game.

The game got tetchier as it went on and an eye-watering 92 penalty minutes were handed out overall – 68 to Altrincham and 24 to Deeside.

The closing minutes saw a lot of disruption and the match finished in disarray with 4 Altrincham players – including former Duck Alfie Kelly – receiving 10 minute major penalties for misconduct and abusive behaviour, along with Deeside's Rhys Howells, to end the game on a sour note.

The Ducks have another home game this Saturday 8th February when they take on Nottingham Lions for the first time this season at Deeside Leisure Centre, 5pm face off.

Andrew Chappell (centre) and Rhys Howells (#85) away at Altrincham (Photo by All Sports Photography)

Saturday 1st February 2025 – NIHL Laidler Division
Deeside Ducks 1 – Sutton Sting 9

Scoring Summary

G	Per	Time	Team	Scorer	Assist 1	Assist 2	Str
1	1	08.57	SUT	Ryan Apsley	Ch Saunders	Bailey Templar	E
2	1	12.18	SUT	Joseph Colton	Ryan Apsley	Charles Saunders	E
3	2	34.33	SUT	Charles Saunders	Lawson Glasby	Adam Br-Smith	PP
4	3	46.04	SUT	Adam Br -Smith	Lawson Glasby		E
5	3	46.33	SUT	Lawson Glasby	Jacob Truswell		E
6	3	46.54	SUT	Cameron Glasby	Ch Saunders	Jacob Truswell	E
7	3	47.24	SUT	Ryan Apsley			E
8	3	51.06	SUT	Elliot Meadows	Samuel Colton		E
9	3	53.03	SUT	Morgan Glasby	Lawson Glasby		E
10	3	54.16	DEE	Charlie Nicholson*			E

*Note: EIH Gameday lists the Ducks goal as being scored by Charlie Spridgeon however NIHL North Upates and other social media say that it was Charlie Nicholson.

Penalty Summary

Deeside Ducks				Sutton Sting			
Time	Player	PIM	Off	Time	Player	PIM	Off
03.28	Luke Wainwright	2	SLAS	09.44	Bailey Templar	2	BOAR
24.30	Charlie Spridgeon	2	TRIP	26.57	Jasper Wright	2	DEL-G
33.37	Bench	2	TO-M				
Total		**6**		**Total**		**4**	

Team Summary

Deeside Ducks		G	A	Pts	PIM	Sutton Sting		G	A	Pts	PIM
4	C. Spridgeon				2	2	B. Templar		1	1	2
5	M. Speare					7	A. Br-Smith	1	1	2	
10	S. Cutting					8	S. Colton		1	1	
12	H. Phillips					9	C. Akers				
13	D. Wilkes					11	O. Watson				
18	G. Spofforth					16	C. Saunders	1	3	4	
19	M. Wilkes					17	M. Glasby	1		1	
21	K. Clarkson					18	R. Apsley	2	1	3	
25	L. Yarwood					20	J. Humphreys				
27	O. Booth					48	C. Glasby	1		1	
29	B. Roscoe					72	J. Colton	1		1	
45	C. Nicholson	1		1		78	J. Wright				2
51	C. Swift					80	L. Glasby	1	3	4	
52	G. Dixon					82	J. Hargreaves				
72	C. Jones					86	E. Meadows	1		1	
73	J. Jones					94	J. Truswell		2	2	
91	R. Sillery					99	L. King				
98	L. Wainwright				2						
00	Bench				2						
Totals		**1**	**0**	**1**	**6**	**Totals**		**9**	**12**	**21**	**4**

Netminder Summary

Deeside Ducks		GA / SA				Sutton Sting		GA / SA			
	Mins	1	2	3	Tot		Mins	1	2	3	Tot
Callum Preston						L King	60.00				13
Oliver Booth	60.00				58						

Match details and player stats transcribed into a readable format from EIH Gameday upload data by Paul Breeze

Altrincham Aces 5-3 Deeside Ducks
North 2 Regular Season, Sunday 2nd February
Game 102

Altrincham Aces (11-1-0-10)   (1-1-0-18) Deeside Ducks

SCORING SUMMARY

G	Per	Time	Score	Team	Goal Scorer	Assist	Assist	Str
1	1	3:57	0-1	DEE	Rhys Howells	Andrew Chappell	Rory Sillery	E
2	1	5:05	1-1	ALT	Ollie Gotts (11)	David Kovacs (2)	David Kamenicek (6)	E
3	1	6:16	1-2	DEE	Chris Jones	Rhys Howells	Dalton Thompson	E
4	1	9:44	2-2	ALT	Josh Milnes (11)	Malachi Budd (15)	David Kovacs (3)	E
5	1	15:56	3-2	ALT	Jake Frost (12)			SH
6	1	18:40	4-2	ALT	Kane Morin (4)	Jake Frost (10)		E
7	2	39:26	4-3	DEE	Andrew Chappell	Chris Jones	Ben Roscoe	E
8	3	52:39	5-3	ALT	Ronnie Grimes (6)	Carl Price (10)	Sam Hockey (3)	E

PENALTY SUMMARY

ALTRINCHAM ACES								DEESIDE DUCKS				
#	Per	Time	Player	PIM	Penalty	#	Per	Time	Player	PIM	Penalty	
1	1	15:26	Ronnie Grimes	2	Interference	1	1	16:49	Chris Jones	2	Roughing	
2	1	16:49	Carl Price	2	NM Interference	2	1	19:31	Harry Shearman	2	Interference	
3	2	27:30	Carl Price	2	Tripping	3	2	32:26	Chris Jones	2	Tripping	
4	2	27:30	Carl Price	2	Tripping	4	2	32:26	Chris Jones	2	Interference	
5	2	30:22	Alfie Kelly	2	Tripping	5	2	35:26	Rory Sillery	2	Boarding	
6	2	31:15	Bailey Thomas	2	Interference	6	3	47:14	Rafferty Smith	2	Tripping	
7	2	31:44	Ronnie Grimes	2	Roughing	7	3	59:59	Rhys Howells	2	Cross Checking	
8	3	41:09	Bailey Thomas	2	Delay of Game	8	3	59:59	Rhys Howells	10	Abuse	
9	3	53:16	Jayson Burgess	2	High Sticking	9						
10	3	54:33	David Kamenicek	2	Delay of Game	10						
11	3	58:24	Ronnie Grimes	2	Cross Checking	11						
12	3	58:24	Ronnie Grimes	2	Abuse	12						
13	3	58:46	Alfie Kelly	2	Cross Checking	13						
14	3	58:46	Alfie Kelly	10	Misconduct	14						
15	3	58:46	Jayson Burgess	10	Abuse	15						
16	3	59:59	Kane Morin	2	Cross Checking	16						
17	3	60:00	Sam Hockey	10	Abuse	17						
18	3	60:00	Ronnie Grimes	10	Abuse	18						

TOT (PN-PIM) 18-68	TOT (PN-PIM) 8-24
Power Plays (Goals-Opp) 0-4	Power Plays (Goals-Opp) 0-10

TEAM SUMMARY

		ALTRINCHAM ACES	G	A	P	PN	PIM			DEESIDE DUCKS	G	A	P	PN	PIM
1	NM	Cameron Valentine-Higgs						4	F	Charlie Spridgeon					
5	F	Sam Dunford						5	F	Michael Speare					
8	F	Kane Morin	1		1	1	2	10	F	Stewart Cutting					
14	D	Alfie Kelly				3	14	11	F	Rafferty Smith				1	2
15	F	Jake Frost	1	1	2			13	D	Deacon Wilkes					
16	D	Max Sullivan						16	F	Andrew Chappell	1	1	2		
21	F	Josh Milnes	1		1			19	F	Mackenzie Wilkes					
23	F	C.J Ashton						21	D	Kieran Clarkson					
31	NM	Bayley Hodkinson						25	F	Liam Yarwood					
36	F	Elliot Hunt						27	NM	Oliver Booth					
44	D	Bailey Thomas				2	4	29	F	Ben Roscoe		1	1		
45	D	James Best						44	F	Harry Shearman				1	2
55	D	David Kovacs		2	2			45	F	Charlie Nicholson					
62	F	Sam Hockey		1	1	1	10	47	NM	Callum Preston					
69	D	David Kamenicek		1	1	1	2	51	F	Dalton Thompson		1	1		
75	F	Jayson Burgess				2	12	52	F	Corey Swift					
77	F	Ronnie Grimes	1		1	5	18	72	D	Chris Jones	1	1	2	3	6
90	F	Malachi Budd		1	1			85	D	Rhys Howells	1	1	2	2	12
95	F	Ollie Gotts	1		1			91	D	Rory Sillery		1	1	1	2
96	F	Carl Price		1	1	3	6								
98	F	Billy King													
		Team Penalty								Team Penalty					
		TEAM TOTALS	5	7	12	18	68			TEAM TOTALS	3	6	9	8	24

GOALTENDER SUMMARY

ALTRINCHAM ACES		Goals-Shots Against						DEESIDE DUCKS		Goals - Shots Against				
		TOI	1	2	3	OT	TOT			TOI	1	2	3	OT	TOT
1	Cameron Valentine-Higgs							27	Oliver Booth	60:00	4-12	0-20	1-15		5-47
33	Bayley Hodkinson	60:00	2-10	1-11	0-13		3-34	47	Callum Preston						
	Empty Net								Empty Net						

Source: NIHLStats.wordpress.com (Box Scores)

Dragons' MVI at Blackburn and he claimed one of the goals on the evening.

There were two goals from Jake Witkowski, plus one apiece from Ross Kennedy and Garry Simpson.

Dragons were always playing catch-up in their meeting with Solihull, who were 2-0 to the good at the end of the first period.

Kennedy and Witkowski struck for the home side in the next period, but Barons held a comfortable 7-2 lead at the final break.

They would add four more goals to their tally, while MJ Clancy's strike was Deeside's only response.

"There was so much to be pleased about with the performance in Blackburn," said assistant head coach Matt Compton.

"We had Cody Ogden, a 17-year-old, who played fantastically, scored a goal and did so well.

"There were so many positives to take from Saturday.

"Then, on Sunday, it capitulated pretty quickly. We were losing little puck battles, thinking about ourselves and not the team."

Other results: Leeds 7 Sheffield 0; Solihull 8 Nottingham 6; Widnes 2 Hull 4; Billingham 8 Leeds 4; Sheffield 1 Nottingham 6.

Deeside Ducks had an eventful weekend, losing 9-1 at home to league leaders Sutton Sting on Saturday and then having a much closer game, losing 5-3 away to Altrincham Aces on Sunday.

Sutton had won 20 of their 21 league games so far this season and, while Deeside put in a good showing, they never really looked like beating the title favourites. However, the game was very close in its earlier stages and it took Sutton until a good nine minutes in to open the scoring.

It was 2-0 at the first period break and, with only a single goal scored in the second period, 3-0 at the second interval - leaving Deeside still in with a chance.

Sutton pulled away in the third period, however, with more goals to lead 9-0 with six minutes left to play.

Ducks continued to battle away and their perseverance eventually paid off with a consolation goal from Charlie Nicholson – his first senior goal - on 55 minutes, which also saw off the unwanted spectre of a first ever home shut-out.

Despite the scoreline, Oli Booth,

MVP: Deeside Ducks' star man versus Sutton was Oli Booth. Picture: Maxine Roscoe

playing his first game for the Ducks, put in a good performance in goal, keeping out 49 of the 58 shots that he faced, and he was named MVP for Deeside.

The game at Altrincham was a lot closer and Deeside actually took the lead early on with a goal from Rhys Howells.

The score was a tantalisingly close 4-3 after two periods, with further strikes from Chris Jones

and Andrew Chappell, who was making his Ducks' debut.

The only goal of the third period fell to the Aces on 53 minutes, sealing the win for them but, after conceding 16 goals on their previous visit to Altrincham, Deeside can look upon this as one of their better results of the season.

Other results: Coventry 7 Altrincham 2; Telford 6 Billingham 0; Bradford 3 Coventry 5; Nottingham 5 Sheffield 2.

Ducks In The Newspaper!

There's a summary of the Deeside Ducks' weekend games at home to Sutton Sting and away to Altrincham Aces in today's Flintshire & Wrexham Leader (4th February 2025 - Page 37).

You can read a longer version of the report – along with lots of other fascinating stuff - on the highly informative grass roots Ice Hockey Review website:

https://www.icehockeyreview.co.uk/2025/02/deeside-ducks-weekend-report-1st-2nd.html

#keepquacking   #fowlnotfoul

Ben Roscoe was the Ducks' MVP against Nottingham
(Photo by Paul Breeze)

Saturday 8th February 2025 – NIHL Laidler Division
Deeside Ducks 4 – Nottingham Lions 2

The Deeside Ducks picked up their third win of the season – and their first since November - with a superb 4-2 victory over Nottingham Lions at Deeside Leisure Centre on Saturday.

This was a very closely fought and entertaining game with little to choose between the teams and it remained goal-less at the first period break.

Nottingham finally broke the deadlock 25 seconds into the second period but Deeside equalised 4 minutes later with a goal from Charlie Spridgeon. A further goal on 38 minutes edged the Lions back in front but a powerplay strike from Dalton Thompson for the Ducks with just 10 seconds left on the clock tied the score again at 2-2.

Deeside took the lead for the first time 70 seconds into the third period with Spridgeon's second goal of the game and Nottingham fought back. However, they were unable to breach the stubborn Ducks defence or get past netminder Jace Gledhill, who was in fine form throughout the game.

The Lions withdrew their netminder in favour of an extra attacker for the final minute and put the Deeside goal under siege. The win, however, was secured for the Ducks with a long range Empty Net Goal from James Morgan with 5 seconds left to play.

After the final buzzer, Ducks Head Coach Gary Shaw said: "Both teams played some good hockey throughout the game and I think either could have won - but we prevailed with a great team effort."

The Ducks are at home again this Sunday 16th February when they take on Coventry NIHL Blaze at Deeside Leisure Centre – 5pm face off.

Coach's Comments from Gary Shaw

Talking about the Ducks' win over Nottingham, Head Coach Gary Shaw said:

The Ducks played a team which has the same idea of developing players for the next stage of their careers.

The game started with both teams having some good offensive chances and our defensive shape was a little all over the place and due to this we went behind from a good play by one of their talented forwards.

The chances for both teams kept rising and our goalie Jace (Gledhill) made some great saves to keep us in the game, we put some good pressure on their defence and turned the puck over and Charlie managed to equalise for us and finished the period strongly.

The second period started much of the same of the first, end to end and players of both side had good chances but both goalies playing well. Nottingham took the lead again from a shot from the point which Jace didn't pick up.

The game started to get a bit feisty we a couple of players delivering late hits which the refs didn't pickup, so on a powerplay Dalton (Thompson) equalised with a good shot from the half wall as the netminder was not ready with his stick in the air. So the period ended all square.

During the break we talked about tightening up in our defence zone and making sure we keep their players to the outside and to be more patient in the offensive zone and control the game.

We started well and the players responded well causing Nottingham some defensive problems and their goalie was playing well.

After some strong attacking pressure on their net Charlie managed to score to give us the lead.

Nottingham started to put some strong pressure on our defence and come up with some good chances but Jace pulled off some great saves to keep our lead.

We called a time out to settle the players down and refocus on our goal about us controlling the game, Nottingham pulled their netminder to add an extra attacker in the last minutes of the game and James (Morgan) managed to score an empty net goal to secure the victory.

Both teams played some good hockey throughout the game and I think either could have won - but we prevailed with a great team effort.

Deeside Ducks 4 – Nottingham Lions 2

Fluffy yellow ducklings don't stay little for long
If they play ice hockey an exciting opportunity comes along

Deeside Ducks are a very special team
And their players are living the dream
CONGRATULATIONS Ducks
Just keep icing and pushing those pucks.

Lucy London, 8th February 2025

Deeside Ducks team v Nottingham, 8th February 2025 (Photo by Paul Breeze)

Back Row: Simon Hughes, Callum Preston, Gary Shaw, Corey Swift, Dan Fadejevs, Cody Ogden, Luke Wainwright, Rhys Howells, Chris Jones, Dalton Thompson, Henry Phillips, Stewart Cutting, Kieran Clarkson, Louis Morgan, James Parsons. Front Row: Josh Jones, Deacon Wilkes, Harry Shearman, James Morgan, Andrew Chappell, Rory Sillery, Charlie Spridgeon, Ben Roscoe, Jace Gledhill

Deeside Ducks 4-2 Nottingham Lions NIHL 2

North 2 Regular Season, Saturday 8th February
Game 106

Deeside Ducks (2-1-0-18) (4-1-0-16) Nottingham Lions NIHL 2

SCORING SUMMARY

G	Per	Time	Score	Team	Goal Scorer	Assist	Assist	Str
1	2	20:25	0-1	NOT	Jake Fisher (6)	Charlie Davenport (5)	James Cox (1)	E
2	2	24:40	1-1	DEE	Charlie Spridgeon (3)	Rhys Howells (3)	Chris Jones (7)	E
3	2	38:03	1-2	NOT	Charlie Davenport (10)	Myles Richardson (4)	Jake Fisher (10)	E
4	2	39:50	2-2	DEE	Dalton Thompson (2)	Jace Gledhill (1)		PP
5	3	41:13	3-2	DEE	Charlie Spridgeon (4)	Chris Jones (8)		E
6	3	59:55	4-2	DEE	James Morgan (1)			EN

DEESIDE DUCKS	NOTTINGHAM LIONS NIHL 2

PENALTY SUMMARY

#	Per	Time	Player	PIM	Penalty		#	Per	Time	Player	PIM	Penalty
1	1	15:02	Rhys Howells	2	Holding		1	1	19:46	Harry MacGarvey	2	Roughing
2	1	19:46	Chris Jones	2	Roughing		2	2	38:08	Myles Richardson	2	Hooking
3	2	34:37	Andrew Chappell	2	High Stickin		3					

TOT (PN-PIM) 4-8	TOT (PN-PIM) 2-4
Power Plays (Goals-Opp) 1-1	Power Plays (Goals-Opp) 0-2

TEAM SUMMARY

		DEESIDE DUCKS	G	A	P	PN	PIM			NOTTINGHAM LIONS NIHL 2	G	A	P	PN	PIM
2	F	Harry Shearman						3	F	Brodey Butlin					
4	F	Charlie Spridgeon	2		2			5	D	Josh Rawsthorne					
10	F	Stewart Cutting						10	F	Michael Berehowskyj					
12	F	Henry Phillips						14	NM	Owen Crowder					
13	D	Deacon Wilkes						16	D	Tyler Poole					
16	F	Andrew Chappell				1	2	23	F	Harvey Smith					
18	D	George Spofforth						27	D	Josh Dowds					
21	F	Kieran Clarkson						28	F	Jake Fisher	1	1	2		
29	F	Ben Roscoe						31	F	Edward Bonn					
31	D	James Morgan	1		1			35	D	Ben Bridgett					
40	F	Cody Ogden						36	NM	Joe Nolan					
47	NM	Callum Preston						42	F	Harry MacGarvey				1	2
51	F	Dalton Thompson	1		1			53	D	Andrew Rourke					
52	F	Corey Swift						66	D	Alex Weems					
72	D	Chris Jones		2	2	1	2	80	F	Josh Marsden					
81	F	Daniels Fadejevs						81	D	Myles Richardson		1	1	1	2
85	F	Rhys Howells		1	1	1	2	83	F	Charlie Davenport	1	1	2		
91	D	Rory Sillery						84	D	Jessica Urquhart					
94	NM	Jace Gledhill		1	1			91	F	Ethan Wilcox					
98	D	Luke Wainwright						93	D	James Cox		1	1		
								95		Cody Nurden					
		Team Penalty								Team Penalty					
		TEAM TOTALS	4	4	8	3	6			TEAM TOTALS	2	4	6	2	4

GOALTENDER SUMMARY

DEESIDE DUCKS		Goals-Shots Against						NOTTINGHAM LIONS		Goals - Shots Against				
	TOI	1	2	3	OT	TOT			TOI	1	2	3	OT	TOT
47 Callum Preston								14 Owen Crowder						
94 Jace Gledhill	60:00	0-8	2-25	0-14		2-47		36 Joe Nolan	59:05	0-8	2-6	1-14		3-2
Empty Net								Empty Net	0:55			1-1		1-1

Source: NIHLStats.wordpress.com (Box Scores)

pressure into a leveller from Ross Kennedy when the next period got underway.

A trio of quickfire efforts made sure Nottingham were able to build-up a 4-1 advantage, while Jake Witkowski cut the deficit with Dragons' second goal of the evening.

Lions held a 4-2 advantage when the final period started and they would go on to add a further four goals to their tally. Dragons' solitary response came from Witkowski's second of the evening, while the home MVP on the night was Cody Ogden.

"Again, the scoreline didn't really reflect the game," said Deeside assistant head coach Matt Compton.

"We hit the post five times. Discipline let us down a little bit as well.

"We definitely need to be better with our discipline. We have played well in the first 20 minutes.

"When things aren't going your way, you feel everything's not going your way."

Other results: Blackburn 8 Widnes 2; Leeds 5 Whitley 8; Hull 7 Leeds 1; Solihull 6 Blackburn 5; Whitley 11 Sheffield 4; Widnes 1 Billingham 3.

Deeside Ducks picked up their third win of the season – and their first since November - with a superb 4-2 victory over Nottingham Lions at Deeside Leisure Centre.

This was a very closely fought and entertaining game with little to choose between the teams and it remained goalless at the first period break.

Nottingham finally broke the deadlock 25 seconds into the second period but Deeside equalised four minutes later with a goal from Charlie Spridgeon.

A further goal on 38 minutes

MVP: Ben Roscoe was Deeside Ducks' top performer against Nottingham. Picture: PAUL BREEZE

edged the Lions back in front but a powerplay strike from Dalton Thompson for the Ducks with just 10 seconds left on the clock tied the score again at 2-2.

Deeside took the lead for the first time 70 seconds into the third period with Spridgeon's second goal of the game and Nottingham fought back.

However, they were unable to breach the stubborn Ducks' defence or get past netminder Jace Gledhill, who was in fine form throughout the game.

The Lions withdrew their netminder in favour of an extra attacker for the final minute and put the Deeside goal under siege. The win, however, was confirmed for the Ducks with a long range empty net goal from James

Morgan with five seconds left to play.

After the final buzzer, Ducks head coach Gary Shaw said: "Both teams played some good hockey throughout the game and I think either could have won - but we prevailed with a great team effort."

Other results: Kingston 6 Sheffield 9; Sutton 4 Altrincham 0; Telford 18 Bradford 0; Altrincham 3 Sutton 7; Billingham 3 Kingston 2; Nottingham 1 Coventry 9.

Ducks In The Newspaper!

There's a short report of the Deeside Ducks' home win over Nottingham in today's Flintshire & Wrexham Leader (11th February 2025 - Page 35).

You can read the report – along with detailed comments from Head Coach Gary Shaw - on the highly informative grass roots Ice Hockey Review website:

http://www.icehockeyreview.co.uk/2025/02/match-report-deeside-ducks-4-nottingham.html

#keepquacking   #fowlnotfoul

Laidler Division • January
D-man of the Month

Keith and Jenny Davies

Chris Jones
2 GP • 1g, 1a for 2pts

12th February 2025: Chris Jones Named Defenceman Of The Month

Deeside Ducks senior player Chris Jones has been named the Laidler Division's "Defenceman of the Month" for January 2025 by the influential NIHL North Updates organisation.

NIHL North Updates operate a Facebook page where they post - as is suggested in the title - match updates for games being played in the NIHL North Moralee and Laidler Divisions each weekend.

In fact, during the current – and somewhat elongated - "transition" period while we are all waiting for the EIH(A) to get their new Gameday online scoring and stats system up and running properly, NIHL North Updates is pretty much the only place where you can find an up-to-date and centralised summary of what is happening on match days across the two divisions.

The Player of the Month Awards were launched by NIHL North Updates this season and are based on nominations put forward by fans on the Facebook page, with the instruction: "Players don't need to be flashy goal-scorers ... they can be stay-at-home defencemen, brick wall goaltenders, the lot!"

Regarding Chris Jones' award, NIHL North Updates commented:

"The Deeside Ducks, in their first year, have been far from good. But, when they do have all their men on the bench, one of the side's brightest lights is Chris Jones, who can credibly contribute to the team's offence with (Charlie) Spridgeon but has been defensively instrumental in bringing some games within touching distance of points, or softening the blow in others."

The full list of award winners for January 2025 is as follows:

Moralee Division

Forward: Daragh Spawforth (Blackburn Hawks)

Defence: Matt Cross (Blackburn Hawks)

Netminder: Mark Turnbull (Billingham Stars)

Laidler Division

Forward: Taylor Stanton (Telford Tigers)

Defence: Chris Jones (Deeside Ducks)

Netminder: Chris Outhwaite (Billingham Buccaneers)

You can follow what's going on in the Moralee and Laidler Divisions every weekend on the NIHL North Updates Facebook page at:

https://www.facebook.com/nihlnupdates

The EIHA ran their own Player Of The Month Awards for all 4 NIHL Divisions in seasons 2017/18 and 2019/20, although the shortlists were compiled and the monthly winners picked by a panel of media experts.

The current NIHL North Updates awards differ from this as the shortlists are taken from nominations by the public.

Ducks MVP Jace Gledhill (Photo by Maxine Roscoe)

Sunday 16th February 2025 – NIHL Laidler Division
Deeside Ducks 1 – Coventry Blaze 0

The Deeside Ducks picked up their second win in a row with a close and hard-fought 1-0 victory over Coventry NIHL Blaze at Deeside Leisure Centre on Sunday.

Following on from last week's win over Nottingham and having only lost out by a single goal to Coventry on the Blaze's previous visit, the Ducks were especially keyed up for this game, knowing that a win would significantly boost their chances of qualifying for the end of season play offs.

The early stages of the game were littered with niggly penalties for both sides and, despite numerous chances at both ends, the first period played out goal-less.

The second period was also goal-less as the Ducks battled hard against the team 6 places - and 36 points - above them in the league table, and the score stood at a tantalisingly balanced 0-0 heading into the final 20 minutes.

The breakthrough finally came on 52.45 when former Dragons player Andrew Chappell fired in the only goal of the game, assisted by Dalton Thompson.

Despite late pressure from Coventry, the solid Ducks defence held out to secure the win – backed up by a superb overall display from netminder Jace Gledhill, who registered a 40 shot shut-out and was deservedly named MVP for Deeside.

The Ducks now have a game free weekend and are next in action on Saturday 1st March when they take on Billingham Buccaneers at Deeside Leisure Centre, 5pm face off.

Scoring Summary

G	Per	Time	Team	Scorer	Assist 1	Assist 2	Str
1	3	52.45	DEE	Andrew Chappell	DJ Thompson		E

Deeside Ducks	Coventry Blaze

Penalty Summary

Time	Player	PIM	Off	Time	Player	PIM	Off
05.56	Chris Jones	2	ROUGH	02.00	Jamie Lewis	2	ROUGH
17.25	James Morgan	2	ROUGH	13.18	Dalton Upton	2	TRIP
27.49	DJ Thompson	2	HOOK	13.48	Max Parham	2	X-CH
27.49	Andrew Chappell	2	SLASH	17.25	Tho Br-Smith	2	INTF
34.36	Daniels Fadejevs	2	X-CH	21.15	Connor Mellett	2	HOLD
36.22	Rhys Howells	2	ROUGH	36.22	Ethan Wheeldon	2	ROUGH
36.22	Louis Morgan	2	ROUGH	36.22	Arthur Brookes	2	ROUGH
39.10	Gary Dixon	2	HOLD	36.22	Arthur Brookes	2	UNSP
				42.15	BENCH	2	TOO-M
	Total	**16**			**Total**	**18**	

Team Summary

	Deeside Ducks	G	A	Pts	PIM		Coventry Blaze	G	A	Pts	PIM
4	C. Spridgeon					39	J. Bearman				
5	A. Chappell	1		1	2	34	H. Laverick				
8	L. Morgan				2	10	J. Ald-Smith				
9	G. Dixon				2	95	J. Gavigan				
10	J. Gledhill					49	W. Kibkalo				
12	H. Phillips					18	M. Parham				2
13	D. Wilkes					40	N. Simpson				
21	K. Clarkson					57	D. Upton				2
29	B. Roscoe					87	A. Brookes				4
31	J. Morgan				2	59	O. Harris				
40	C. Ogden					9	J. Lewis				2
44	H. Shearman					12	H. Sumner				
45	C. Nicholson					22	M. Wickens				
47	C. Preston					20	O. Dixon				
51	D. Thompson		1	1	2	8	R. James				
72	C. Jones				2	37	C. Mellett				2
73	J. Jones					93	S. Prosser				
81	D. Fadejevs				2	21	C. Wheeldon				
85	R. Howells				2	19	T. Bro-Smith				2
91	R. Sillery					25	D. Kent				
98	L. Wainwright					24	E. Wheeldon				2
0	Bench					0	Bench				2
	Totals	**1**	**1**	**2**	**16**		**Totals**				**18**

Netminder Summary

Deeside Ducks		GA / SA				Sutton Sting		GA / SA			
	Mins	1	2	3	Tot		Mins	1	2	3	Tot
Callum Preston						Bearman	60.00				22
Jace Gledhill	60.00				40	Laverick					

Match details and player stats transcribed into a readable format from EIH Gameday
upload data by Paul Breeze

"It was fairly sort of comfortable, I would say," said Dragons' assistant head coach Matt Compton.

"At no point we felt in any danger. We played really well, but there's still room for improvement."

"We mixed the lines up a little bit with the forwards.

"Every line produced and every line scored, which we haven't had for a while, and we were happy with the performance."

While the MVP award went to two-goal Simpson, it was Hajek who claimed the Deeside hard worker belt thanks to his goal and two assists.

This accolade is handed out after a Dragons' win and it is voted for by the previous winner.

"Captain James Parsons handed it out and said Hajek works hard every game," added Compton.

Other results: Billingham 6 Nottingham 3; Whitley 5 Blackburn 9; Blackburn 4 Hull 0; Nottingham 4 Billingham 11; Solihull 12 Widnes 5, Whitley 7 Leeds 1.

Deeside Ducks picked up their second Division Two win in a row with a close and hard-fought 1-0 victory over Coventry Blaze at Deeside Leisure Centre.

Following on from the previous week's win over Nottingham and having only lost out by a single goal to Coventry on the Blaze's previous visit, the Ducks were especially keyed up for this game, knowing that a win would significantly boost their chances of qualifying for the end of season play-offs.

The early stages of the game were littered with niggly penalties for both sides and, despite numerous chances at both ends, the first period played out goal-less.

The second period was also goal-less as the Ducks battled hard against the team six places - and 36 points - above them in the league table, and the score stood at a tantalisingly balanced 0-0 heading into the final 20 minutes.

The breakthrough finally came on 52.45 when former Dragons player Andrew Chappell fired in the only goal of the game, assisted by Dalton Thompson.

Despite late pressure from Coventry, the solid Ducks' defence held out to secure the win - backed up by a superb overall display from netminder Jace Gledhill, who registered a 40-shot shut-out and was deservedly named MVP for Deeside.

The Ducks now have a game-free weekend and are next in action on Saturday, March 1 when they take on Billingham Buccaneers at Deeside Leisure Centre (5pm face-off).

Other results: Coventry 9 Sheffield 2; Kingston 9 Bradford 3; Nottingham 0 Billingham 2; Billingham 1 Telford 6; Sheffield 2 Altrincham 6.

STAR: Deeside Ducks' MVP Jace Gledhill. Picture: MAXINE ROSCOE

Jonny wants England recall

JONNY BAIRSTOW is not ready to accept his status as England's forgotten man and remains determined to revive his international career, according to his Yorkshire coach Anthony McGrath.

Bairstow found himself edged out in all three formats last year and despite having a central contract that runs until October, it is almost eight months since he last represented his country.

An injury to Jacob Bethell ahead of the Champions Trophy might have opened the door for a player whose powerful hitting helped England to World Cup glory in 2019 but despite a dreadful run of results in India the selectors instead brought another wicketkeeper-batter, Tom Banton, in from the cold.

McGrath's first season back at Headingley would be made a lot easier with a player of Bairstow's vast experience at his disposal, but he has not given up on wearing an England shirt again.

"Having Jonny with us at Yorkshire would be transformational, he improves everything we do on and off the field, but he still has ambitions to play for England," said McGrath.

Ducks In The Newspaper!

There's a report of the Deeside Ducks' home win over Coventry in today's Flintshire & Wrexham Leader (18th February 2025 - Page 35).

You can read the report – along with lots more fascinating stuff – on the highly informative grass roots Ice Hockey Review website:

http://www.icehockeyreview.co.uk/2025/02/match-report-deeside-ducks-1-coventry.html

#keepquacking   #fowlnotfoul

*Chris Jones in action for the Deeside Ducks
(Photo by All Sports Photography).*

Chris Jones Named Defenceman Of The Month

Deeside Ducks senior player Chris Jones has been named the Laidler Division's "Defenceman of the Month" for January 2025 by the influential NIHL North Updates organisation.

NIHL North Updates operate a Facebook page where they post match updates for games being played in the NIHL North Moralee and Laidler Divisions each weekend.

The Player of the Month Awards were launched by NIHL North Updates this season based on nominations put forward by fans on the Facebook page and provide for an award for the top forward, defenceman and netminder in each division.

Regarding Chris Jones' award, NIHL North Updates commented:

"The Deeside Ducks, in their first year, have been far from good. But, when they do have all their men on the bench, one of the side's brightest lights is Chris Jones, who can credibly contribute to the team's offence with (Charlie) Spridgeon but has been defensively instrumental in bringing some games within touching distance of points, or softening the blow in others."

The Ducks were without a game at the weekend but are back in action this Saturday 1st March when they take on Billingham Buccaneers at Deeside Leisure Centre, 5pm face off.

Top honour for Deeside's Chris

WHAT a start to the year it has been for Chris Jones!

The Deeside Ducks senior player has been named the Laidler Division's defenceman of the month for January by the the NIHL North Updates organisation.

NIHL North Updates operate a Facebook page where they post match updates for games being played in the NIHL North Moralee and Laidler Divisions each weekend.

The player of the month awards were launched by NIHL North Updates this season based on nominations put forward by fans on the Facebook page and provide for an award for the top forward, defenceman and netminder in each division.

Regarding Chris Jones' award, NIHL North Updates said: "The Deeside Ducks, in their first year, have been far from good. But, when they do have all their men on the bench, one of the side's brightest lights is Chris Jones, who can credibly contribute to the team's offence with (Charlie) Spridgeon but has been defensively instrumental in bringing some games within touching distance of points, or softening the blow in others."

Deeside Ducks, who have won their last two matches, were without a game at the weekend.

They are back in action this Saturday when they take on Billingham Buccaneers at Deeside Leisure Centre (5pm face-off).

BACK PAGE DUCK!

The Deeside Ducks make the back page of the Flintshire & Wrexham Leader today for the first time (25th February 2025 – page 40) with the story about Chris Jones being named Laidler Division Defenceman of the month for January.

You can read a longer version of the story – along with lots more fascinating stuff - on the highly informative grass roots Ice Hockey Review website.

https://www.icehockeyreview. co.uk/2025/02/chris-jones-named-defenceman-of-month.html

Henry Phillips was MVP for the Ducks against Billingham
(Photo by Chris Jones)

Saturday 1st March 2025 – NIHL Laidler Division
Deeside Ducks 1 – Billingham Buccaneers 3

The Deeside Ducks put in a spirited performance against top-3 side Billingham Buccaneers but eventually lost out 1-3 at Deeside Leisure Centre on Saturday.

The game was closely fought throughout and could easily have gone either way for much of its duration.

Billingham took the lead on 13 minutes and, despite chances at both ends, the score remained 0-1 at the first period break.

Following an incident in the last minute of the period, a patch on the ice surface behind the Ducks' goal was damaged and the referee decided to take the break early to allow this to be fixed.

This meant that the remaining 25 seconds of the first period were finished off when the players came out after the break. The buzzer then sounded, the teams changed ends and then started the second period.

Deeside equalised just 2 minutes into the second period with a goal from Dalton Thompson but, unfortunately, they got into penalty trouble and Billingham retook the lead on 25 minutes, taking advantage of a 5-on-3 powerplay.

At 1-2 at the second interval, the game was still anyone's for the taking but Billingham scored another powerplay goal on 45 minutes to double their lead.

The Ducks were unable to make the most of a 5-on-3 powerplay of their own late in the game and the match finished 1-3 to the visitors.

The Ducks play their last home game of the season this Saturday when they take on Telford Tigers 2 at Deeside Leisure Centre, 5pm face off.

They then finish off their debut league campaign with away trips to Sutton Sting and Nottingham Lions.

You did your best Ducks
Against Billingham Buccs
But, if you want to win
Stay out of the Sin Bin

Lucy London, 2nd March 2025

Deeside Ducks 1-3 Billingham Buccaneers

North 2 Regular Season, Saturday 1st March
Game 120

Deeside Ducks (3-1-0-19)   (16-0-0-7) Billingham Buccaneers

SCORING SUMMARY

G	Per	Time	Score	Team	Goal Scorer	Assist	Assist	Str
1	1	13:22	0-1	BIL	Josh Nertney (7)	Tom Cummings (2)		E
2	2	21:42	1-1	DEE	Dalton Thompson (3)	Rafferty Smith (1)	Rhys Howells (4)	E
3	2	25:14	1-2	BIL	Sam Dowd (14)	Tom Wakefield (7)	Lennon Thomas (7)	PP
4	3	43:53	1-3	BIL	Stephen Wallace (14)	Sam Dowd (10)	Callum Clark (11)	PP

PENALTY SUMMARY

DEESIDE DUCKS

#	Per	Time	Player	PIM	Penalty
1	1	10:49	Dalton Thompson	2	Elbowing
2	1	19:35	Harry Shearman	2	Roughing
3	1	19:35	Harry Shearman	2	Roughing
4	2	23:32	Cody Ogden	2	Illegal Equipment
5	2	24:33	Rhys Howells	2	Tripping
6	3	41:53	Henry Phillips	2	Holding

TOT (PN-PIM) 6-12
Power Plays (Goals-Opp) 0-3

BILLINGHAM BUCCANEERS

#	Per	Time	Player	PIM	Penalty
1	1	13:46	Ethan McLaughlin	2	High Sticking
2	1	19:35	Josh Nertney	2	Cross Checking
3	1	19:35	Josh Nertney	2	Roughing
4	3	52:30	Tom Wakefield	2	Cross Checking
5	3	53:20	Simon Geldart	2	Interference
6					

TOT (PN-PIM) 5-10
Power Plays (Goals-Opp) 2-4

TEAM SUMMARY

	DEESIDE DUCKS	G	A	P	PN	PIM
1	NM	Jace Gledhill					
4	F	Charlie Spridgeon					
10	F	Stewart Cutting					
11	F	Rafferty Smith		1	1		
12	D	Henry Phillips				1	2
16	D	Andrew Chappell					
21	D	Kieran Clarkson					
29	F	Ben Roscoe					
31	D	James Morgan					
40	F	Cody Ogden				1	2
44	F	Harry Shearman				2	4
45	D	Charles Nicholson					
51	F	Dalton Thompson	1		1	1	2
52	F	Corey Swift					
72	D	Chris Jones					
81	F	Daniels Fadejevs					
85	F	Rhys Howells		1	1	1	2
88	D	Kenny Williams					
91	D	Rory Sillery					
		Team Penalty					
		TEAM TOTALS	1	2	3	6	12

	BILLINGHAM BUCCANEERS	G	A	P	PN	PIM
4	F	Josh Nertney	1		1	2	4
10	F	Tom Fraser					
11	D	Andrew Finn					
13	D	Callum Clark		1	1		
14	F	Stephen Wallace	1		1		
16	F	Michael Plant					
17	F	Kieran Wrench					
22	F	Sam Dowd	1	1	2		
25	F	Tom Cummings		1	1		
27	D	Luke Burdon					
30	NM	Ronald Pierce					
33	NM	Chris Outhwaite					
35	F	Tom Wakefield		1	1	1	2
36	F	Kyle Black					
40	D	Ethan McLaughlin				1	2
44	F	Anthony Price					
45	F	Simon Geldart				1	2
48	F	Abi McCourt					
66	F	Jamie Pattison					
71	D	Lennon Thomas		1	1		
		Team Penalty					
		TEAM TOTALS	3	5	8	5	10

GOALTENDER SUMMARY

DEESIDE DUCKS		TOI	1	2	3	OT	TOT
1	Jace Gledhill	60:00	1-15	1-11	1-9		3-35
	Empty Net						

Goals-Shots Against

BILLINGHAM BUCCANEERS		TOI	1	2	3	OT	TOT
30	Ronald Pierce	60:00	0-7	1-15	0-18		1-40
33	Chris Outhwaite						
	Empty Net						

Goals - Shots Against

Source: NIHLStats.wordpress.com (Box Scores)

STAR PLAYER: Henry Phillips was Deeside Ducks' MVP against Billingham. Picture: CHRIS JONES

Ducks impress in close clash

"But, we got the goal in the end, so happy."

Although Deeside were never ahead until overtime, assistant head coach Matt Compton says he was never concerned about the outcome.

"Again, I didn't feel we were in trouble at any time," he said.

"We still had plenty left to go and I had confidence in the lads they would come back into it."

There are just three weekends of the regular season remaining. Deeside are away to Sheffield this Saturday, before they play host to Leeds the following day.

Other results: Blackburn 9 Solihull 4; Leeds 2 Billingham 9; Nottingham 9 Whitley 2; Nottingham 4 Blackburn 6; Whitley 3 Billingham 4; Widnes 5 Leeds 4 (overtime).

DEESIDE DUCKS put in a spirited performance against top-three side Billingham Buccaneers but they eventually lost out 3-1.

The game was closely fought throughout and could easily have gone either way for much of its duration.

Billingham took the lead on 13 minutes and, despite chances at both ends, the score remained 1-0 at the first period break.

Deeside equalised just two minutes into the second period with a goal from Dalton Thompson but, unfortunately for them, they got into penalty trouble and Billingham retook the lead on 25 minutes, taking advantage of a five-on-three powerplay.

Billingham scored another powerplay goal on 45 minutes to double their lead. The Ducks were unable to make the most of a five-on-three powerplay of their own late in the game.

Deeside Ducks play their last home game of the season this Saturday when they take on Telford Tigers (5pm face-off).

Other results: Altrincham 3 Sheffield 4; Billingham 5 Sutton 4; Telford 3 Kingston 0.

Ducks In The Newspaper!

There's a short report about the Deeside Ducks' home game against Billingham in today's Flintshire & Wrexham Leader (4th March 2025 - Page 34).

You can read a longer version of the report – along with lots more fascinating stuff – on the highly informative grass roots Ice Hockey Review website:

http://www.icehockeyreview.co.uk/2025/03/match-report-deeside-ducks-1-billingham.html

Jace Gledhill (Photo by Keith & Jenny Davies)

Jace Gledhill Named Netminder Of The Month

Rather like buses, you hang around waiting for ages and then two come along in quick succession.

Following on from Chris Jones's Player of the Month Award for January, the Ducks can boast another accolade winner in Jace Gledhill, who has been named as Netminder of the Month for the Laidler Division for February 2025 by NIHL North Updates.

Regarding Gledhill's award, NIHL North Updates commented:

"This goaltender of the month award cannot go to anyone else. Having stepped down from the Dragons to fill in an incomplete Ducks tandem, Jace Gledhill has had one of the best netminding performances in the NIHL this season.

"Jace netted Deeside two momentous upset victories (half of the team's total wins this season), including a 40-save shutout — his first as a senior — against the 4th-placed Coventry Blaze who have been a force to be reckoned with in 2024/25."

Josh Jones was the MVP for the Ducks (Photo by Paul Breeze)

Saturday 8th March 2025 – NIHL Laidler Division
Deeside Ducks 2 – Telford Tigers 7

The Deeside Ducks put in a creditable performance against league champions in waiting Telford Tigers, ending up with a 2-7 defeat at Deeside Leisure Centre on Saturday.

The Ducks actually had the puck in the net first with a Dan Fadejevs strike after 4½ minutes but the goal was disallowed by the referee due to an infringement and the score remained at a finely balanced 0-0 at the first period break.

Telford eventually opened the scoring three minutes into the second period and went 0-2 up 35 seconds later. Josh Jones broke the Ducks' duck on 28 minutes but another Telford goal 90 seconds later restored the two-goal advantage, and two more unanswered goals saw the Tigers leading 1-5 at the second interval.

Former Dragons' favourite Paul Davies put Telford further ahead on 42 minutes but Stewart Cutting scored a superb goal for the Ducks on 52 minutes to keep the game interesting. A last minute Tigers goal with just 12 seconds left on the clock rounded off the scoring and gave Telford a 2-7 victory.

The final result meant that Telford clinched the Laidler Division title and the league trophy and medals were awarded by England Ice Hockey officials on the ice after the game.

This was the Ducks' final home game in their roller-coaster debut season. They have two away games left and are back in action away to Sutton Sting this Saturday.

*****

The MVP awards were presented by Ducks match volunteer Andy Brown and went to #73 Josh Jones for Deeside and #26 Paul Davies for Telford.

Andy was ably assisted by EIH Director Martin Peters and NIHL General Manager Haydn Hunter, who had come to Deeside to present the Laidler Division trophy and medals to the Tigers for winning the league title.

Saturday 8th March 2025 – NIHL Laidler Division
Deeside Ducks 2 – Telford Tigers 7

Scoring Summary

G	Per	Time	Team	Scorer	Assist 1	Assist 2	Str
1	2	23.29	TEL	Daniel Mitchell	Vladimir Luka		E
2	2	24.04	TEL	Vladimir Luka	Taylor Stanton	Daniel Retter	E
3	2	28.01	DEE	Josh Jones	Ben Roscoe		E
4	2	29.33	TEL	Ben Washburn	Callum Griffin		E
5	2	34.25	TEL	Vladimir Luka			E
6	2	39.56	TEL	Daniel Harrison			E
7	3	42.28	TEL	Paul Davies	Taylor Stanton	Robert Oxley	E
8	3	52.22	DEE	Stewart Cutting	Rafferty Smith	Dan Fadejevs	E
9	3	59.48	TEL	Josef Lauder			E

Penalty Summary

Deeside Ducks				Telford Tigers			
Time	Player	PIM	Off	Time	Player	PIM	Off
17.14	Rafferty Smith	2	TRIP	27.10	Kyle Watt	2	HOOK
36.39	James Morgan	2	HI-ST	36.39	Simon Harrison	2	X-CHE
54.32	Josh Jones	2	HOOK	46.25	Vladimir Luka	2	ROUGH
Total		**6**		**Total**		**6**	

Team Summary

Deeside Ducks		G	A	Pts	PIM	Telford Tigers		G	A	Pts	PIM
4	C. Spridgeon					5	R Oxley		1	1	
5	M Speare					8	S Harrison				2
10	S. Cutting	1		1		10	D Harrison	1		1	
11	R Smith		1	1	2	15	D Retter		1	1	
13	D Wilkes					18	J Hustwick				
16	A. Chappell					25	S Crowe				
18	G Spofforth					26	P Davies	1		1	
21	K. Clarkson					27	C Griffin		1	1	
27	O Booth					29	C Keyes				
29	B. Roscoe		1	1		31	M Byrne				
31	J. Morgan				2	36	J Lauder	1		1	
44	H. Shearman					39	C O'Reilly				
47	C Preston					40	B Washburn	1		1	
52	C Swift					50	H Griffiths				
72	C. Jones					59	C Bennett				
73	J. Jones	1		1	2	61	K Watt				2
81	D. Fadejevs		1	1		71	T Stanton		2	2	
91	R. Sillery					88	D Mitchell	1		1	
98	L. Wainwright					94	V Luka	2	1	3	2
						95	C MNaughton				
0	Bench					0	Bench				
	Totals	**2**	**3**	**5**	**6**		**Totals**	**7**	**6**	**13**	**6**

Netminder Summary

Deeside Ducks	Mins	GA / SA				Sutton Sting	Mins	GA / SA			
		1	2	3	Tot			1	2	3	Tot
Preston						Byrne	60.00	9	14		
Booth	60.00	20	24			Griffiths					

Match details taken from own notes and players details taken from paper team lists.
Transcribed by Paul Breeze

IT'S a ton-up for Jake Witkowski following another successful spell for Deeside Dragons.

They defeated Sheffield Scimitars 10-4 margin and followed it up with a 9-3 outcome against Leeds Knights, making it six victories on the bounce.

In the second game, Witkowski's stellar season continued as he managed to surpass 100 points for the campaign.

He found the target twice on the evening and a pleasing aspect for the Dragons must be the fact the goals were shared around. Garry Simpson, Marc Lovell, Ross Kennedy, Alex Parry, skipper James Parsons, MJ Clancy and Cody Ogden also struck.

"There are so many positives to take from the weekend," said assistant head coach Matt Compton. "That win (over Leeds) was really good.

"When we went through the patch of losing games, we only produced from one line. Now it's spread through the lines."

Deeside Dragons put on an offensive clinic in Sheffield, overpowering the Scimitars 10-4.

Brodie Jesson hit a hat-trick for the visitors and he was joined on the scoresheet by Jakub Hajek, Kennedy, Ogden, Witkowski, MVP Parsons and Charles Phillips.

Other results: Hull 4 Blackburn 5; Widnes 8 Nottingham 4; Sheffield 1 Blackburn 7; Solihull 4 Billingham 8; Whitley 9 Nottingham 4.

Deeside Ducks put in a creditable performance against league champions-in-waiting Telford Tigers, ending up losing 7-2.

STAR: Josh Jones was Deeside Ducks' MVP. Picture: PAUL BREEZE

The Ducks actually had the puck in the net first with Dan Fadejevs' disallowed strike.

Telford eventually opened the scoring three minutes into the second period and went 2-0 up 35 seconds later.

Josh Jones broke Ducks' duck on 28 minutes, but Telford led 5-1 at the second interval.

Former Dragons' favourite Paul Davies put Telford further ahead but Stewart Cutting scored a superb goal for the Ducks on 52 minutes. Tigers added another with 12 seconds left.

Other results: Billingham 4 Sheffield 1; Kingston 5 Coventry 4; Bradford 1 Billingham 8; Coventry 2 Nottingham 3 (overtime).

Ducks In The Newspaper!

There's a – somewhat edited - report about the Deeside Ducks' home game against Telford in today's Flintshire & Wrexham Leader (11th March 2025 - Page 35).

You can read the full version of the report on the highly informative grass roots Ice Hockey Review website:

http://www.icehockeyreview.co.uk/2025/03/match-report-deeside-ducks-2-telford.html

#keepquacking #fowlnotfoul

Telford Tigers 2 celebrate winning the Laidler Division title, with the Ducks players in attendance (Photo by Billie Jane Photography)

How The League Was Won

This isn't about the Deeside Ducks *per se* – but it did happen at a Ducks' game, and the Ducks did play their part in the whole affair, so it is certainly worth mentioning here.

Plus, it's not every day that you get to witness the presentation of the league championship trophy – even if it did go to the opposing team..!

Saturday 8th March was the Ducks' last home game of their eventful debut season and they were at home to "champions elect" Telford Tigers, who needed to win the game in order to be assured of finishing clear of fellow challengers Sutton Sting and securing the league title.

While the Ducks still had two more away games to play, this was the Tigers' last game of the regular season so it had been arranged that they would be presented with the league trophy and players' medals on the ice afterwards, and some league officials from England Ice Hockey had come along especially for this purpose.

A bit presumptuous, possibly, but the Ducks had lost all three meetings with the Tigers thus far in the season so, from a "league form" point of view, it did seem highly likely that Telford would win the game and that the festivities could follow.

Now, Deeside obviously hadn't read the script here as they – rather stubbornly – played out of their skins and, at the end of the first period, the score remained at a rather worrying (for the Tigers, at least – and the EIH visitors...) 0-0.

Telford eventually got into their stride and, driven on by their Czech superstar Vladimir Luka, managed to build up a 1-5 lead by the second interval.

Collective breath ceased to be held at this point and the somewhat relieved EIH guys came out to set up the goodies on a table that we had brought round earlier.

I went through the running order with them for the presentations and, with the game finishing as a creditable (from a Ducks point of view) 2-7, the Tigers title party was able to get under way.

EIH Director Martin Peters and NIHL General Manager Haydn Hunter presented the awards - firstly medals to all the players and team staff and then the Laidler Division league trophy to Tigers captain Oliver Hunt.

Dalton Thompson was the Ducks' MVP away at Sutton
(Photo by Sutton Sting IHC)

Saturday 15th March 2025 – NIHL Laidler Division
Sutton Sting 20 - Deeside Ducks 0

The Deeside Ducks slumped to a 20-0 defeat away at league runners up Sutton Sting in Sheffield on Saturday.

Sutton were on top pretty much from the start and ran up an 8-0 lead by the end of the first period. At the second interval, the score was 12-0 and the final score of 20-0 equals the Ducks' heaviest margin of defeat in their debut season when they lost 24-4 away at league champions Telford back in October.

Despite the obviously one-sided scoreline, not helped by travelling with a short bench, the Ducks' heads did not drop and they continued to battle throughout the whole 60 minutes.

The result means that the Ducks can no longer qualify for the end of season play offs and are resigned to finishing in bottom spot in the Laidler Division table.

They still have the chance to finish their rollercoaster first season of league competition on a high note, however, as they face Nottingham Lions – who they have already beaten once this season – in their final game of the campaign away in the Lace City this Sunday 23rd March, face off 7.20pm.

That will be at home to Hull Jets on Sunday.

It's a crucial contest to decide who will finish in the top-four heading into the play-offs. Dragons currently occupy fourth position, but they're only a point ahead of the Jets, who have two games left to play.

It looks likely that Deeside and Hull will then meet in the opening stage of the play-offs. **Other results:** Leeds 0 Hull 4; Whitley 3 Widnes 1; Blackburn 7 Whitley 1; Hull 7 Widnes 5; Sheffield 3 Solihull 8.

Deeside Ducks slumped to a 20-0 defeat away at league runners-up Sutton Sting in Sheffield.

Sutton were on top pretty much from the start and they ran up an 8-0 lead by the end of the first period.

At the second interval, the score was 12-0 and the final score of 20-0 equals Ducks' heaviest margin of defeat in their debut season, when they lost 24-4 away at league champions Telford back in October.

Despite the obviously one-sided scoreline, not helped by travelling with a short bench, Ducks' heads did not drop and they continued to battle throughout the whole 60 minutes.

The result means that the Ducks can no longer qualify for the end of season play-offs and are resigned to finishing in bottom spot in the Laidler Division table.

They still have the chance to finish their rollercoaster first season of league competition on a high note, however, as they face Nottingham Lions – who they have already beaten once this season – in their final game of the campaign away in the Lace City this Sunday (face-off 7.20pm). **Other results:** Sheffield 4 Nottingham 5; Altrincham 5 Coventry 8; Bradford 5 Sutton 3.

Ducks In The Newspaper!

There's a short report about the Deeside Ducks' away game at Sutton in today's Flintshire & Wrexham Leader (18th March 2025 - Page 34).

You can read the same report – along with lots of other interesting stuff - on the highly informative grass roots Ice Hockey Review website.

Sutton Sting 20-0 Deeside Ducks

North 2 Regular Season, Saturday 15th March
Game 131

Sutton Sting (23-0-0-2)   (3-1-0-21) Deeside Ducks

SCORING SUMMARY

G	Per	Time	Score	Team	Goal Scorer	Assist	Assist	Str
1	1	3:23	1-0	SUT	Will Stennett (3)	Cameron Glasby (19)	Calum Russell (8)	E
2	1	6:06	2-0	SUT	Charlie Saunders (10)	Joe Colton (23)	Cameron Akers (3)	E
3	1	11:05	3-0	SUT	Joe Colton (16)	Charlie Saunders (21)	Cameron Akers (4)	E
4	1	12:43	4-0	SUT	Oliver Watson (2)	Bailey Templar (4)	Cameron Kushnirenko (5)	E
5	1	12:54	5-0	SUT	Ben Crowther (2)	Morgan Glasby (27)		E
6	1	14:17	6-0	SUT	Morgan Glasby (28)	Elliott Meadows (4)		E
7	1	15:45	7-0	SUT	Morgan Glasby (29)	Elliott Meadows (5)		E
8	1	16:58	8-0	SUT	Calum Russell (11)	Adam Brooke-Smith (12)		E
9	2	26:28	9-0	SUT	Joe Colton (17)	Lawson Glasby (26)	Morgan Glasby (28)	PP
10	2	34:21	10-0	SUT	Calum Russell (12)	Josh Humphreys (5)		E
11	2	34:54	11-0	SUT	Bailey Templar (4)	Alex Williams (2)		E
12	2	38:26	12-0	SUT	Cameron Akers (5)	Jacob Truswell (16)		E
13	3	42:13	13-0	SUT	Morgan Glasby (30)	Elliott Meadows (6)	Jamie Scott (5)	E
14	3	47:18	14-0	SUT	Elliott Meadows (9)	Morgan Glasby (29)	Cameron Akers (5)	E
15	3	47:39	15-0	SUT	Elliott Meadows (10)	Morgan Glasby (30)	Lawson Glasby (27)	E
16	3	50:33	16-0	SUT	Adam Brooke-Smith (17)	Jasper Wright (3)	Josh Humphreys (6)	E
17	3	51:57	17-0	SUT	Morgan Glasby (31)	Cameron Kushnirenko (6)	Jacob Truswell (17)	E
18	3	53:15	18-0	SUT	Elliott Meadows (11)	Jamie Scott (6)	Lawson Glasby (28)	E
19	3	55:11	19-0	SUT	Calum Russell (13)	Joe Colton (24)	Matt Jeffcock (1)	E
20	3	59:14	20-0	SUT	Lawson Glasby (10)	Elliott Meadows (7)		E

PENALTY SUMMARY

			SUTTON STING						DEESIDE DUCKS		
#	Per	Time	Player	PIM	Penalty	#	Per	Time	Player	PIM	Penalty
1						1	2	26:15	Rafferty Smith	2	Boarding

TOT (PN-PIM) 0-0	TOT (PN-PIM) 1-2
Power Plays (Goals-Opp) 1-1	Power Plays (Goals-Opp) 0-0

TEAM SUMMARY

	SUTTON STING		G	A	P	PN	PIM			DEESIDE DUCKS		G	A	P	PN	PIM
2	F	Bailey Templar	1	1	2				1	NM	Oliver Booth					
7	F	Adam Brooke-Smith	1	1	2				4	F	Corey Swift					
9	F	Cameron Akers	1	3	4				5	F	Michael Speare					
10	D	Will Stennett	1		1				10	F	Andrew Chappell					
11	F	Oliver Watson	1		1				11	F	Rafferty Smith				1	2
16	F	Charlie Saunders	1	1	2				18	D	George Spofforth					
17	F	Morgan Glasby	4	4	8				19	F	Mackenzie Wilkes					
19	F	Matt Jeffcock		1	1				25	F	Liam Yarwood					
20	D	Josh Humphreys		2	2				44	F	Harry Shearman					
25	F	Callum Russell	3	1	4				47	NM	Callum Preston					
33	F	Alex Williams		1	1				51	F	Dalton Thompson					
46	D	Cameron Kushnirenko		2	2				72	F	Josh Jones					
48	F	Cameron Glasby	1	1					91	D	Rory Sillery					
65	D	Jamie Scott		2	2				98	D	Luke Wainwright					
72	F	Joe Colton	2	2	4											
78	D	Jasper Wright		1	1											
80	F	Lawson Glasby	1	3	4											
82	NM	Jack Hargreaves														
83	D	Ben Crowther	1		1											
86	F	Elliot Meadows	3	4	7											
94	F	Jacob Truswell		2	2											
		Team Penalty									Team Penalty					
		TEAM TOTALS	20	32	52						TEAM TOTALS				1	2

GOALTENDER SUMMARY

SUTTON STING		TOI	Goals-Shots Against							DEESIDE DUCKS		TOI	Goals - Shots Against				
			1	2	3	OT	TOT					1	2	3	OT	TOT
82	Jack Hargreaves	60:00	0-3	0-6	0-5		0-14		1	Oliver Booth	31:38	8-37	1-18			9-55
									47	Callum Preston	28:22		3-18	8-33		11-51
	Empty Net									Empty Net						

Source: NIHLStats.wordpress.com (Box Scores)

*Kieran Clarkson scored the Ducks' goal away at Nottingham
(Photo by All Sports Photography)*

Sunday 23rd March 2025 – NIHL Laidler Division
Nottingham Lions 9 - Deeside Ducks 1

The Deeside Ducks rounded off their debut Laidler Division season with a 9-1 defeat away to Nottingham Lions on Sunday.

Having already beaten the Lions at home in Deeside a few weeks earlier, there were hopes that the Ducks might finish the season on a high note, but it was not to be.

Nottingham were on top pretty much from the start and led 3-0 at the first period break. It was 5-0 after two periods and 8-0 before Kieran Clarkson fired in a consolation strike for Deeside on 47 minutes.

A late goal for Nottingham finished off the scoring for the game and the Ducks' first season of league competition was brought to a close.

They finish in 10th place in the Laidler Division table with 3 regulation wins and an overtime win from their 26 games.

Jesson grabs key goal in Dragons' overtime win

DEESIDE DRAGONS enter the end-of-season play-offs with a win under their belts.

Dragons claimed a thrilling 9-6 overtime triumph over Hull Jets in their final regular season match of the campaign, which made sure of a fourth-placed finish in the Division One North table.

With Hull concluding the campaign in fifth place, the two sides will clash again in a two-legged play-off encounter this weekend.

"Actually, once we got to overtime, that secured fourth place for us," said assistant head coach Matt Compton.

It was Hull who claimed an early lead, but this was soon cancelled out by James Parsons' response.

Henry Phillips and Alex Parry added further goals, but Jets were 4-3 ahead at the end of an all-action first period.

After Hull stretched their lead further, Jake Witkowski's 50th goal of the season dragged Deeside back into it.

Jets were 5-4 ahead with one period remaining, but Parsons soon levelled things up once more.

Brodie Jesson and a Witkowski brace moved Dragons clear, but Hull struck three times in the closing stages to tie things up.

It was Jesson who grabbed the overtime winner for Deeside.

Other results: Billingham 8 Whitley 2; Hull 7 Solihull 2; Sheffield 6 Leeds 2; Widnes 7 Nottingham 5; Leeds 4 Nottingham 3 (overtime); Solihull 10 Sheffield 0; Whitley 2 Blackburn 5.

Deeside Ducks rounded off their debut Laidler Division season with a 9-1 defeat away to Nottingham Lions.

Having already beaten the Lions at home in Deeside a few weeks earlier, there were hopes that the Ducks might finish the season on a high note, but it was not to be.

Nottingham were on top pretty much from the start and led 3-0 at the first period break. It was 5-0 after two periods and 8-0 before Kieran Clarkson fired in a consolation strike for Deeside on 47 minutes.

A late goal for Nottingham finished off the scoring for the game and the Ducks' first season of league competition was brought to a close.

They finish in 10th place in the table with three regulation victories and an overtime win from their 26 games.

Other results: Billingham 3 Bradford 1; Sheffield 8 Kingston 2.

ON TARGET: Deeside Ducks' Kieran Clarkson scored against Nottingham. Picture: All Sports Photography

Ducks In The Newspaper!

There's a short report about the Deeside Ducks' away game at Nottingham in today's Flintshire & Wrexham Leader (25th March 2025 - Page 36).

You can read the same report – along with lots of other interesting stuff - on the highly informative grass roots Ice Hockey Review website.

https://www.icehockeyreview.co.uk/2025/03/match-report-nottingham-lions-9-deeside.html

#keepquacking #fowlnotfoul

Sunday 23rd March 2025 – NIHL Laidler Division
Nottingham Lions 9 - Deeside Ducks 1

Scoring Summary

G	Per	Time	Team	Scorer	Assist 1	Assist 2	Str
1	1		NOT				
2	1		NOT				
3	1		NOT				
4	2		NOT				
5	2		NOT				
6	3		NOT				
7	3		NOT				
8	3		NOT				
9	3	47.00	DEE	Kieran Clarkson			
10	3		NOT				

Penalty Summary

Nottingham Lions				Deeside Ducks			
Time	Player	PIM	Off	Time	Player	PIM	Off
Total				Total			

Team Summary

Nottingham Lions	G	A	Pts	PIM	Deeside Ducks		G	A	Pts	PIM
					4	C. Spridgeon				
					85	R Howells				
					11	R Smith				
					13	D Wilkes				
					10	A. Chappell				
					19	G Spofforth				
					21	K. Clarkson	1			
					25	L Yarwood				
					31	J. Morgan				
					44	H. Shearman				
					47	C Preston				
					14	C Swift				
					91	R. Sillery				
					45	C. Nicholson				
					51	D Thompson				
Totals	9				Totals		1			

Netminder Summary

Nottingham Lions	Mins	GA / SA				Deeside Ducks	Mins	GA / SA			
		1	2	3	Tot			1	2	3	Tot
					1/?	Preston	60.00	3/?	2/?	4/?	

Full match details not available. Transcribed as far possible from minimal Gameday data by Paul Breeze

NIHL Laidler Division – Season 2024/25

Final Table	GP	W	OTW	OTL	L	GF	GA	Pts
Telford Tigers	26	25	0	0	1	212	54	75
Sutton Sting	26	23	0	0	3	171	48	69
Billingham Buccanrs	26	19	0	0	7	109	66	57
Coventry Blaze	26	15	1	1	9	120	63	48
Altrincham Aces	26	12	1	0	13	119	116	38
Kingston Sharks	26	8	1	3	14	101	130	29
Nottingham Lions	26	6	2	0	18	94	142	22
Sheffield Titans	25	6	0	1	18	62	134	19
Bradford Bulldogs	25	6	0	1	18	83	159	19
Deeside Ducks	26	3	1	0	22	55	214	11

Top Points Scorers

Player	Team	GP	G	A	Pts	PIM
Morgan Glasby	Sutton Sting	25	32	32	64	2
Taylor Stanton	Telford Tigers 2	25	30	33	63	8
Oliver Hunt	Telford Tigers 2	25	24	32	56	14
Thomas Humphries	Kingston Sharks	26	27	24	51	22
Ryan Apsley	Sutton Sting	21	21	20	41	6
Joseph Colton	Sutton Sting	18	17	24	41	0
Connor Mellett	Coventry Blaze	25	16	25	41	79
Filip Supa	Telford Tigers 2	14	22	17	39	10
Karol Jets	Telford Tigers 2	16	16	22	38	2
Lawson Glasby	Sutton Sting	24	10	28	38	12

Top Netminders (minimum 10 games)

Netminder	Team	GPI	Mins	SA	GA	GAA	SV%	SO
Lewis King	SUT	19	978	380	27	1.66	92.9	3
Matthew Byrne	TEL	19	1018	476	34	2.01	92.9	2
Chris Outhwaite	BIL	21	1188	706	54	2.73	92.4	2
Hayden Laverick	COV	25	1415	698	55	2.34	92.1	2
Hal Griffiths	TEL	11	497	186	16	1.94	91.4	1
Dominic Smith	KIN	15	741	502	48	3.89	90.4	0
Jack Hargreaves	SUT	10	340	146	15	2.25	89.7	1
Nathaniel Bell	SHE	16	904	659	68	4.51	89.7	1
Bayley Hodkinson	ALT	17	819	472	56	4.11	88.1	2
Michael Rogers	ALT	12	578	392	49	5.09	87.5	0

Laidler Cup 2024/24

Group A	GP	W	OTW	OTL	L	GF	GA	Pts
Sutton Sting	8	8	0	0	0	51	10	24
Billingham Buccaneers	8	6	0	0	2	37	21	18
Kingston Sharks	8	2	1	0	5	31	38	8
Nottingham Lions	8	2	0	0	6	30	43	6
Sheffield Titans	8	1	0	1	6	12	49	4

Group B	GP	W	OTW	OTL	L	GF	GA	Pts
Telford Tigers	8	8	0	0	0	74	19	24
Altrincham Aces	8	5	0	0	3	43	28	15
Coventry NIHL Blaze	8	5	0	0	3	33	19	15
Bradford Bulldogs	8	1	0	1	6	22	46	4
Deeside Ducks	8	0	1	0	7	22	82	2

Note: no qualifying games were played for the Laidler Cup. The results from the first two league meetings between each of the teams were used instead to make up the final group table.

As no separate cup matches were played in the group stage, no individual player stats are awarded for those games. Player stats are, however, awarded for the semi final and final matches.

Laidler Cup Semi Finals

Semi Final 1	Semi Final 2
18th Jan : Telford 10 –Billingham 3	18th Jan: Altrincham 6 – Sutton 10
19th Jan: Billingham 7 – Telford 4	9th Feb: Sutton 4 – Altrincham 0
Telford win 14-10	*Sutton win 14-6*

Laidler Cup Final

Final - First Leg	Final - Second Leg
22nd Feb: Telford 5 – Sutton 4	23rd Feb: Sutton 2 – Telford 4

Telford win 9-6 on aggregate

Deeside Ducks Fixtures & Results – 2024/25

Date	Home		Away		WDL	Ducks Scorers
31/08/2024	Ducks *	6	Not Ducks	8	L	J Jones, Spridgeon (2), Davies (2), C Jones
15/09/2024	Deeside	4	Kingston	5	L	Milnes, C Jones, Ogden 2
21/09/2024	Coventry	13	Deeside	1	L	Speare
28/09/2024	Kingston	5	Deeside	0	Ab^	
29/09/2024	Deeside	4	Sheffield	3	W	K Clarkson 2, Ogden, C Jones
05/10/2024	Deeside	3	Bradford	4	L	Speare, J Jones, Spridgeon
20/10/2024	Sheffield	6	Deeside	0	L	-
26/10/2024	Telford	24	Deeside	4	L	Ogden 3, Davies
03/11/2024	Bradford	5	Deeside	6	WPS	Cutting, Fadejevs, K Clarkson, Milnes, Speare 2 (1PS)
17/11/2024	Deeside	1	Telford	11	L	Wainwright
23/11/2024	Coventry	17	Deeside	2	L	Spridgeon, Wainwright
30/11/2024	Deeside	2	Coventry	3	L	C Jones, Cutting
08/12/2024	Altrincham	16	Deeside	4	L	J Jones, K Clarkson, Fadejevs, Dixon
14/12/2024	Deeside	5	Bradford	6	L	R Smith, C Jones, Dixon, Cutting, Sillery
15/12/2024	Billingham	12	Deeside	0	L	-
21/12/2024	Deeside	1	Altrincham	6	L	Howells
05/01/2025	Deeside	2	Altrincham	4	L	Ogden Fadejevs
12/01/2025	Bradford	9	Deeside	1	L	C Jones
26/01/2025	Telford	11	Deeside	2	L	Cutting, Thompson
01/02/2025	Deeside	1	Sutton	9	L	Nicholson
02/02/2025	Altrincham	5	Deeside	3	L	Howells, C Jones, Chappell
08/02/2025	Deeside	4	Nottingham	2	W	Spridgeon (2), Thompson, J Morgan
16/02/2025	Deeside	1	Coventry	0	W	Chappell
01/03/2025	Deeside	1	Billingham	3	L	Thompson
08/03/2025	Deeside	2	Telford	7	L	J Jones, Cutting
15/03/2025	Sutton	20	Deeside	0	L	-
23/03/2025	Nottingham	9	Deeside	1	L	K Clarkson

Notes: *Not an official game – included here for information purposes only. No player stats included in the records.*

^ Game was abandoned after 1 period following problems with the ice surface. Result awarded as a 5-0 win to Kingston (the score at the time of the abandonment). No official explanation about this decision has been received from the EIH(A)

Deeside Ducks Player Statistics
Laidler Division - Season 2024/25

Player	GP	G	A	Pts	PIM
Charlie Spridgeon	23	4	13	17	21
Chris Jones	15	6	8	14	29
Cody Ogden*	16	7	4	11	43
Kieran Clarkson	20	5	4	9	2
Stewart Cutting	19	5	4	9	0
Daniels Fadejevs	13	3	4	7	12
Ben Roscoe	22	0	6	6	29
Josh Jones	20	3	3	6	10
Gary Dixon	13	2	4	6	18
Rhys Howells	8	2	4	6	46
Michael Speare*	17	4	2	6	2
Dalton Thompson	7	3	3	6	6
Thomas Milnes	8	2	3	5	39
Rafferty Smith	9	1	2	3	6
Andrew Chappell	7	2	1	3	4
Rory Sillery	23	1	1	2	8
James Morgan	18	1	1	2	23
Luke Wainwright	14	2	0	2	6
Louis Ellwood*	12	0	0	0	2
Louis Morgan	6	0	2	2	33
Liam Yarwood	15	0	1	1	2
Henry Phillips	12	0	1	1	2
Charles Nicholson	9	1	0	1	0
Alfie Kelly	9	0	1	1	45
Jack Davies	7	1	0	1	2
Jace Gledhill	7	0	1	1	0
Callum Preston	24	0	0	0	2
Deacon Wilkes	19	0	0	0	0
Mackenzie Wilkes	19	0	0	0	24
George Spofforth	16	0	0	0	0
Harry Shearman	12	0	0	0	12
Paul Jones	11	0	0	0	0
Corey Swift	9	0	0	0	0
Kenny Williams	8	0	0	0	4

Oliver Booth	4	0	0	0	0
Heather Clarkson	3	0	0	0	0
Callum Garwell	1	0	0	0	0

Based on information provided by NIHLstats.wordpress.com

Note*: NIHL Stats have incorrectly recorded 2 goals for Louis Ellwood which were actually scored by Cody Ogden. Michael Speare also has an extra goal for the Penalty Shot win away at Bradford. The above table shows the corrected figures for all three players and may. therefore, differ from official tables published elsewhere. Player appearances include the abandoned away game at Kingston.

Netminder Statistics – Season 2024/25

Netminder	GPI	Mins	SA	GA	GAA	SV%	SO
Callum Preston	15	684:10	602	115	10.09	81.00%	0
Jace Gledhill	7	364:56	270	27	4.56	90.00%	1
Paul Jones	6	263:51	271	43	9.78	84.00%	0
Oliver Booth	4	211:38	212	30	8.51	86.00%	0

Player Stats Leaders – Season 2024/25

Most Games 2024/25	GP
Callum Preston	24
Charlie Spridgeon	23
Rory Sillery	23
Ben Roscoe	22
Kieran Clarkson	20
Josh Jones	20

Most Goals 2024/25	GP	G
Cody Ogden	16	7
Chris Jones	15	6
Kieran Clarkson	20	5
Stewart Cutting	19	5
Charlie Spridgeon	23	4
Michael Speare	17	4
Josh Jones	20	3
Daniels Fadejevs	13	3
Dalton Thompson	7	3

Most Assists 2024/25	GP	A
Charlie Spridgeon	23	13
Chris Jones	15	8
Ben Roscoe	22	6
Kieran Clarkson	20	4
Stewart Cutting	19	4
Cody Ogden	16	4
Daniels Fadejevs	13	4
Gary Dixon	13	4
Rhys Howells	8	4

Most PIMs 2024/25	GP	PIM
Rhys Howells	8	46
Alfie Kelly	9	45
Cody Ogden	16	43
Thomas Milnes	8	39
Louis Morgan	6	33
Ben Roscoe	22	29
Chris Jones	15	29

Deeside Ducks - Highs & Lows (2024/25)

Biggest Win - Home

+/-	Date	Comp	Home			Away
2	08/02/2025	Laidler	Deeside Ducks	4	2	Nottingham Lions
1	29/09/2024	Laidler	Deeside Ducks	4	3	Sheffield Titans
1	16/02/2025	Laidler	Deeside Ducks	1	0	Coventry Blaze

Biggest Win - Away

+/-	Date	Comp	Home			Away
1	03/11/2024	Laidler	Bradford Bulldogs	5	6	Deeside Ducks

Heaviest Defeat - Away

+/-	Date	Comp	Home			Away
-20	26/10/2024	Laidler	Telford Tigers	24	4	Deeside Ducks
-20	15/03/2025	Laidler	Sutton Sting	20	0	Deeside Ducks
-15	23/11/2024	Laidler	Coventry Blaze	17	2	Deeside Ducks
-12	21/09/2024	Laidler	Coventry Blaze	13	1	Deeside Ducks
-12	08/12/2024	Laidler	Altrincham Aces	16	4	Deeside Ducks
-12	15/12/2024	Laidler	Billingham Buccs	12	0	Deeside Ducks

Heaviest Defeat - Home

+/-	Date	Comp	Home			Away
-10	17/11/2024	Laidler	Deeside Ducks	1	11	Telford Tigers
-8	01/02/2025	Laidler	Deeside Ducks	1	9	Sutton Sting

Highest Scoring Game - Home

+/-	Date	Comp	Home			Away
12	17/11/2024	Laidler	Deeside Ducks	1	11	Telford Tigers
11	14/12/2024	Laidler	Deeside Ducks	5	6	Bradford Bulldogs
10	01/02/2025	Laidler	Deeside Ducks	1	9	Sutton Sting

Highest Scoring Game - Away

+/-	Date	Comp	Home			Away
28	26/10/2024	Laidler	Telford Tigers	24	4	Deeside Ducks
20	15/03/2025	Laidler	Sutton Sting	20	0	Deeside Ducks
20	08/12/2024	Laidler	Altrincham Aces	16	4	Deeside Ducks
19	23/11/2024	Laidler	Coventry Blaze	17	2	Deeside Ducks
14	21/09/2024	Laidler	Coventry Blaze	13	1	Deeside Ducks
12	15/12/2024	Laidler	Billingham Buccs	12	0	Deeside Ducks

Lowest Scoring Game – Home

+/-	Date	Comp	Home			Away
1	16/02/2025	Laidler	Deeside Ducks	1	0	Coventry Blaze
4	01/03/2025	Laidler	Deeside Ducks	1	3	Billingham Buccs
5	30/11/2024	Laidler	Deeside Ducks	2	3	Coventry Blaze

Lowest Scoring Game – Away

+/-	Date	Comp	Home			Away
5	28/09/2024	Laidler	Kingston Sharks	5	0	Deeside Ducks
6	20/10/2024	Laidler	Sheffield Titans	6	0	Deeside Ducks
8	02/02/2025	Laidler	Altrincham Aces	5	3	Deeside Ducks

Charlie Spridgeon was the Ducks' top points scorer with 4+13=17
(Photo by Keith & Jenny Davies)

Deeside Ducks' Satisfying Season

Despite finishing in 10th place in the final league table, the Deeside Ducks team can look back with an air of satisfaction over their debut season in the NIHL Laidler Division.

The Ducks team was formed last summer with the specific aim of providing a stepping stone between the Deeside junior programme and the senior Dragons team - and they have achieved just that by giving over 20 promising young local players the chance to play regular competitive league hockey.

In addition, Cody Ogden, Henry Phillips, Daniels Fadejevs, Dalton Thompson, Oli Booth and Jace Gledhill have all made appearances for the Dragons senior team this season as well as playing for the Ducks, showing that the Deeside development pathway from juniors to seniors is working well.

The Ducks team won four of their 26 league games – four more than Head Coach Gary Shaw admitted that he had expected for their first season of league competition – and lost 4 more matches by a single goal margin, any of which – on another day with the rub of the green - could easily have been a win instead.

Cody Ogden finished as the Ducks' top goal scorer for the season with 7 goals in 16 games. Dragons veteran Chris Jones was second with 6 strikes, while Stewart Cutting and Kieran Clarkson each contributed 5.

Charlie Spridgeon was the leading playmaker with 13 assists in 22 games and was also the Ducks' overall top points scorer with 4+13=17. Chris Jones finished second overall in the Ducks' point standings with 6+8=14.

Jace Gledhill had the best netminding figures from the four goalies used over the course of the season, finishing up with a 90.00% Save Percentage and a shut out from the 1-0 home win over Coventry Blaze.

Coach's Comments

By Gary Shaw

Deeside Ducks Head Coach Gary Shaw has given his verdict on the team's debut season in the Laidler Division.

Looking back on their first season of league competition, he said:

"The Ducks season - if you look at the league table - seems not to have been a good one. But you have to remember that this team was put together from a range of different abilities - with players playing at rec and Under 19 level and a few older players to help out.

"The goal was to enhance the development of the younger players into senior. We had 16, 17, 18 year olds who had never played at this level and the key was to have the selection of older experienced players help nurture this raw talent and keep them safe on the ice.

"The Ducks had some poor losses but also had some very close games and as the season progressed we were becoming more confident and had started to compete with the other teams that are well established and had players that were very comfortable playing at this level of hockey.

"When we started the season, my only goal was to get them playing together as a unit and be competitive as a team, which we achieved and had as a bonus that the players actually won games.

"The strategy was to develop players and get through the season - which we achieved. We now have 4 or 5 players training with the Dragons each week, as well as the three already signed for them."

"So, as the first season for the team closes, we now have a group of players that we can progress onto the Dragons in a few years time."

"From my point of view the season was a success. Looking at the results, maybe not - and I hate to lose - but the amount of players that have improved this year is a big plus. They have earned the wins they achieved, and they have competed all year."

"I am very happy with how the team has done this season, and looking forward to carry on the progression of these young players and the future Dragons players."

Shaw also revealed that plans are already well under way for next season:

"We now already have more players interested in playing for the Ducks and some stronger developed experienced players are interested who will enhance the squad and help develop the young talent further."

"The squad next year should be stronger in terms of quality and depth and will compete from the very start of the season."

Let's go Ducks!

Deeside Ducks – Season Review, 2024/25

Written for inclusion in the NIHL Stats Yearbook

The Deeside Ducks were formed in the summer of 2024 to play in the NIHL Laidler Division (North 2).

The Ducks team is part of the Deeside Junior Club and it has been put in place to provide a stepping stone between the junior development programme and the senior Dragons team, who play in the higher Moralee Division.

Open player trials were held during June and, as well as many Deeside-based hopefuls, attracted players from around the northwest, including Widnes and Altrincham.

A coaching team was put in place under the leadership of long-time Deeside player and coach Gary Shaw as Head Coach with Peter Bleackley as Lead Coach, Simon Hughes as Assistant Coach and Stewart Cutting as Player / Assistant Coach.

Under England Ice Hockey's rules about young players "playing up" to gain experience at a higher level, all Deeside juniors over the of 16 are technically eligible to play for the Ducks team, but an initial core of promising youngsters was initially named as regular members of the squad for the season.

These were joined by a number of former junior players who had "aged out" during the Covid closedowns - thus interrupting their development - and who had since mostly been playing recreational hockey.

In order to add some senior league experience to this fledgling side of youngsters, a number of older established Dragons players were signed – notably Chris

Jones, Kenny Williams and Gary Dixon – and a few other recent or former Dragons were also added to the mix.

An informal practice match was arranged at short notice for 31st August where the new Ducks team could have a decent run out before the start of the league season.

The much anticipated league opener on 14th September at Deeside Leisure Centre saw a narrow 4-5 defeat at the hands of the Kingston Sharks -with the official first ever goal coming from Thomas Milnes at 12.32 - and the Ducks then suffered a heavy 13-1 loss away to Coventry.

An eventful weekend saw the away game at Hull abandoned after one period due to safety concerns about the ice surface - and the Ducks picked up their first ever win with a 4-3 home victory over Sheffield the next day.

They only won one more game during the calendar year of 2024 with a 5-6 victory on Penalty Shots away to Bradford - and the rest of the results were a mixture of drubbings against the top sides and some close run things against the rest.

The second half of the season saw an overall improvement in performances – and back to back victories over Nottingham Lions (4-2) and Coventry Blaze (1-0) in consecutive home games during February.

True, the Ducks did finish in 10th place in the Laidler Division table but it is still comparatively early days in their development as a fully fledged league team and they can look back upon their first year as a club with some satisfaction, having already achieved much of what they set out to achieve at the start of the season.

They have given over 20 promising young local players the chance to play regular competitive league hockey at a senior level that they might never have achieved otherwise – or only after weeks of bench warming in the hope of the odd shift with a higher league team.

And Cody Ogden, Henry Phillips, Daniels Fadejevs, Dalton Thompson, Oli Booth and Jace Gledhill have all made appearances for the Dragons senior team this season, as well as playing for the Ducks, showing that the Deeside development pathway from juniors to seniors is working well.

The team won four of their 26 league games – four more than Head Coach Gary Shaw admitted that he had expected for their debut league season – and, added to that is the fact that they lost 4 more matches by a single goal margin, any of which – on another day with the rub of the green, or better player discipline, in some cases - could easily have been a win instead.

Cody Ogden finished as the Ducks' top goal scorer for the season with 7 goals in 16 games. Dragons veteran Chris Jones was second with 6 strikes, while Stewart Cutting and Kieran Clarkson each contributed 5.

Charlie Spridgeon was the leading playmaker with 13 assists in 22 games and was also the Ducks' overall top points scorer with 4+13=17. Chris Jones finished second overall in the Ducks' point standings with 6+8=14.

Jace Gledhill had the best netminding figures from the four goalies used over the course of the season, finishing up with a 90.00% Save Percentage and a shut out from the 1-0 home win over Coventry Blaze.

Despite their lowly overall league position, Ducks' players' efforts were recognised in the various league awards that were announced over the course of the season.

Chris Jones was named as Laidler Division Defenceman of the Month for January 2025 in the Player Of the Month Awards organised by NIHL North Updates, while Jace Gledhill was named as Netminder of the Month for February.

Jones was also named as a defenceman in the Laidler Division All Stars team on NIHL North Updates, selected by fellow players.

Looking back at the Ducks' debut season in the Laidler Division, Head Coach Gary Shaw said:

"When we started the season, my only goal was to get the team playing together as a unit and be competitive. We achieved that and, as a bonus for the players, actually won some games."

"The strategy was to develop players and get through the season. We now have 4 or 5 players training with the senior Dragons each week, as well as the three already signed for them."

"From my point of view was the season a success, looking at the results maybe not - and I hate to lose - but the amount of players that have improved this year is a big plus. They have earned the wins they achieved, and they have competed all year.

"I am very happy with how the team has done this season, and looking forward to carry on the progression of these young players and the future Dragons players."

Deeside Ducks already planning ahead

THOUGHTS have already turned to the future following a promising first season of ice hockey action for Deeside Ducks.

The youthful Ducks won four of their 26 games in their debut Laidler Division season.

Head coach Gary Shaw has revealed that plans are already well underway for next season.

He said: "We now already have more players interested in playing for the Ducks and some stronger developed experienced players who will enhance the squad and help develop the young talent further.

"The squad next year should be stronger in terms of quality and depth and will compete from the very start of the season."

Cody Ogden finished as the Ducks' top scorer for the season with seven goals in his 16 games. Deeside Dragons' veteran Chris Jones was second with six strikes, while Stewart Cutting and Kieran Clarkson contributed five apiece.

Charlie Spridgeon was the leading playmaker with 13 assists in 22 games and he was also the Ducks' overall top points scorer, with four goals added into the mix. Chris Jones had six goals and eight assists.

Looking back on a first season of league competition, Shaw said: "When we started the season, my only goal was to get them playing together as a unit and be competitive as a team, which we achieved and had as a bonus that the players actually won games.

"The strategy was to develop players and get through the season - which we achieved. We now have four or five players training with the Dragons each week, as well as the three already signed for them.

"So, as the first season for the team closes, we now have a group of players that we can progress onto the Dragons in a few years' time.

"From my point of view the

season was a success. Looking at the results, maybe not - and I hate to lose - but the amount of players that have improved this year is a big plus. They have earned the wins they achieved, and they have competed all year.

"I am very happy with how the team has done this season, and looking forward to carry on the progression of these young players and the future Dragons players."

Billingham Stars, who defeated Deeside Dragons in the semi-finals of the Division One North play-offs, have enjoyed double joy.

They defeated Blackburn Hawks 5-3 in the final, before securing a 5-4 overtime win against Slough Jets to take the national Division One title.

Meanwhile, Cardiff Devils beat Coventry Blaze 8-3 on aggregate to make sure of their place in the Elite League play-off finals weekend, where they will face league winners Belfast Giants in the last-four.

GOOD SEASON: Charlie Spridgeon.
Picture: Billie Jane Photography

Ducks In The Newspaper!

There's a brief summary of the Ducks' debut season in today's Flintshire & Wrexham Leader (15th April 2025 - Page 36), along with Head Coach Gary Shaw's comments.

You can read the original reports in full – along with lots of other interesting stuff - on the highly informative grass roots Ice Hockey Review website.

Season Review: http://www.icehockeyreview.co.uk/2025/03/deeside-ducks-satisfying-season-202425.html

Coach's Comments:
http://www.icehockeyreview.co.uk/2025/04/deeside-ducks-coachs-comments-on-debut.html

#keepquacking #fowlnotfoul

(Source: NIHL North Facebook group)

(Source: NIHL North Updates (Facebook))

Deeside Ducks' Gary Shaw receives the Laidler Coach of the Year award from NIHL General Manager Haydn Hunter (Photo by Ryan Gleeson / RDG Digital)

April 2025: Ducks' Coach Shaw Named Coach Of The Year

Deeside Ducks Head Coach Gary Shaw has been named Coach Of The Year for the Laidler Division in the official NIHL awards, sponsored by The Ice Barn.

Shaw made the 3-name shortlist along with Ian Weedall of Billingham Buccaneers who finished 3rd in the Laidler Division and Ian Brown of Bradford Bulldogs who finished just above the Ducks in 9th place.

The choice is notable because there was no room for the coaches of the top two teams in the Division – Sutton Sting, who were runners up, and Telford Tigers who went on to win the league, cup and play offs – and clearly demonstrates that, at this level, the development and progression of younger players is just as highly valued as winning trophies.

In contrast, the shortlist for the Moralee Division comprised of Stephen Foster from Billingham Stars, Dominic Osman from Blackburn Hawks and Andy Daintith & Mike Roddy from Hull Jets - and the nod eventually went to Foster, who guided his team to an historic treble of league, cup and play off titles.

The award was presented to Shaw at the NIHL Play Off Weekend in Sheffield and came as a complete surprise to him, as he explains:

"When attending the NIHL Play Offs, I was asked to drop the puck for the Division 2 game for which I was glad to accept the honour. While we were waiting, they announced that there was a presentation award they had to give out."

"They announced that it was for Coach of the Year and I had no idea that I was there for the award as they had kept it under wraps really well and I was shocked that the announcement was made for me."

"I never thought that I would be nominated for an award like this - I have always maintained that it's always been about the players' development throughout my coaching career, and I have never been one to take the accolades for their accomplishments on the ice."

"I have coached at a few different clubs and have had the enjoyment of starting kids at novice level to players representing England and Great Britain, and this is why I have kept coaching for so long in the game I love so much."

"I am humbled and proud to be named Coach of the Year, especially for representing my home club at Deeside where I have played and coached for over 40 years."

Deeside Ducks In The Newspaper!

The story about Gary Shaw receiving the Laidler Division Coach Of The Year is in today's Flintshire & Wrexham Leader (29th April 2025 - Page 34).

You can read the original report – along with lots of other interesting stuff - on the highly informative grass roots Ice Hockey Review website.

https://www.icehockeyreview.co.uk/2025/04/deeside-ducks-head-coach-gary-shaw.html

ALL CHANGE...

At the end of April, the Deeside club decided to do away with the Ducks name for the Laidler Division team and rebrand it under the "Dragons" banner.

This move was explained in the following announcement that was published on the hitherto Ducks – now "rebranded" - Facebook page on 28th April 2025:

> *Exciting News from Deeside Hockey!*
>
> *We've absolutely loved being known as the Ducks during our first season. However, to help bring the whole club together, we're proud to announce that we will be rebranding as the Deeside Dragons for our 2nd season in NIHL2!*
>
> *This change ties us closer to the Deeside Dragons pathway — from our Junior Dragons, right through to the Senior Dragons. Last year, we were thrilled to see some of our players step up and make an impact with the Senior team, and we can't wait to see even more of our Junior Dragons following in their footsteps!*

Thus the fascinating roller-coaster experience that was the Deeside Ducks came to an abrupt end.

And you now hold in your hands the complete record of the shortlived Deeside Ducks Laidler Division team.

And – one last Ducks poem from Lucy:

Can you hear all that quacking -
Deeside Ducks have turned into Dragons!

Deeside Ducks no longer exist
They will be very greatly missed
They're now known as Deeside Dragons Nihl 2
As there is another Deeside team called Dragons too
If you read Nihl incorrectly you get the Latin word nihil
I hope they retain the Ducks' uniqueness still ...

Lucy London, 29th April 2025

DUCKS GALLERY

A to Z

Index to Photo Credits:
A = All Sports Photography (Mark Ferriss)
B = Karen Booth / Kazzabooth Photography
D = Keith & Kenny Davies
J = Billie Jane Photography
M = Maxine Roscoe
P= Paul Breeze / Ducksmedia
R = Jake Renzi @renzimedia
W= Angela Wilkes

Oliver Booth (M)

Andrew Chappell (B)

Kieran Clarkson (A)

Heather Clarkson (P)

Stewart Cutting (B)

Jack Davies (P)

Gary Dixon (A)

Louis Ellwood (A)

Dan Fadejevs (A)

Callum Garwell

Jace Gledhill (D)

Rhys Howells (A)

Chris Jones (A)

Josh Jones (A)

Paul Jones (R)

Alfie Kelly (B)

Thomas Milnes

James Morgan (P)

Louis Morgan (P)

Charlie Nicholson (A)

Cody Ogden (W)

Charlie Phillips (B)

Callum Preston (D)

Ben Roscoe (A)

Harry Shearman (D)

Rory Sillery (B)

Rafferty Smith (A)   *Michael Speare (P)*

George Spofforth (P)   *Charlie Spridgeon (B)*

Corey Swift (P)   *Dalton Thompson (D)*

Luke Wainwright (B)   *Mackenzie Wilkes (D)*

Deacon Wilkes (A)

Kenny Williams (A)

Liam Yarwood (A)

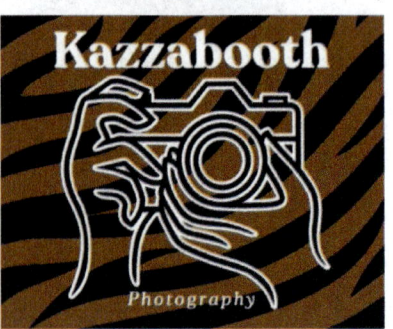

A 24-4 trouncing away at Telford! (Photo by Karen Booth)

Away at Billingham (Photo by Paul Ali Photography)

National Anthem line-up against Nottingham (Photo by Paul Breeze)

Ducks in action away at Altrincham
(Photo by All Sports Photography

Callum Preston makes a great save away at Billingham
(Photo by Paul Ali Photography)

Ditto Paul Jones at Telford (Photo by Karen Booth)

Jace Gledhill between the pipes away at Telford
(Photo by Keith & Jenny Davies)

Oli Booth away at Altrincham (Photo by All Sports Photography)

Above: Chris Jones
(Photo by Chris Jones – the
other one...)

Left: Gary Dixon
(Photo by Paul Breeze)

ROLL OF HONOUR-2024/25

Here is a list of team staff, off-ice officials and other volunteers who all played their part in the Deeside Ducks' debut season.

Team Staff

Head Coach: Gary Shaw

Lead Coach: Peter Bleackley

Assistant Coaches: Simon Hughes, Stewart Cutting

Bench Coaches: James Parsons, Steve Fellows, Bruce Morton

Team Manager: Angela Wilkes, Maxine Roscoe

Equipment Manager: Danny Kelly, Harry Shearman

Off Ice Volunteers

Volunteer Coordinator: Paul Breeze, Angela Wilkes, Maxine Roscoe

Scorer: Paul Simon, Angela Wilkes, Dan Edward

Timekeeper: Dave Billingsley, Morgan Collins

Goal Judges: Dave Jones, Andy Jones, Guntars Fadejevs, Eve Brown, Bernadette Bryce, Andy Howells.

Penalty Boxes: Chris Jones, Dan Roscoe, Bernadette Bryce, Andy Howells, Ellie Baker, Guntars Fadejevs

Penalty Runner: Paul Breeze

Match Announcer: Noah Deverowe, Paul Breeze, Richie Amos

Music: Maxine Roscoe

Presentations MC: Paul Breeze

Photos: Paul Breeze, Maxine Roscoe, Noah Deverowe, Chris Jones

Merchandise / Sales: Andrea Petrie, Andy Brown, Eve Brown, Bernadette Bryce, Ellen Bryce, Olivia Crofts, Benita Petrie, John Petrie, Julie Sharp

Stewarding: Jayne Kushnirenko, Bernadette Bryce, Lauren Kushnirenko, Kat Litherland, Adam Dutton, Andy Howells, Geraint Hughes-Warr, Andy Brown, Hayley.

Match Video Technician: Bruce Morton

Match Reports & Press Liaison: Paul Breeze

Social Media Content: James Parsons, Angela Wilkes, Paul Breeze

Match Night Updates: Lesley Theresa

Poet: Lucy London

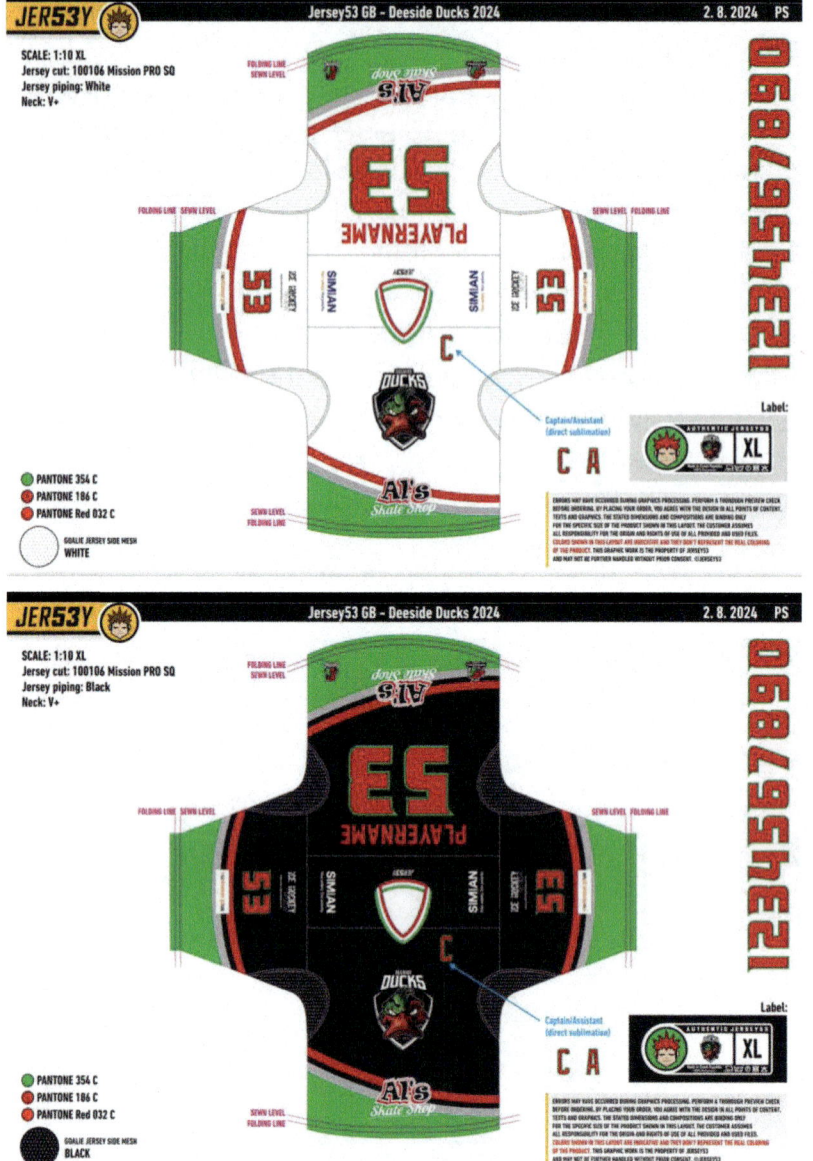

Home and away shirt designs for the Ducks' debut 2024/25 season.

A selection of graphics that were used on the Ducks' social media pages during the 2024/25 season.

BOOK REVIEW
"Ice Hockey In Wales" by Stuart Latham

(Originally published on icehockeyreview.co.uk on 15th February 2025)

Well – what can I say?

Stuart Latham has done it again – with another huge book about British ice hockey - this time all about "Ice Hockey in Wales".

Now, if you are a regular reader of my previous random ramblings on this subject (did you notice my double alliteration of the r-words there…?), you will know that I have already gone on at great length about the huge-ness of his previous Manchester ice hockey book "On Thin Ice" (that's the one that you couldn't read while riding no-handed on a bike – no, please, don't try that yourself - it would be reckless and dangerous, and I only mention it for historical context)…

Well, this latest offering - "Ice Hockey In Wales" - comes from the same stable, and it really is pretty much what it says on the tin. Although you couldn't creosote your fence with it in authentic Karate Kid style, you would certainly know a lot more about the subject matter than the average unassuming oriental martial arts tutor by the time you have finished reading this fascinating book.

As with all of Stuart's other ice hockey books, this one is packed with interesting facts, league tables, players stats and personal stories from people who have been involved with the clubs concerned.

From a Deeside point of view, we have the various incarnations over the years of the Deeside Dragons, there is also the Flintshire Freeze who operated in the ENL in Deeside instead of the Dragons from 1998 to 2012 and an interesting piece by current Dragons GM Shaun Bebbington about the post-Covid period return of ice hockey in Deeside.

There is also a wealth of information about the Deeside second teams, covering the historical Deeside Demons, the short lived Dragons 2 and a very well written and informative (ahem...) piece about the new Deeside Ducks team that just started this season.

There's no mention of the Clwyd Flames, unfortunately, who were the Deeside second team for a couple of seasons in the early 1980s, although – to be fair - detailed information about them is pretty hard to track down.

The other ice hockey venue in Wales – down in the Welsh capital - gets similar treatment and we have year by year league tables, player stats, stories and photos (as available) about Cardiff Devils, Cardiff Rage, Cardiff Capitals, Cardiff Fire, Cardiff Fire 2, Cardiff Bears, Cardiff Satans and the new Cardiff Canucks team.

If you are a keen collector of ice hockey books in general - and Stuart Latham's books in particular - you will probably have come across a lot of this material before as he has previously produced separate volumes about the Deeside Dragons (in 2020) and Cardiff Devils (2021) but, even so – it's nice to have all this stuff together in one tidy edition and with everything brought right up to date.

So, if you want vital statistics, I'll give you some vital statistics. "Ice Hockey In Wales" is a whopping 630 pages in length - not quite as huge as "On Thin Ice"s 734 pages but it is still a heavyweight hardback.

In fact, it weighs 1.25kg, is 260mm high, 180mm wide and has a spine width of 38mm and it will stand bold and proud on your bookshelf next to the rest of your Stuart Latham ice hockey book collection.

For orders, drop Stuart a line via Facebook or send him an email to stuartlatham65@sky.com

- and get him to tell you about his other books as well.

"Lucy Match Scorer" caricature by Manga Mark

BOOK REVIEW

"On Thin Ice"
By Stuart Latham

(Originally published on icehockeyreview.co.uk on 25th June 2024)

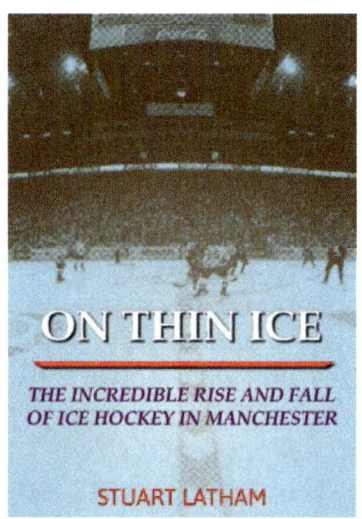

When I was a young lad growing up in Stanground - which, if you don't happen to know it, is a pleasant leafy suburb of the historic cathedral city of Peterborough – I once saw a very odd sight which has stayed in the back of my mind all these years.

I was walking to the sweet shop when I saw a chap – maybe late teens / early 20s (when you are 9 or 10, everybody else just looks "old" to you...) – ride by on a bike. BUT he was riding no-handed and reading a book at the same time.

Now, this was back in the mid 1970s in the days when the liberal consensus and permissive society and everything else were all in full swing and nobody had ever heard of "Health & Safety" but even then, I figured this might have been a bit of a dangerous thing to do.

As far as I can remember, he had a small paperback book balanced against the handlebars held loosely in position by his thumbs, so may well have had a modicum of control over his machine, but he certainly wasn't looking where he was going.

I don't know who he was, where he was going or what happened later – he could have come to a sticky end a bit further up the road for all I knew – but the vision of this bloke on this bike with this book has always stuck with me.

So – why am I telling you this? Well, not that I would EVER encourage or condone anybody attempting to doing anything quite so dangerous and illegal on a public road, putting themselves and others in harm's way, and however clever this particular bloke was with reading books on bicycles, I bet that he would NOT have been able to do it with Stuart Latham's new publication "On Thin Ice" – which is a fascinating comprehensive account of ice hockey in Manchester from 1961 onwards.

I have commented before on the "huge-ness" of some of Stuart's other books – the Alloa Athletic one still lays stubbornly where I first put it down because it is too heavy for me to pick up and put away anywhere - and this is another very impressive example of literary huge-ity. It is certainly too big to prop up against the handlebars and read while you are pedalling along.

If you want facts and figures to back up this assertion – or "stats", as we like to call them in the ice hockey world – I will give you some.

"On Thin Ice" has a whopping 734 pages and weighs 1.3kg! It is a hardback, which gives it that nice classic quality feel and, as the spine is 4.5cm wide, it will stand nicely on your bookshelf without falling over or flopping. It is 26.5cm tall – which is actually 1cm taller than most of Stuart's other B5 format ice hockey books – but that just means that it is easier to find on the shelf in the dark.

Now, if you are a keen collector of ice hockey books in general - and Stuart Latham's books in particular - you will probably have come across a lot of this material before as he has previously produced separate volumes about the Altrincham Aces, Manchester Phoenix and Manchester Storm teams but, even so – it's nice to have all this stuff together in one tidy edition.

This book goes right back to the early days when the original Devonshire Road rink in Altrincham first opened and boasts such well known names of the day as Chick Zamick and Art Hodgins on the Aces bench.

We then navigate through the Trafford Metros era of the late 1980s and early 90s, the first Manchester Storm team in the Superleague, the Manchester Phoenix period from 2002 to 2017 and finish up with the modern Storm and Aces teams.

As you'd expect from a Stuart Latham publication, it is packed with league tables, stats and photos. There are loads of player profiles and some great memories from people who were involved, such as

Daryl Lipsey, Hilton Ruggles and John Lawless (Storm)

Neil Morris, Tony Hand and Peter Hagan (Phoenix)

Tom Revesz, James Ashton and Sarah Hutchinson (Aces)

and there's even a bit from me in there as well…

So, there we have it: "On Thin Ice – The Incredible Rise And Fall Of Ice Hockey In Manchester".

BOOK REVIEW

Gone But Not Forgotten

(Originally published on icehockeyreview.co.uk on 20th December 2024)

I have said, in the past, that you can "never have too many ice hockey books". And, while I WOULD say that because I do, occasionally, sell the odd one or two to help fund my Twiglet habit, this book is not one of mine.

Yep, just when I was wondering how I was going to cope over the festive period without any NIHL hockey to watch or report on (we in the lower reaches don't have Boxing Day games etc like the "Elite" boys and National Division do...) this latest offering from the fine stable of Stuart Latham ice hockey club histories has landed on the doormat.

"Gone But Not Forgotten" is an interesting book as it covers a number of different teams from different eras.

Depending on how old you are and how much you might have read about past glories in British ice hockey, you may have heard of a lot of these teams already, but it is nice to see so much information all gathered up in one place.

And what we have here covers:

Kensington Corinthians (1930s)

Richmond Hawks (1930s)

Earls Court Royals (1930s)

Grosvenor House Canadians (1930s)

Wembley Canadians (1930s)

Wembley Monarchs (1930s & 40s)

Wembley Vets (1970s)

London Phoenix Flyers (Richmond – 1970s)

Richmond Flyers (1980s)

Earls Court Rangers (1930s & 40s)

London Lions (1920s & 30s)

London Lions (1970s - exhibition team)

Wembley Lions (1930s, 40s & 50s)

Milton Keynes Kings (1990s & 00s)

Ashfield Islanders (1980s & 90s)

Bournemouth Stags (1980s & 90s)

As you'd expect with a Stuart Latham compilation, the book is packed with league tables, player statistics and fascinating photos and is bound to be of interest to ice hockey fans of all the various eras.

Now if I were being picky here, (picky – moi? shurely not...) - but if I WAS being picky, I would have expected the 1980s London All Stars team (Dave Richards, Bob Mitura et al) to be worthy of a page or two in this as well. Ice hockey fans of a particular vintage may well recall that they won the 1984/85 British League Division 2 South title.

That was quite an achievement for them because – like Ashfield Islanders - they had to play all of their games away for double points, as their home ice at the Sobell Centre in Islington wasn't suitable for playing league matches.

There was, actually, quite a lot of that went on during those halcyon Heineken-fuelled "expansion" days of the mid 80s – check out Brighton and Hastings as well (oops! - he hasn't included them, either...)

But I am not being picky today. The last train to Picky-Ville has departed "ohne mich" - so I won't mention any of them...

Anyway, despite that, this book is all very interesting and represents a very good record of a lot of teams that have fallen by the wayside over the years.

So, there we have it: "Gone But Not Forgotten.

To order your copy, drop Stuart a line via Facebook or send him an email to stuartlatham65@sky.com - and get him to tell you about his other ice hockey books as well.

MORE ICE HOCKEY BOOKS BY STUART LATHAM

  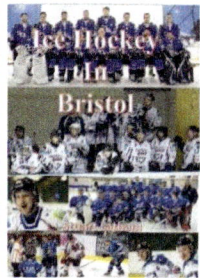 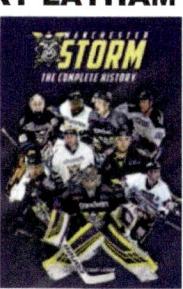

ISBN	Title	RRP £
9781838116507	60 Years Of The Altrincham Aces	£15.99
9781838116521	Ice Hockey in Bristol	£15.99
9781838116538	The Deeside Dragons	£15.99
9781838116545	The Manchester Storm	£15.99
9781838116569	The Rise and Fall of the Manchester Phoenix	£15.99
9781838116590	The Cardiff Devils	£16.99
9781838332808	Ice Hockey Memories	£18.99
9781838332822	The History of the Slough Jets	£17.99
9781838332846	More Ice Hockey Memories	£17.99
9780953060863	Blood Sweat and Tears Ice Hockey in Peterborough	£24.99
9780953060870	Swindon Wildcats 1986-2016	£22.99
9780953060887	The History of the Bracknell Bees	£24.99
9781838332853	Ice Hockey in Edinburgh	£18.99
9781838332891	Stars Wars - The Oxford City Stars	£16.99
9781838460907	Swindon Ice Hockey Statistically Speaking 1986-2021	£17.99
9781838460914	In Their Own Words - Swindon Ice Hockey Memories	£16.99
9781838460938	Hockey in Haringey	£17.99
9781838460952	Ice Hockey In Solihull	£18.99
9781838460983	The NHL IN The UK	£19.99
9781915697042	Ice Hockey In Guildford	£21.99

Available by mail order from Waterstones.com, brownbfs.co.uk, foyles.co.uk and other major outlets.

**For more details, contact
stuartlatham65@sky.com or tel: +44 7702035951**

ICE HOCKEY BOOKS
by Michael A Chambers

THE COMPLETE WORKS: Compendium of the Nottingham Panthers Ice Hockey Team

This is the third book on the Nottingham Panthers and is an extension to the two previous about the club with additional statistics and facts. It is an update of the recent seasons 2007-08 to 2022-23 and is filled with lots of player pictures or events not published before.
Also a complete list and register of every player to have put on the Panthers jersey from 1946 – this has never been documented until now.
It's a complete history of all of the competitions in all the seasons. Cartoons, drawings and more.

300 Pages A4 Paperback - ISBN: 979-8365711198

UK ICE HOCKEY - *Featuring:*

History of English & Scottish Leagues, Season By Season League Tables, Cup And Play Off Competitions,

Full Lists of Title & Trophy Winners, UK clubs in European Competitions, Great Britain National Team, All Star Teams

226 pages A4 paperback - ISBN: 978-0-9539398-4-8

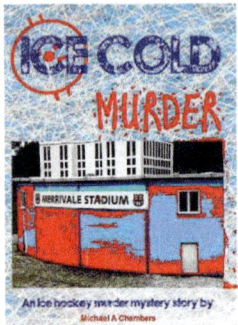

ICE COLD MURDER –

an ice hockey murder mystery

ISBN: 978-0953939831

When a body is found within hockey owner Mark Atkin's establishment, Inspector Dilley has to unravel this terrible scene in order to find out what happened. Amongst a complexity of doors, keys and camera pictures which have much to do with it all.

Many people have much to do with the events that occur this day which puts them 'in the frame' within this much troubled club. Who did it?

Copies available from the author. Contact Michael via e-mail at: spikc2004@yahoo.co.uk

ICE HOCKEY REVIEW

www.icehockeyreview.co.uk

ICE HOCKEY POEMS 2013-2023

by Lucy London

THE SEAGULL HAS LANDED!

ICE HOCKEY (1936)
by Major BM Patton
Annotated & Illustrated 2020

A facsimile reprint of the original 1936 edition with new introduction, author biography and appendices

NORTH DIVIDE SOUTH

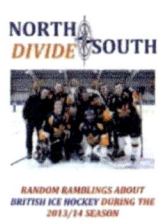

RANDOM RAMBLINGS ABOUT BRITISH ICE HOCKEY DURING THE 2013/14 SEASON

By Paul Breeze

NORTH / SOUTH DIVIDE

Volume 2: Ice Hockey And Me

WIGHTLINK RAIDERS
SIMPLY THE BEST

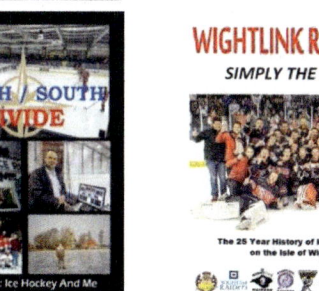

The 25 Year History of Ice Hockey on the Isle of Wight

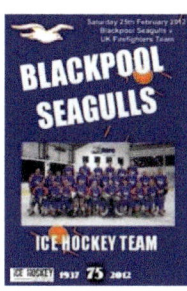
BLACKPOOL SEAGULLS
ICE HOCKEY TEAM
1937 75 2012

ICE HOCKEY review

LEGENDS GAME 2013

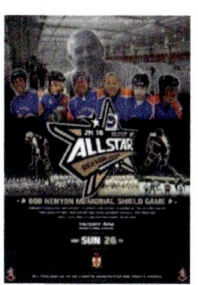
ALLSTAR

*Available by mail order from www.poshupnorth.com, **Amazon**, icehockeyreview.co.uk and other quality outlets*

FYLDE FLYERS
A Complete Record

The Fylde Flyers ice hockey team only existed for two seasons but they reignited interest in a sport that has a proud history in Blackpool dating back to the 1930s.

Their legacy goes on even though the team does not.

Here is the fascinating story of the Fylde Flyers.

Full Contents List:

Acknowledgements
About The Author
Historical Timeline
The SubZero Story
The "Small Ice Rink" Dilemma

2011/12 Season Summary
*News Stories, Match Reports &
Gamesheets
End Of Season Awards*

2012/13 Season Summary
*News Stories, Match Reports &
Gamesheets
End Of The Line For Flyers*

Fylde Flyers Fact File
*Summary Of Player Statistics
Most Points
Most Goals
Most Assists
Most Appearances
Most Penalties
Netminder Statistics
Summary Of All Time League
Results*

Player Directory A - Z

ISBN: 9781909643130

Available by mail order from www.poshupnorth.com, Amazon, icehockeyreview.co.uk and other quality outlets

10 YEARS IN THE WILD
2013 to 2023

10 YEARS

In The Wild

Season summaries, articles, photos and statistics for the
Widnes Wild NIHL team from 2013 to 2023
With all-time Player A to Z and 10-Year Playing Record

ICE HOCKEY
REVIEW

To celebrate the 10th anniversary of the founding of the Widnes Wild ice hockey team, we thought we'd gather up all the material that we have collected over the years and put it together in one single volume.

ISBN: 978-1-909643-54-3

Full Contents List:

Introduction

New Ice Rink Opens In Widnes

Widnes Wild Team Launch

How It All Began!

Widnes Wild's First Ever Game

Richard Charles Looks Back At The First Widnes Game

Craig Williams And The First Ever Widnes Wild Goal

Season by Season: 2013/14, 2014/15, 2015/16, 2016/17, 2017/18, 2018/19, 2019/20, 2020/21, 2021/22, 2022/23

10 Year Records

Roll Of Honour

Playing Record

Wild Player Top 10s

Head to Head Playing Records

Wild Player A To Z

Pukka Penguin

Team Staff, Off Ice Officials & Match Volunteers

Long Service Awards

Wild Shirt Retirements

NIHL Player Award Winners

Lucy London – Poet In Residence

Bookshelf

Various mail order options available
Visit www.icehockeyreview.co.uk for more details

RAPTORS, EAGLES & HAWKS 2 TOO...

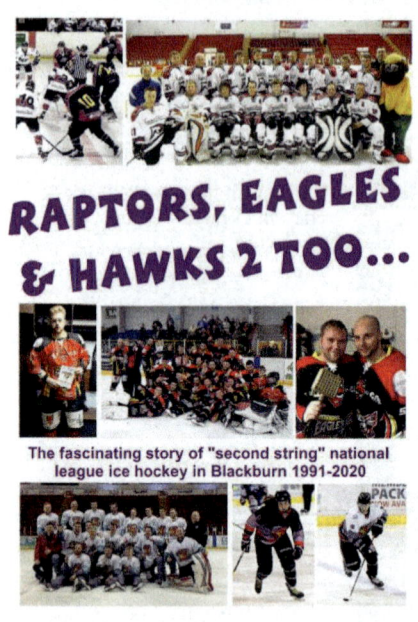

RAPTORS, EAGLES & HAWKS 2 TOO...

The fascinating story of "second string" national league ice hockey in Blackburn 1991-2020

The fascinating story of "second string" national league ice hockey in Blackburn 1991-2020

ISBN: 978-1-909643-63-5

Full Contents List:

Introduction

Ice Hockey Arrives In Blackburn

1991-93: Blackburn Falcons

1993-97: Blackburn Seagulls

1997-98: Blackburn Phoenix

2007-12: Lancashire Raptors
Introduction
Season By Season
All Time Player Records

2012-17: Blackburn Eagles
Season By Season
All Time Player Records

2017-20: Blackburn Hawks 2
Season By Season
All Time Player Records

Overall Playing Record
– All Teams

A to Z Players Records
– All Teams

Bookshelf

Please note: the full colour version is available direct from the publisher via eBay. A budget black and white version is available via Amazon. Apart from colour photos, the actual content is the same in both versions.

Mail order links can be found on
www.icehockeyreview.co.uk

Check out our audio and video archive in our dedicated "Paul & Lucy's Best Kept Secrets" YouTube channel at www.youtube.com.

CONNAH'S QUAY COBRAS

Recreational ice hockey team based at Deeside Leisure Centre, Queensferry, CH5 1SA

Training time: 8.30 to 10.30pm Sunday Evenings

E-mail:
enquiries@cobras.hockey

Website:
https://cobras.hockey/

Facebook:
Cobras Hockey

POEMS FROM MY NOTEBOOKS

by
Daisy Minnie
Hannah Cook

Introduction & Concept by Lucy London
Edited by Paul Breeze

ISBN: 9781909643581

Concept and introduction by Lucy London

Biography and additional research by Paul Breeze

Additional background, biography and photos
by Dave Barlee

Coming Soon...

Keep a check on
www.icehockeyreview.co.uk
for details!

Printed in Dunstable, United Kingdom

64134518R00147